Successful Fundraising for Arts and Cultural Organizations

Second Edition

Karen Brooks Hopkins
Carolyn Stolper Friedman

ORYX PRESS

1997

The rare Arabian oryx is believed to have inspired the myth of the unicorn. This desert antelope became virtually extinct in the early 1960s. At that time several groups of international conservationists arranged to have 9 animals sent to the Phoenix Zoo to be the nucleus of a captive breeding herd. Today the oryx population is over 1,000, and over 500 have been returned to the Middle East.

© 1997 by The Oryx Press
4041 North Central at Indian School Road
Phoenix, Arizona 85012-3397

Published simultaneously in Canada
Printed and bound in the United States of America

∞ The paper used in this publication meets the minimum requirements of the American National Standard for Information Sciences—Permanence of Paper for Printed Library Materials, ANSI Z39.48-1984.

Library of Congress Cataloging-in-Publication Data
Hopkins, Karen Brooks.
   Successful fundraising for arts and cultural organizations / Karen Brooks Hopkins, Carolyn Stolper Friedman. — 2nd ed.
      p. cm.
   Rev. ed. of: Successful fundraising for arts and cultural organizations / Carolyn L. Stolper. 1989.
   Includes bibliographical references and index.
   ISBN 1-57356-029-4 (pbk.)
      1. Arts fund raising—United States—Handbooks, manuals, etc.
   2. Arts publicity—United States—Handbooks, manuals, etc.
   I. Friedman, Carolyn Stolper. II. Friedman, Carolyn Stolper.
   Successful fundraising for arts and cultural organizations.
   III. Title.
NX765.S78 1996
700'.68'1—dc20   96-43146
                                                          CIP

CONTENTS

• • • • • • • • •

LIST OF CHARTS

· · · · · · · · · ·

PREFACE

· · · · · · · · ·

Fundraising for arts and culture in the United States today is a challenging and increasingly complex process. Because of the uncertain economic climate, Americans are reexamining their charitable contributions and are tightening their belts in all areas of support for nonprofit institutions, including those dedicated to arts and culture. Today's citizens are experiencing a period of overwhelming change—corporate downsizing, reductions in government programs, demands for reduced taxes, a technology boom, education reform, and an overhaul of the social welfare system. In this shifting environment, arts institutions cannot assume that fundraising practices that have been successful in the past will continue to work. They must be more creative, resourceful, and assertive than ever in meeting their financial needs.

When we wrote the first edition of *Successful Fundraising for Arts and Cultural Organizations* in 1989, our purpose was to present the fundraising process as a series of practical steps for conducting a successful annual fundraising campaign. That purpose remains important, and part of this second edition covers similar ground, using updated materials that address the dramatically changed fundraising environment of the last several years.

As in the earlier version of the book, we discuss the fundraising roles of the senior staff, volunteers, and board of trustees in a nonprofit organization for culture or the arts, and we include chapters on each of the major funding-source categories: businesses, foundations, individuals, and government agencies. Annual fundraising is discussed in detail, as is the successful development of fundraising special events. There is a new chapter on capital and endowment campaigns, and increased coverage throughout of fundraising for small organizations. Charts in many chapters present details that augment the text.

A set of appendixes provides a wide range of supplementary materials: lists of books and periodicals useful to fundraisers; an article on some of the most popular World Wide Web sites for fundraising professionals; an annotated bibliography of fundraising research resources; state foundation directories and where to obtain them; addresses of national, state, and regional arts councils and humanities councils; addresses of fundraising and management organizations; and a discussion of sponsorship versus advertising, from the viewpoint of a corporation. Two appendixes include examples of fundraising materials such as proposals, invitations, and annual reports; taken exclusively from the institutions for which we work, they illustrate this book's approach to fundraising. Although some of the examples may not immediately appear relevant to your own organization, we urge you to look at them closely and adapt them to the needs of your institution. An appendix also has been included for arts administration students and instructors, which suggests review questions and projects pertaining to fundraising, based on the text.

Organizations vary substantially in size, discipline, location, and resources, but the fundraising process is essentially the same for all of them. You need to identify the most promising donor prospects for your organization, which involves an understanding of the community in which it operates. A small organization in a rural community will have a different prospect pool than a large urban institution—but both need to identify and cultivate donors. The urban institution may focus closely on the nearby corporate community, while the rural organization may run a series of small special events hosted by friends from local neighborhoods.

As you develop a fundraising strategy, it is important not to waste time on "fantasy" prospects, but to focus first and foremost on the funding sources that are most accessible to your organization. Each funding proposal, whether for a small or large organization, must carefully define the institution's mission, explain the project or other reason for requesting funds, ask for commitment, and define the impact of the grant on the donor.

Ultimately, however, successful fundraising requires more than an awareness of techniques. The talented fundraiser will be attentive to changes affecting his or her organization, will modify the tools presented in this book to work most effectively in each specific situation, and will invest time and energy where the potential return is the greatest. Good luck!

ACKNOWLEDGMENTS

• • • • • • • • • •

We have both had the good fortune of working for cultural organizations that have given us the opportunity to develop our skills as managers and fundraisers. We would like to express our deep gratitude to Harvey Lichtenstein and Bruce C. Ratner of the Brooklyn Academy of Music, and to Kevin E. Consey, Allen M. Turner, and Jerome H. Stone of Chicago's Museum of Contemporary Art.

The fundraising climate in America is particularly difficult right now, and we wish to acknowledge with tremendous appreciation the many corporations, foundations, and individuals that have continued to support artists and arts and cultural organizations. We also wish to recognize the government agencies that continue to provide support for culture under mounting pressure to abandon the field.

To make the second edition of *Successful Fundraising for Arts and Cultural Organizations* as relevant and informative as possible, we asked some of our staff specialists to help make revisions. We wish to acknowledge their skills and professionalism and to thank them for contributing to this book: Daniel Goldberg and Richard Larter (Chapter 6), Richard Serrano (Chapter 3 and Appendixes A–C and E–I), and Jacqueline Kravetz (Chapter 7) from the Brooklyn Academy of Music. We would like to sincerely thank Lisa Rodriguez (also from BAM) for her tremendous effort on behalf of this project and Julie Moller (from the Museum of Contemporary Art) for her additional assistance in preparing the manuscript. We have had the experience of working with many talented professionals, both staff colleagues, board members, and friends, who have helped make the job more interesting and more effective. We wish to thank these individuals: Denis Azaro, Bettina Bancroft, Ken Bloom, Gorel

Bogarde, Gaile Burchill, Bob Curley, Alan Fishman, Stephanie French, Jonathan Gross, Brian Grundstrom, Jane Gullong, Ellen Hollander, I. Stanley Kriegel, Stephen Langley, Arthur Levitt Jr., David R. Luckes, Erica Marks, Lourdes Marquez, Joseph Melillo, Don Mohanlal, Carla Perlo, E. Arthur Prieve, Ann Shillinglaw, Lisa Sommers, Lynn Stirrup, Herb Weissenstein, and James D. Yunker.

Finally, we wish to express our gratitude to our loved ones: Paula and Howard Brooks, Matthew Hopkins, Ronald E. Feiner, David S. Friedman, and Jane and Warren Stolper.

INTRODUCTION

• • • • • • • • •

Philanthropy, the giving of one's resources to benefit another, is the life-blood of the hundreds of thousands of nonprofit organizations in America, which in 1991 had assets exceeding $750 billion. The nearly 600,000 nonprofit organizations in this country are dependent upon the support of businesses, foundations, individuals, and the government to survive and function.

Philanthropy in the United States is unique. No other nation in the world has as large a number and as great a diversity of not-for-profit organizations— including hospitals, religious organizations, universities, colleges, social service agencies, and cultural organizations. Nearly all Americans believe it is their obligation to support charitable causes. This altruistic philosophy stands in marked contrast to that of most other countries, where philanthropic giving is often exclusively the government's responsibility. The democratic ideal that each person should do his or her fair share, combined with the more contemporary notion of income-tax incentives, has encouraged a wide range of U.S. citizens to become philanthropists. In fact, more than 80 million Americans contribute time and money to the not-for-profit sector.

Our nation's earliest donors were individuals contributing to religious organizations that had established programs to alleviate human suffering. Many of these organizations exist to this day. Due in part to their charitable activities, religious bodies were granted tax exemption. By the beginning of the twentieth century, however, secular organizations had begun to take over many of the charitable functions once performed by religious institutions.

At the same time, individuals such as Andrew Carnegie and John D. Rockefeller had amassed great fortunes. These and other wealthy individuals were instrumental in establishing a new vehicle for philanthropic purposes: the general-purpose private foundation. In that period, health care and education were the primary beneficiaries of foundation funds.

With the outbreak of World War I, Americans for the first time began to make individual contributions on a massive scale. Four hundred communities throughout the United States established war chests, and the American Red Cross astonished the nation by raising $115 million in one month in 1917. World War I also served as a catalyst for the first substantial giving by American corporations.

The Depression of the 1930s created a new role for government as the primary provider of human services. Private philanthropists turned their attention to seeking remedies for human suffering. Corporate giving to charitable causes was encouraged by the passage of the 1935 Revenue Act, which authorized companies to deduct these contributions from their taxable profits.

In the aftermath of World War II and during the 1950s, both incomes and taxes skyrocketed; the result was a proliferation of family- and company-sponsored foundations established to gain tax advantages. At the same time, Americans began to contribute substantially to the arts and humanities. In the 1960s, Lyndon Johnson's Great Society initiatives laid the groundwork for widespread support of culture. The establishment of both the National Endowment for the Arts and the National Endowment for the Humanities in 1965, coupled with increased foundation and individual giving, enabled culture in America to flourish.

The sheer number and diversity of today's cultural organizations are a testament to our nation's creative spirit. There are currently thousands of arts and cultural organizations in the United States, including dance companies, museums and other exhibition spaces, orchestras, zoos, choruses, jazz ensembles, botanical gardens, and theater companies. As the number of cultural organizations has grown, so have their audiences.

Today, despite the expanded audience, the income earned from sales of tickets, merchandise, and services covers only 50 to 60 percent of the operating expenses of a typical cultural organization. Arts and cultural organizations must rely on voluntary contributions for the balance of their funds, as do health care organizations and educational institutions. In addition, since the early 1990s, government agencies have come under mounting pressure to decrease, and in some cases entirely eliminate, support for arts and culture. The controversy in the federal government began in 1994 when a small group of senators and representatives singled out a few NEA-funded exhibitions that they believed contained objectionable material and were therefore inappropriate recipients of government funds (even though the amounts of these grants were extremely small). A political storm around the issues of government funding and censorship ensued, and by 1995, the budget for the National

Endowment for the Arts had been cut by 40 percent for the following year. Because of this and federal downsizing in general, the NEA's future (along with that of the National Endowment for the Humanities) is uncertain. This upheaval in government funding has resulted in intense competition for the contributed dollar, forcing cultural organizations to develop extremely aggressive fundraising operations in order to continue their work.

The cuts to the NEA represent more than a loss of funds. For fundraisers in arts institutions all over the country, the diminished enthusiasm of the federal government to support culture increases the difficulty of the "sell" to the private sector and to state and local government agencies. Thus, arts organizations no longer defend their existence based solely on the programs and services they provide to their communities. To bolster their cause, these organizations now cite studies showing that arts and culture stimulate tourism, jobs, and economic development. The new fundraising strategies of nonprofit cultural organizations, large and small, often focus on the benefits a corporation will receive in return for support, rather than appealing exclusively to the satisfaction of being a good corporate citizen. Individual donors, rather than simply responding to requests for charity, are asking for—and receiving— more services from the organizations they support.

Fundraisers for arts and cultural organizations need new strategies, as well as a continued substantial effort, creativity, and responsiveness, to succeed in the contemporary climate of reduced government funding and the attitude that regards support of the arts as an investment requiring a substantial return to the donor, rather than simply as an act of giving.

CHAPTER

••••••••••

Institution Building

A n *institution* may be defined as an establishment founded with authority and intended to be permanent. This definition applies well to cultural organizations that are established with a clear artistic or programmatic purpose and with the goal of becoming a permanent part of the communities in which they are located. To fulfill this purpose and meet this goal, raising funds is essential. Because fundraising requires a certain level of organizational development, arts or cultural organizations must make a commitment to the process of institution building.

Institution building is an organic process through which organizations evolve from newly formed entities into mature organizations. The use of the word *institution* is not meant to apply only to 100-year-old museums and well-endowed symphony orchestras. All types of arts and cultural organizations, large and small, experimental and traditional, can establish themselves as institutions. The more advanced the organization's institution-building process is, the greater its fundraising capability will be.

This process involves defining the purpose and programs of the organization, putting in place and nurturing a board of trustees and a professional staff, and developing a long-range plan. Institution building is necessary for success, but it also can be difficult and often tedious, and the need for it continues throughout the life of an organization.

Simply stated, the process begins with a group of individuals dedicated to an artistic or programmatic vision; these individuals form the nucleus of a board of trustees and make the first contributions to the organization. Gradually, as the vision is communicated to more and more people and as it becomes realized in the programs themselves, the organization's audiences will grow, board membership will expand, and the donor base will increase. Although this is an idealistic description of the shell of the building process, each piece—the formation of a clear artistic concept, the creation of a board, the growth of an audience, and the establishment of a group of donors—adds the bricks and mortar that make the organization viable and worthy of support. There are four broad categories into which funding sources can be grouped: individuals, businesses, foundations, and government agencies. Typically, a newly formed small- or medium-sized organization raises funds most easily from individuals and local arts and humanities agencies, as well as from certain foundations that make grants to start-up projects. As the organization continues its institution-building process, funding from businesses, foundations, and state and federal agencies becomes available. Many businesses and foundations require grantees to have a certain minimum budget size, audience size, and level of program activity to be eligible for support.

The first step, then, in preparing to raise funds is for management to articulate clearly the artistic or programmatic purpose of the organization. This articulation should be in the form of a written statement of mission. Then, the organization must work to develop an effective leadership body—consisting of a board of trustees and a professional staff capable of defining the direction of the organization, developing long-range plans that include information about funding and how it will be used, and delivering what the organization promises.

If the organization is just beginning, it must incorporate itself as a not-for-profit, tax-exempt corporation under section 501(c)(3) of the Internal Revenue Code. Organizations must be set up in this way to legally apply for and receive grants. It is best to seek an attorney's counsel in filing the necessary documents.

The organization's bylaws are drawn up at the time of incorporation. Bylaws are the written rules that set forth the structure of the organization's corporate operations. Bylaws specify such information as the official name of the corporation; its purpose; and the powers, duties, and terms of office of the trustees. The bylaws of an organization can be amended only by action of the board and must not violate any state laws governing not-for-profit corporations.

ARTICULATING A STATEMENT OF MISSION

The statement of mission should succinctly define the organization's purpose and programs. The statement should be carefully thought out; it is an important tool for planning, recruiting board members, raising funds, and communicating with the public. The basic mission statement (which is very brief) should answer the following questions:

- What are the services and programs of the organization?
- For whom are the services and programs intended?
- Which geographic area(s) is (are) served by the organization?

The statement should be worded so as to remain relatively unchanged from year to year; it should be broad enough to allow organizational growth, but not so broad as to allow wholesale changes in direction. It is essential that the leadership understand the purpose of the organization and be able to articulate its programs. The following examples are statements of mission written for hypothetical cultural organizations:

> The Children's Theatre Company is a professional theater company that produces classical fairy tales, fables, and exceptional contemporary plays for children, parents, and educators in the greater Philadelphia area.

> The purpose of the Chamber Music Ensemble is to present to St. Louis audiences a distinctive and varied repertoire of both contemporary and classical music performed by a unique combination of established and emerging artists.

> It is the purpose of the Artists' Collective of Washington, D.C., to facilitate the creation of new American drawing, painting, and sculpture by providing studio space to artists and by exhibiting their works in various locations throughout the nation's capital.

> The Ballet Company exists to perform a wide range of classical and modern ballets created by the world's finest choreographers, past and present, in the greater Minneapolis-St. Paul area, and to tour these works throughout the upper Midwest.

An expanded statement, consisting of a few paragraphs, is often used in fundraising to establish the credibility of the organization. Information about the history, leadership, and goals of the institution embellishes the basic statement of mission. Even this expanded material should be succinct, to give the potential donor a quick profile of the institution's purpose. The following is an example of an expanded statement:

> The Brooklyn Academy of Music (BAM), America's oldest performing arts center, was established in 1861 and has become one of the nation's most significant forums for innovation in the arts. BAM is a national model of an urban arts center in the nineties, addressing both global issues in the arts and local community needs.
>
> The Academy's primary mission is to develop and present new work in the performing arts; to encourage innovative approaches to the traditional repertory of dance, opera, music, and theater; to promote unusual collaborations with visual artists; and to reach out to the local community through educational activities and multicultural experiences that specifically serve the interests of a culturally diverse, urban population.

BAM achieves this mission through four basic programming initiatives: the Next Wave Festival, an annual contemporary performing arts festival; BAM Opera, which features alternative approaches to opera production in the United States; BAM Theater and other special international events; and the Academy's various educational and community programs, which include one of the nation's largest performing-arts programs for young people.

DEVELOPING EFFECTIVE MANAGEMENT

Effective management—that is, management that provides the leadership and guidance necessary to direct the growth of the organization and to achieve its potential—depends on a hard-working and committed board of trustees and a skilled professional staff. Although it is beyond the scope of this volume to discuss this facet of organization building extensively, competent institutional leadership must be in place for successful fundraising. The ability of managers to assess realistically the conditions facing the organization is absolutely essential. Pragmatic and imaginative problem solving is necessary to meet the challenge of presenting programs that not only advance the artistic mission of the organization but also fit within its budget limitations.

FORMULATING A LONG-RANGE PLAN

A long-range plan is a written document that defines the goals of the organization and the steps for achieving them. It is a blueprint the board uses to direct and monitor the growth of the organization. It is an institution-building tool, one that not only provides internal direction and focus for the organization, but also inspires confidence in funders.

An organization with a plan is one that indeed intends to be permanent. Donors, board members, and the general public feel secure about investing their time and money in an organization whose management has a sense of where it is heading. Sharing plans for the future can motivate community members and funding agencies to support the organization. Small organizations, often rejected by donors because of their limited resources, appear much stronger to the funding world when they have a long-range plan and clear sense of direction.

An organization without a long-range plan may be diverted from its original purpose and may be crippled by time and money wasted dealing with unanticipated problems. Program quality often suffers during crisis periods, and valuable opportunities for institutional growth may be sacrificed. Planning does not preclude risk taking but instead helps in calculating risks and determining which should be taken and when.

It is the job of the board and staff to formulate the long-range plan. The general guidelines and overall philosophy, however, must be provided by the organization's leaders: the artistic or program director, the managing director, and the board chair.

The long-range-planning process involves systematic consideration of the current and foreseeable factors that influence the way the organization conducts its business. The process begins with an examination of the strengths and weaknesses of the organization's staff, board, audience or customer size and composition, physical plant, image, reputation, and policies. This enables the executive staff to assess the resources available to the organization and to determine those that need to be improved or acquired.

The organization's role in the community must then be appraised realistically by analyzing the community's needs, its interest in the arts and culture, and its ability to support the organization by participating in its programs and making donations. Demographic and economic trends, as well as the strengths and weaknesses of competing organizations, should be examined.

In considering all these issues, both internal and external, it will become clear that although some factors can be controlled completely by the organization, others can be controlled only partially or not at all. Having taken an inventory of the organization's strengths and weaknesses and having pinpointed where it stands with respect to the community and its competition, the executive staff can identify the issues most critical to the survival and growth of the organization. Long-range goals addressing each of the critical issues can then be established.

At this point, the organization's leaders should examine the statement of mission in light of what has been learned. Does it still hold up? Does it clearly and accurately describe the purpose, programs, audiences, and geographic boundaries of the organization? If not, modifications should be made. Next, objectives and timetables for accomplishing each of the goals should be determined and the means of meeting the objectives should be defined. This means defining specific tasks and who will undertake them, when they will be undertaken, and what resources will be used. Finally, the organization should design methods for evaluating progress toward achieving the objectives outlined in the plan. Chart 1.1 shows one institution's goal and the related objective and tasks.

It is possible that after objectives and tasks have been determined, it will become apparent that the goal is unreachable or too expensive and should be rejected. This evaluation stage is very important to the planning process and helps ensure a realistic long-range plan. Small organizations especially are advised to make their long-range plans ambitious—but not grandiose. In a tough fundraising climate, donors will be "reality checking" institutions even more carefully than usual before making a commitment.

When the planning process has been completed, a long-range plan should be written that consists of the following sections:

- Statement of mission
- Assumptions: internal and external strengths and weaknesses
- Goals
- Objectives and tasks
- Evaluation procedures
- Supplemental information

The supplemental information should include a description of current operations: staff and board responsibilities, facilities, programs, and financial position. Budgets and audited financial statements for the past three years and budget projections for the coming three years should also be included.

Having a long-range plan is no guarantee that an organization will survive and prosper; the plan is only as good as the thinking that went into constructing it and the ability of managers to carry it out. If the plan is realistic, it will provide a blueprint for growth and a tool for evaluating the feasibility of new ventures, enabling the organization to face the future confidently.

An organization with creative leadership, a clear statement of mission, and a sound long-range plan is in a good position to deliver programs of consis-

---

Goal: To develop a more effective board of trustees.

Objective: To identify three potential new board members, each with expertise in one of three areas: fundraising, marketing, and public relations. Candidates will be presented for election to the board of trustees at the annual meeting in December.

Tasks:

1. The managing director will solicit names of potential board members from current board members, staff, donors, and colleagues and will draw up a list of these candidates by May 30.

2. The development director will research the list of candidates and determine, with the managing director, five of the most promising by July 30.

3. An informal luncheon will be set up by the development director for each of the five candidates selected. A nominating committee member, the artistic or program director, and the managing director will attend. The luncheons will be held on September 15 and 16, October 1 and 2, and October 15. The budget for each luncheon will be $100.

4. The managing director will arrange a meeting by November 1 with top management and the nominating committee to discuss the candidates. Three candidates will be selected for nomination to the board of trustees.

Outlining the Steps toward Accomplishing a Long-Range Goal

CHART 1.1

tently high quality. Such an organization can be relied upon to use funds contributed by outside sources in a responsible and professional way. Donors will be more willing to invest in such an organization than in one without a fully thought-out purpose and direction.

CHAPTER 2

Leadership

BOARD OF TRUSTEES

A respected, prominent, and hard-working board of trustees is a very important ingredient in successful fundraising. Persons of high professional caliber with stature in the community are best able to raise the funds needed to ensure the long-term financial health of an organization. In order to attract such individuals for board membership, it is necessary to define clearly the board's

- Composition
- Structure
- Recruiting procedure
- Responsibilities
- Fundraising participation

Composition of the Board

To be effective, a board of trustees should comprise a balanced mix of individuals who can

- Contribute funds
- Obtain funds from other sources
- Provide professional expertise
- Lend credibility to the organization
- Represent the diverse interests and ethnic composition of the community

Often, individuals with these abilities are wealthy and socially prominent members of the community. This is not to suggest that all board members should be wealthy or that all institutions can have access to the wealthiest, most prestigious individuals. Ideal board members are persons who can provide social and business connections; who have professional expertise in accounting, advertising, finance, law, management, marketing, or public relations; and who are sympathetic to the aims of the organization and the community. Chart 2.1 is a practical tool organizations can use in evaluating the strengths of both current and prospective board members.

Field	Current Trustees	Prospects
Accounting		
Advertising/Marketing/PR		
Arts/Artists		
Banking		
Closely Held Business		
Community Leader		
Design		
Education		
Financial Services		
Fortune 500		
Insurance		
International		
Law		
Media/Entertainment		
Medical		
Real Estate/Construction		
Retail/Fashion		
Service/Consultants/Search		
Technology		
Tourism/Travel		
Utilities		
Venture Capital		
Wall Street (Investment)		

BOARD MEMBERS' SPHERES OF INFLUENCE

CHART 2.1

Printed with permission from H. F. Weissenstein & Co., Inc.

It is wise to think about community concerns when developing board membership. For example, an orchestra located in a steel-mill town may consider asking a representative of that industry to serve. Ethnic diversity on boards has become extremely important as institutions seek to expand their programs and audiences.

There are a few pitfalls organizations should avoid in composing their boards. First, they should be wary of individuals who may want to use the organization to further their own ambitions. The interests of an individual board member should never override the interests of the organization. Second, organizations should be careful not to overload their boards with staff members. An organization may believe it cannot attract qualified individuals to its board, or its staff may feel it needs to exert influence through participation on the board. However, professionals and community leaders will not take seriously and will have no interest in joining a board composed largely of staff members. In addition, conscientious nonstaff board members may object to staff board members' attempts to wield power, and may tire of the politics and resign. It is better to keep the size of the board small than to encumber it with staff simply to create a larger body.

Whether the program director and managing director should serve on the board is a matter of policy to be decided by the board. In cases where senior staff do serve, it is crucial that they be willing to accept the authority of the board president or board chair and to uphold decisions made by the board.

Ultimately, the most effective board is one that is multicultural and made up of individuals who believe in the mission and goals of the organization and are willing to work to accomplish them.

Structure of the Board

The structure of the board (officers, committees, meetings, and terms of office), as well as its responsibilities and procedures, are outlined in the organization's bylaws. The board's structure allows it to conduct the business of the organization in an orderly and efficient manner.

It is usual for boards to have the following officers:

- Chair or president
- Vice-chair or vice-president
- Secretary
- Treasurer

The *chair* (or *president*) is elected as head of the organization by action of the full board. The responsibilities of the chair are to conduct board meetings according to accepted rules of parliamentary procedure, to appoint board members to committees, and to work closely with senior staff. The *vice-chair* (or *vice-president*) should be familiar with the duties of the chair and should be able to assume them in the chair's absence. The *secretary's* major responsibility is to keep accurate records or minutes of the proceedings of each board meeting. The responsibility for overseeing the financial operations of the organization belongs to the *treasurer*.

Terms of office ideally should be three years (but can sometimes be much longer, depending on the individuals involved), with an annual review to remove those members who are not participating fully. A one-year term usually is not long enough to enable an individual to function with maximum effectiveness. Any change in the trustees' term of office requires official amendment of the bylaws by the full board.

Board meetings should be scheduled well in advance and should take place at approximately the same time every month, two months, or quarter, depending on the needs of the organization. Meetings can take place at the organization's offices or in the business office of a board member. Under normal circumstances, meetings should not exceed two hours. Employing strict parliamentary procedure at meetings is a matter of choice, but some type of established voting procedure is needed. Agendas and materials requiring close scrutiny, such as budgets, should be sent to board members at least a week in advance of the scheduled meeting.

As organizations grow in size and sophistication, the in-depth work of the board often is accomplished by committees. Committees, being smaller and more narrowly focused, can concentrate on solving specific problems, freeing the full board of trustees to deal with major policy issues. The following is a list of commonly constituted committees and their responsibilities:

- *Executive committee.* This committee is generally made up of the board's officers—chair, vice-chair, secretary, and treasurer—and the chairs of the standing committees. It formulates institutional policies and consults closely with senior staff.
- *Nominating committee.* This committee works closely with other trustees and with the organization's managing director to recommend and recruit prospective board members. It also assesses each member's participation on the board at the end of his or her term and either recommends reelection or termination.
- *Development committee.* This committee works with the organization's development director to formulate fundraising strategies and to supervise campaigns. Whenever possible, the board treasurer should attend meetings of this committee.
- *Finance committee.* This committee oversees the financial-planning process, audit procedures, and the fiscal-management practices of the organization. The board treasurer should serve as chair of this committee.
- *Long-range planning committee.* This committee monitors the implementation of long-range plans.
- *Ad hoc committee.* This type of committee is set up and disbanded as needed to supervise specific projects, such as a review of real-estate issues or the planning of fundraising benefits and other special events.

Trustee Recruiting Procedure

Recruitment of board members is an ongoing process that requires careful thought and constant attention. The process begins when the first individual agrees to serve on the organization's board. In the case of a small or new organization, sometimes a relative or close friend of the artistic director is first board member. It may also happen that an enthusiastic audience member will want to get more involved and will approach the artistic leadership about volunteering to serve on the board. Social engagements, community events, and programs to meet attendees face to face are all opportunities for cultivating board prospects.

Organizations seek to recruit outstanding individuals as board members, and usually board members want to serve with individuals of similar caliber. If they have a positive experience with the organization, both managerially and programmatically, they will recruit other talented individuals for board membership. Through this slow process of one board member recruiting another, it is possible to form a cohesive and effective leadership body. Management can stimulate this process by regularly asking board members for names of colleagues who may be suitable board candidates—as well as for suggestions about the proper approach to take in contacting these prospects.

Senior staff and the nominating committee chair must continually search for individuals who are interested in the organization's programs and who possess the necessary talents for board membership. The organization's donor, participant, membership, and subscriber lists are good sources of information about the business affiliations and special interests of likely candidates. By following social and business activities in the news media and by attending community and social events, senior staff and board members can meet and identify individuals who have both interest in the organization's programs and high profiles in the community.

Once a group of prospective board candidates has been identified, an effective procedure for recruiting must be established. This procedure includes

- Familiarizing the candidate with the organization
- Asking the candidate to serve on the board
- Electing the candidate to the board
- Orienting the new board member

One way to familiarize candidates with the organization is to host a reception for prospective board members. A simple reception might include refreshments followed by a brief performance, demonstration, facility tour, or slide show. This enables the organization's leaders to introduce themselves and the programs in a hospitable and festive atmosphere. The cultivation process can also be implemented with individual candidates if the institution prefers not to deal with prospective members *en masse*. One way or another, senior staff must have the opportunity to become acquainted with all candidates and to assess their levels of interest in the organization. However, the candidates should *not* be asked to serve on the board at this stage.

Following the reception or the individual meetings, the nominating committee should determine who will be asked to serve. Representatives of the board should then meet with candidates individually to discuss the responsibilities of board membership and the ways in which they feel the particular candidate's qualifications would benefit the organization. Candidates should also be encouraged to indicate their areas of interest and what they would like to accomplish as board members.

Once the board's representatives are ready to recommend candidates to the full board, members of the nominating committee and the executive committee should be polled for their opinions on each candidate. Then the nominating committee should convene and draw up a final slate of nominees to present to the board for consideration.

At the next board meeting, the chair of the nominating committee or the chair of the board should nominate the candidates for election to the board of trustees for the term specified in the organization's bylaws. If the nominating committee has done its job, the election will be essentially a formality. Once

---

Mission Statement
History of the Organization
Organizational Chart
Board of Trustees Affiliation List
Board of Trustees Contact Information
Schedule of Board Meetings for the Fiscal Year
Board Committees List
Names and Phone Numbers of Key Staff
Annual Program Schedule
Articles of Incorporation
Bylaws
Review of Board Members' Liability Insurance
Criteria for Board Membership and Responsibilities
Institutional Budget/Year-to-Date Financial Analysis
Annual Report/Press
Endowment Earnings and Financial Report
Minutes from Previous Board Meeting
Selected Press and Brochures

MATERIAL TO INCLUDE IN A BOARD ORIENTATION MANUAL

CHART 2.2

the new trustees have been elected, the board chair should send official letters and make phone calls notifying them of their election.

An orientation manual should be prepared and mailed to each new board member with the letter. The manual should be as thorough as possible. Chart 2.2 gives a suggested list of items to include in such a manual.

Board Responsibilities

The major responsibilities of the board are to maintain the organization's financial solvency and to uphold its programmatic mission. The board carries out these responsibilities by

- Developing sound management policies and practices
- Participating actively in fundraising
- Recruiting qualified board members
- Hiring qualified senior staff
- Representing the organization in the community

In addition, the board's role with respect to programming is to provide responsible counsel, raise pertinent questions about the organization's financial commitment to its programs, and support programmatic experimentation and creative development. Boards of trustees should not make decisions about day-to-day matters.

Trustee Participation in Fundraising

Board members are the most important participants in the development and execution of annual fundraising campaigns. Board members involve themselves in fundraising by

- Making personal donations
- Enlisting support from others
- Attending special fundraising events and openings

All board members should contribute to the organization. While personal donations need not be extravagant, they should be as generous as possible. A donation from every trustee is important psychologically to the success of the campaign; however, in some cases, donations of in-kind goods and services are as valuable as money. For small organizations (and often large ones as well), a donation of time and expertise can be of tremendous value. Each institution must evaluate its needs to determine the types of board-member contributions that can best serve it. Funding agencies are favorably impressed by an organization all of whose board members have made a financial contribution. A board composed of individuals who are both donors to the organization and participants in its activities delivers the message that theirs is a well-supported and professionally run organization. It is the board chair who should, once a year, solicit individual board members for their contributions. A solicitation by the highest-ranking member of the board is far more effective and appropriate than one initiated by a staff member.

Board members should provide the names of contacts at foundations and in the business sector, as well as among private citizens, to the development director. The development director should then determine whom each board member will solicit for a contribution on behalf of the organization and work with the board member to make the appeal.

Board members are expected to attend premieres, openings, and special fundraising events at which donors and prospective donors will be present. In addition to lending considerable credibility to the organization, the atten-dance of board members at these events is helpful to the organization's fundraising efforts because it facilitates personal relations with those who support the organization.

SENIOR STAFF

The senior staff is as important as the board of trustees in determining the health and growth of the organization. To ensure that the organization prospers, the board of trustees and senior staff must work together, sharing their sense of pride and ownership with donors, audience members, and the community.

The senior staff of an arts or cultural organization usually includes an artistic or program director, a managing director, a development director, a finance or business manager, and a marketing director. Other positions may be created as an organization grows and becomes more sophisticated. These additional positions may entail responsibilities previously included in the job descriptions of the original senior staff members, or they may involve new areas of responsibility.

The artistic or program director is often hired by the board of trustees. The selection of the development director, although usually made by the top artistic and administration directors, is influenced by the board because of the close relationship between it and the development director.

To hire qualified individuals, the board must clearly define the responsibili-ties of each position and the attributes and qualifications required of its incumbent. The board must then take time to search for, interview, and check the references of qualified candidates. When an individual is hired, the board should communicate to him or her a timetable for performance review (such as every six months or once a year) and, if appropriate, a letter of agreement should be signed.

Artistic or Program Director

The primary responsibility of a program director is to establish and carry out the programs of the organization. He or she must also be willing to participate in fundraising and in the recruitment of board members.

Good program directors must not only be skilled in their field, but they must also be able to inspire the board and the staff. They should both understand the process of creating artistic and cultural programs and have a working knowledge of fundraising, marketing, and financial management in order to select programs compatible with the mission and financial capabilities of the organization.

Program directors are typically the most effective spokespersons for the organization. They must be able to share their vision with their colleagues, staff, board, audience, and community. This is important not only in raising funds and recruiting board members, but also in generating goodwill in the community. Future board members and representatives of funding agencies often become acquainted with the organization through a one-to-one relationship with the person who is directly responsible for its programs. The artistic or program director can reinforce the organization's presence in the community by attending community functions that do not necessarily involve the organization.

Managing Director

Managing directors are responsible for the administration of the organization in realizing its artistic or cultural goals. They must work in partnership with the board of trustees and the program director, supporting programs and maintaining realistic fiscal and management policies. If the organization has no development director, the managing director assumes the duties of development director (discussed below).

Just as program directors must strive to understand the business practices of the organization, managing directors must be knowledgeable about the art form or program thrust that is the raison d'être for the organization.

Marketing Director

Marketing directors are responsible for planning and implementing earned income campaigns to sell the organization's products and services. These products or services can include tickets, subscriptions, publications, tours, admissions, programs, courses, or merchandise. To this end, marketing directors oversee promotion and advertising, group sales, press relations, audience development, telemarketing and direct-mail campaigns, and promotional events. They must be energetic, creative, and able to find new ways to focus the attention of key markets on the organization and its products and services.

Finance Director

Finance directors manage the organization's cash and see that bills are paid and receipts collected. Responsibilities usually include preparing financial reports, cash flow statements, and budgets; submitting federal, state, and local tax forms; monitoring accounting systems; and administering health, welfare, and pension plans for employees.

Finance directors must understand the principles of accounting and be skilled in money management. They must also be able to work with each department in the organization to set up systems flexible enough to meet each department's cash needs in a timely way and to provide an accurate record of the department's business transactions.

Development Director

Development directors are responsible for planning and implementing annual fundraising campaigns. They must be energetic and capable of sustaining the momentum of these campaigns.

Development directors work closely with board members and senior staff to determine fundraising goals and to create an ambitious yet realistic fundraising plan that will enable the organization to undertake challenging projects. This cooperation helps ensure the success of fundraising campaigns because it leads to realistic and well-coordinated programmatic and financial plans. Development directors often have a support staff that carries out specific aspects of the campaigns. This staff may include grant writers, prospect researchers, special events planners, sponsorship specialists, and membership directors who oversee direct mail and telefundraising efforts. The size of the staff and the functions it performs are determined by the needs and assets of individual institutions.

VOLUNTEERS

According to a study published in 1986 by Independent Sector (see Appendix H), entitled "The Charitable Behavior of Americans," people who volunteer for an organization contribute more funds to that organization than those who do not directly participate. Giving and volunteering go hand in hand. It is wise for an arts or cultural organization to devise ways of incorporating volunteers into its fundraising strategy. Volunteers not only carry out the actual work of many not-for-profit organizations; they can also be instrumental in helping the organization raise funds. They do this by making contributions themselves, becoming board members, asking others to contribute, conducting small fundraising events, working at galas or phonathons, and providing expertise and information that can enhance the fundraising campaign.

According to Independent Sector, in 1993 an estimated 89.2 million Americans from all walks of life volunteered a total of 15 billion hours in both formal and informal settings ("Giving and Volunteering in the United States in 1994," published in 1994 by Independent Sector; see Appendix H). Part of this trend is due to corporations encouraging their employees to do volunteer work. The 1995 issue of *Giving USA* (see Appendix A) reported that many companies facilitate and promote volunteerism among employees because it builds teamwork skills, improves morale, and attracts better employees. Volunteering is clearly a national pastime.

Volunteers can make the difference between a successful campaign and one that never reaches its full potential. To incorporate volunteers successfully into fundraising, organizations should

- Clearly outline their responsibilities
- Train them to carry out these responsibilities
- Prepare them to solicit funds effectively
- Monitor their progress and reward successful performance

Outlining Volunteer Responsibilities

Because volunteers do not receive salaries for their work, organizations often do not clearly outline their particular responsibilities or what is expected of them. Organizations should interview potential volunteers with an eye to the skills needed for the job at hand—in much the same way as they would interview candidates for salaried positions. Establishing an acceptable work schedule, defining the bounds of the volunteers' responsibilities, and clarifying which decisions must be made by staff and which may be made by volunteers should all be done at the outset, to avoid problems. It would be a good idea to draw up volunteer job descriptions or to have volunteers sign an informal letter of agreement. All workers—including volunteers—perform better when they know how their performance will be judged.

Training Volunteers

All volunteers, regardless of the particular jobs they perform, require a general introduction to the organization and its programs. This could be accomplished simply by offering them a packet of information on the organization, including an annual report and program brochures, and by giving them a tour of the facility. Additional training needs will depend on the jobs they are assigned to do.

In this discussion, the focus will be on training key volunteers to solicit funds in face-to-face meetings. Not all volunteers will participate in solicitation because it is a delicate process. To be successful, the volunteer must be extremely well informed and well prepared. Training volunteers to solicit funds generally involves educating them about the motivations behind giving, preparing them for face-to-face visits, and providing a forum for practicing before they have to ask "for real." The volunteers who do solicit funds are often board members; individuals who are deeply involved in the institution and who are participating specifically because their connections and status in the community increase the chances of the solicitation's success. Using volunteers for telefundraising and special events is discussed later—in Chapters 6 and 8, respectively.

Generally, it is assumed that tax benefits are the main reason people contribute to charity. Although this is certainly an important factor in giving, it is rarely a primary motivation. Individuals give because

- They are committed to the mission of the organization and believe in its programs and activities
- They are involved directly in the organization as participants, subscribers, or volunteers
- They wish to be recognized publicly for their good deeds and have a certain sense of community responsibility
- They are asked to contribute by someone they respect

Thus, in setting the stage for volunteer solicitation, it is helpful to shift the emphasis from asking for money (which is a terrifying prospect to many people) to offering donors an opportunity to become involved in the fine work of the cultural organization.

Preparing Volunteer Solicitors

Because an organization usually gets only one shot at asking an individual for funds, it should muster the best possible effort. If it has been decided that a volunteer or board member is the best person to do the asking, it is incumbent upon the development director to train the volunteer thoroughly. It is recommended that trainers read Chapter 3 (which describes how to implement an annual fundraising campaign) in its entirety before undertaking the task of preparing a volunteer to solicit.

Preparing the volunteer or board member to solicit involves developing research profiles of the assigned prospects and going over the information with the solicitor. Because the intent here is to minimize surprises, the profiles should present pertinent facts about the prospects' (and their families') past involvement with the organization, as well as their financial situation and general philanthropic activities. (See Chapter 3 for an introduction to the various information sources that are available in preparing a research profile.) The solicitor should also be instructed about the various forms contributions may take, such as cash grants or gifts of stock or real estate. Lastly, the solicitor must be knowledgeable about the history, goals, and current programs of the organization. It is highly recommended that training include conducting some practice sessions with the volunteer.

Monitoring Volunteers' Progress and Rewarding Success

Because volunteers receive no wages for their services to an organization, they should be paid with respect and prompt service. The best volunteer/staff relationships are built on mutual trust and respect. Staff members should call key volunteers often to let them know the organization is counting on them and to offer to prepare letters, materials, or special visual aids for them. This kind of service not only fosters a positive relationship, but it also ensures a certain consistency and standard of professionalism in the documents and letters that represent the organization. Phone calls can also help uncover any real or potential problems that might prevent the volunteer from following through on solicitations.

When volunteers succeed, they should be duly honored and recognized. Special events and social get-togethers honoring volunteers should be planned as a regular part of the organization's activities. Volunteers should receive personal thank-you letters from the senior staff, and successful volunteers can be featured in the organization's newsletter. Many organizations present a special award to the volunteer who contributed the most service.

CHAPTER

••••••••

The Annual Fundraising Campaign

A n annual fundraising campaign is a step-by-step process of raising a specific amount of money over a set period of time. The annual campaign should run for a span of one year, corresponding to the organization's fiscal year, and should begin again at the start of the next fiscal year. This regular annual cycle enables the organization to monitor its relationship with each funding source, to track progress toward reaching fundraising goals, and to evaluate the success of each fundraising effort in comparison with past campaigns. A pattern of carefully orchestrated fundraising campaigns conducted on an annual basis leads an organization gradually to build a base of support with a broad range of donors.

It is a far healthier strategy to seek grants (both large and small) from many different sources than to pursue only large grants from just a few. An organization puts itself at risk by counting on the generosity of a small number of donors.

The annual-fundraising-campaign approach also helps the organization avoid the damaging situation of having to appeal for emergency financial support. Funding agencies typically do not respond positively to appeals from organizations in financial crisis. They are reluctant to risk funding an organization with serious financial difficulties; even if they decide to do so, however, they are often unable to respond quickly enough to be of assistance. Most importantly, an organization's credibility in the philanthropic sector diminishes substantially when it appeals for emergency support. It can often take years to rebuild a damaged reputation.

Nonetheless, in certain disastrous situations, it is appropriate to seek support if the crisis is not the obvious consequence of mismanagement. For example, an organization that suffers extensive damage as the result of a flood or fire may successfully raise funds to rebuild by making an emergency appeal.

A successful fundraising effort depends on a well-conceived and well-executed campaign. To achieve this, the organization must do the following:

- Determine goals, strategies, and timetables
- Establish an information and record-keeping system
- Research renewals and prospects
- Develop cultivation plans
- Solicit funding sources
- Build a sense of ownership

DETERMINING GOALS, STRATEGIES, AND TIMETABLES

The goals of a fundraising campaign can be determined once the programs for the coming year have been selected. A strong artistic program is a great advantage in raising funds. Therefore, it is essential that the programs and their costs be known far enough in advance of the new fiscal year—usually from six months to a year ahead, or more for larger initiatives—to allow adequate time to plan and implement the fundraising campaign.

Determining the programs is an exercise of considering potential projects, estimating income and expenses for each of the projects, and then selecting the programs that have both artistic or cultural merit and financial viability. In most cases, the artistic or program director, in consultation with the managing director and other senior staff members, makes the program selections, which are subsequently approved by the board. Once the programs have been approved in concept by the board and senior staff, the development director devises a fundraising strategy to meet the financial needs of the programs. A useful device for determining the fundraising potential of a particular project is the fundability index (see Chart 3.1).

The development director and his or her staff should prepare materials that present the history of the organization, its program and senior personnel, and its tour or exhibition schedules. Press reviews and other documents should be gathered as well. The development director may elect to produce special fundraising brochures aimed at a particular funding-source category, such as the business community.

Based on the costs of the programs, the development director determines contributed-income goals; the marketing director, who is responsible for sales fees and admissions, determines earned-income goals. The final program decisions are based on a realistic analysis of the contributed-income and earned-income projections.

Program _____

Person Responsible _____

Rating Key   5 = Excellent   2 = Needs Work
              4 = Good   1 = Weak
              3 = Fair   0 = Nonexistent

External Need   Rating: _____
Does the program meet existing social, economic, educational, and cultural priorities? (Delineate reasons why program is important.)

Internal Need   Rating: _____
Is the organization's mission and number of participants or audience numbers enhanced? (How will this be achieved?)

Uniqueness   Rating: _____
Is a similar program already in operation by another organization? (How is the program unique? Does it represent an innovative solution to a problem?)

Endorsement   Rating: _____
Has the program received educational or cultural endorsements at national, state, and/or local levels in cities where program activity will be taking place? (Are these available to include in proposals?)

Impact   Rating: _____
How many people are expected to benefit from the program, and how will they benefit?

Measurable Results   Rating: _____
Does the program have an evaluation mechanism built into it to measure how the program has met the internal and external needs?

Fundraising Sources   Rating: _____
Is there a sufficient number of interested prospective donors in the city where program activity will be taking place? Do you know actual names of corporations, foundations, and individuals with an interest in the program?

Visibility/Public Relations   Rating: _____
Do opportunities exist for providing PR and visibility for the organization and the sponsor in the city where program activity will be taking place?

FUNDABILITY INDEX

CHART 3.1

The contributed-income projections must take into account the fundraising history of the organization, the economic climate, changes in patterns of donor contributions, the number of past appeals made to a particular donor, and the attractiveness of the programs to specific donors. It should be kept in mind that, because fundraising depends heavily on personal contacts developed over time, it can often take two to three years of repeated appeals to a likely prospect before a grant is received.

The development director determines contributed-income goals by projecting the amount of contributed support in the last fiscal year in each of four categories: businesses, foundations, individuals, and government agencies. Contributions should be projected at 90 percent of the previous year's level, since there is always the possibility that some gifts will not be renewed or will be renewed at a lower amount.

The development director should then project the number and amount of new gifts in each of the four major contributor categories. The director should use a conservative percentage—generally between 35 and 50 percent—in estimating the amount of money that will be received from currently identified prospects (compared with the amount requested).

Currently identified prospects include sources that have been identified and contacted but have not yet been approached through the formal solicitation process, as well as those that have received proposals from the organization and have expressed an interest in making a grant. Also included in this category are sources that have discontinued their support for a period of time and are now likely to give again.

Finally, a conservative estimate should be made of proceeds from special events, such as gala benefits, to be undertaken during the year.

The campaign goal equals the amount of money already in hand or pledged at the beginning of the fiscal year, plus the funds expected from renewals (projected at 90 percent), plus a percentage of currently identified prospects (projected at 35 to 50 percent), plus a conservative estimate of proceeds from special events. Chart 3.2 gives an illustration of such a campaign support plan.

The development director also constructs a campaign timetable. This timetable outlines the dates of special events and the deadlines for appeals to businesses, foundations, individuals, and government agencies. Deadlines are important: Because many funding agencies prepare their contribution budgets well in advance of the actual funding year, the organization's appeals must be submitted at the appropriate time to ensure eligibility for these funds.

When all projections, goals, and timetables have been established, the development director reviews them with the managing director and the board's development committee, the latter of which examines them in detail. At its next meeting, the full board reviews and approves the campaign plan and strategy. The development director then implements the plan, enlisting the help of board members and the staff, as needed. Regular meetings involving the managing director, development director, and development committee should be held throughout the year to track the campaign's progress.

	Total Funds Received (actual)	Total Funds Pledged (actual)	Total Funds Expected (projected at 90%)	Total Funds Projected from Currently Identified Prospects (projected at 35%–50%)	Campaign Goal*
Private					
Foundations					
Businesses					
Individuals					
• Patrons					
• Lower Level					
Special Events					
Subtotal					
Public					
Federal					
State					
Municipal					
Other					
Subtotal					
TOTAL					

CAMPAIGN SUPPORT PLAN

CHART 3.2

*The campaign goal equals the total funds received, pledged, and expected, plus the amount projected from currently identified prospects.

In addition to meeting fundraising goals, the development director is responsible for running the fundraising campaign efficiently and within certain budget restrictions. As a rule of thumb, no more than 20 or 30 cents should be spent to raise each dollar. There may be circumstances that require organizations to exceed this rule of thumb, such as the need for large-scale donor acquisition telefundraising campaigns, a changeover to new computer systems, or the hiring of a consulting firm for major endowment or special capital campaigns. It is important that funds support *programs*, not fundraising. On the other hand, the institution must ensure that its fundraising staff has adequate equipment and personnel to meet its goals.

ESTABLISHING A RECORD-KEEPING SYSTEM

Arts and cultural organizations need the support of a comprehensive information system to store and retrieve facts pertaining to donors and new prospects and to track the progress of various campaigns. The success of any information system depends on the accurate and prompt recording of information. All the hard work put into cultivating a prospect or donor can be totally undone if a slip-up occurs as a result of incorrect information. An information system also can provide continuity in conducting the campaign from year to year and can facilitate transitions when personnel changes occur.

There is a wide variety of computer software for development available off the shelf, as well as many custom applications. The choice of software is a complex one that requires a whole-organization approach, analyzing the information needs of all departments—especially the accounting or business office. The needs of each organization or type of organization will be unique. It could be helpful to turn to management information specialists for guidance in making these decisions.

Regardless of the specific computer system chosen by an organization to support its development projects, records must include the following basic elements:

- Principal records
- Gift processing transaction histories
- Permanent hard-copy files
- Current campaign tracking
- Campaign status reports

Principal Records

The principal computer record comprises the main name and address record for an individual, company, foundation, or government agency. When the record is first entered, each donor is typically assigned an identification number that stays with the record. The following information is kept in the system for each donor:

- Full name, including title (Mr., Mrs., etc.), first name, middle initial, last name, suffix (Jr., III, etc.), and salutation. Organizations often keep records of nicknames, spouse name (which may include a different last name), and names and nicknames of children. If the record is for a corporation, it may include the names of several different subsidiary firms through which it makes contributions to your organization.
- Address and telephone number. This may include information for the principal residence only, or for summer/winter houses or weekend houses as well. The telephone numbers may include phones at all the above addresses along with fax and car-phone numbers.
- Names, business titles, and telephone and fax numbers of the primary contacts (those individuals with whom the development officer builds an ongoing relationship) at a corporate, foundation, or government funding source.
- Names, titles, and addresses of top officials at a corporation,

foundation, or government agency. (The addresses may be different from the address of the primary contact at the same firm.)

- A set of codes that can describe donor attributes that are unique with respect to your organization. Examples of possible attributes include level of membership (regular, supporting, etc.), type of subscriber or level of contributor (guarantor, pacesetter, etc.), and category of contributor (individual, corporate, foundation, or government). Certain institutions also have auxiliaries and various support groups. There should be a code associated with each of these groups, and the code should appear as appropriate in each member's principal record. Coding helps in the process of sorting and selecting lists.

The information in each file needs to be updated whenever there is a change. Be sure to assign to a specific staff member the responsibility of updating name and address changes. An important feature of any development database is the ability to link individual donor files with corporate and foundation records. This is often referred to as a relational database system. This is useful, for example, when an official in a company is also a personal contributor, subscriber, or member. The ability to call up complete information on a donor's affiliations with the institution allows the development officer to take the best possible approach with that donor.

Gift Processing Transaction Histories

When a contribution is received, the development department is responsible for graciously acknowledging it and thanking the donor. This communication provides another opportunity to move the relationship with the donor to another level. An entry recording the acknowledgement is then placed in the donor's transaction history file. Data related to the gift—such as the amount of the gift, the date received, the purpose for which the gift was given, and the appeal the donor responded to—need to be recorded accurately. Typically, the contributions need to be reconciled with the accounting office on a monthly basis to ensure the totals recorded in development and in accounting are consistent.

Transaction histories also record other types of communication. At the beginning of the fiscal year, organizations often prepare a set of thank-you letters to fit situations that typically arise as the year develops—letters thanking donors who increase their gifts or renew at the same level, for example. Other situations might require a letter to donors who respond to an appeal for a special project or a letter from the institution's chairman to those who have donated above a certain dollar level. The number and type of basic thank-you letters vary depending on the type of fundraising programs and the level of personalization incorporated in the letters. The greater the degree of personalization in the letter, generally the better. But personalization takes staff time, and it may make most sense to personalize only those letters acknowledging gifts above a certain level.

Not-for-profit organizations are required to send donors of $250 or more a receipt acknowledging their contribution and disclosing if there were any goods or services given in exchange for the gift. It is important that an organization check with an attorney regarding these and any other disclosure requirements.

Permanent Hard-Copy File

A permanent file should be maintained to store hard copies of all correspondence, proposals, and reports sent by the development office to the donor. This file can also contain pertinent newspaper and magazine clippings, annual reports (in the case of corporate, foundation, and government funding sources), and other file memos. Copies of any receipts sent to a donor, as well as a copy of the donor's check, should be filed in the donor's hard-copy file. This file, together with the principal record and the transaction history, provides an in-depth, chronological record of the organization's relationship with a funding source or donor. The organization may want to keep individual files for each board member as well. Board members' files should contain correspondence, official biographies, and lists of their funding and community contacts.

Current Campaign Tracking

Campaign tracking is accomplished best by a computerized system that tracks active campaign appeals. It helps the development officer determine the appropriate next step to be taken with an existing donor or a new prospect in order to close the gift. A tracking document should contain the name of the donor or funding source; the amount requested; the date of the request; the purpose, if other than for general funds; and the name of the referee. (The referee is the individual—usually a board member—who knows the prospect or donor personally and is making the contact for the institution.) A comments section should also be included in each document. In the comments section, the development officer records interactions with the donor or prospect, such as follow-up phone calls, requests for additional information by the donor or prospect, decision dates for grant awards, or reminders of important information related to the donor. By reviewing this document regularly, the development officer can keep on top of each request and do what is necessary to bring in the contribution. Once the donation is received, the development officer can strike the donor's name from the tracking list and concentrate on securing the other gifts.

Campaign Status Report

The campaign status report enables the development director to track the progress of the campaign against the goal. The detailed report, which can be set up on the computer at the beginning of the campaign, lists the amount requested of each source within each of the funding categories—businesses, foundations, individuals, and government agencies. As the campaign progresses, the amount actually pledged and then received is pulled in from the database. It is a good idea to include special events as a separate funding source category, because funds generated through these events are often given in addition to general or project funding contributed by the funding source. At the end of each month, the development director runs the detailed report showing each gift in relation to what was requested. A summary report (see Chart 3.3), which indicates by category the totals of gifts received and pledged as compared to the campaign goals, is also run. The summary report is a useful tool for reporting progress in the campaign to board members and senior staff.

	Total Funds Received (actual)	Total Funds Pledged (actual)	Total Funds Received and Pledged	Campaign Goal
Private				
Foundations				
Businesses				
Individuals				
• Patrons				
• Lower Level				
Special Events				
Subtotal				
Public				
Federal				
State				
Municipal				
Other				
Subtotal				
TOTAL				

CAMPAIGN STATUS REPORT SUMMARY

CHART 3.3

RENEWING GIFTS

The most important step to be taken at the beginning of a new annual campaign cycle is to select, sort, and print out a list of all the individuals, governmental agencies, corporations, and foundations that contributed to the organization the year before. The individuals and firms on this list represent the best prospects for support. Accurate lists of renewals should be developed in each of the four major contributor categories.

Each list should include the names of the donors and the amount of their contributions in each of the last three or four years. From this list, the development officer can see the pattern of giving and determine whether a funding source or individual is likely to renew at the same level or at an increased level. If the gift history of a donor is spotty, then the likelihood of renewal is not certain, and the donor is not a good prospect for an increased gift. Before assigning a request amount to the donor's record, the development officer should consult the donor's hard-copy file to see if there are any memos or correspondence that bear on the donor's inclination and ability to renew.

Once the request amounts are assigned, the information needs to be merged into a request for renewed or increased support. The letter of request should be personalized to include the full name and address of the donor or funding source.

RESEARCHING NEW PROSPECTS

Researching is an extremely important step in the fundraising process. It allows the development director to identify those businesses, foundations, individuals, and government agencies that have not contributed before but are the most likely to support the organization. Rather than wasting energy on prospects that have no interest in the organization, the development office should pursue more promising funding sources. Researching new prospects is helpful in other ways, too: it helps discover potential board members and it increases overall understanding of the workings of the philanthropic sector.

Lists of new prospects should be assembled in each of the four contributor categories: businesses, foundations, individuals, and government agencies. Each list should include the full name and address of each prospective donor or funding source; if the potential contributor is an agency or firm, the names of the contact person and of trustees or top officials should also be included.

There are many directories, Internet resources, organizations, and individuals that can be consulted during the research process (see Appendixes C–G). A useful device for recording the information gathered is the research profile (see Charts 3.4 and 3.5).

RESEARCH DATE: 9/95

BRI CORPORATION

Address: **HQ:** 1234 Vanguard Avenue
                 Roswell, MA 56789
                 (800) 555-1212
                 NYC Office: 4321 Harbor View Street
                 New York, NY 98765
                 (212) 555-1212

Business: BRI Corporation is a public company founded in 1929 by the
                 late F. A. Thornton that conducts business under the name of
                 Bay Ridge Investments. BRI provides investment advisory
                 services, mutual fund management on a contract or fee basis,
                 security brokerage services, and real estate management. BRI,
                 which is half owned by Katherine A. Thornton and her family, is
                 the seventh-largest mutual fund company in the United States.
                 The company is also involved in venture capital investing
                 through its Bay Ridge Capital subsidiary. In 1987 Bay Ridge
                 Capital purchased Colonial Art Gallery, a chain of art galleries,
                 and expanded the chain from 5 stores to 17 stores in 1994.
                 Although BRI is based in Roswell, MA, the company also has
                 operations in New York City. The company's NYC-based
                 securities clearing operation serves BRI brokerage customers and
                 handles back-office work for over 150 other brokerage firms.

Company Data, YE 12/94:
                 Revenue: $5.2 billion (up 46%)
                 Net Income: $510 million (up 80%)
                 Assets Under Management: $380 million (up 36%)
                 Employees: 5,000

Officers: Katherine A. Thornton   Chair, President, and CEO
                 David X. Smith, III   Vice Chair
                 Edward Rivera, Jr.   CFO and Sr. VP
                 Dorothy Dudley   Executive VP
                 Maria Ruiz   Managing Director
Directors: Robert Boyd   President, Bay Ridge
                                                   Capital Corporation
                 Lisa Rodriguez   Vice President, Micro-
                                                   computer Data, Inc.
                 Pamela Gill   President, Bay Ridge
                                                   Management Co.
                 Joan Rowland   Founder & President,
                                                   Four Hands Piano Co.
                 John M. Thornton   Chair, Pres. & CEO,
                                                   Woodbridge Lane, Inc.

HYPOTHETICAL CORPORATE RESEARCH PROFILE

CHART 3.4

Philanthropy:	The Bay Ridge Investments Foundation
	1234 Vanguard Avenue
	Roswell, MA 56789
	(800) 555-1212
Contact:	Cynthia Stokes, Executive Director
Donor:	Established in 1955 in MA with funds donated by the BRI Corp.
Directors:	Katherine A. Thornton President
	Joan Rowland Vice President
	James Coppola Director
	Hugh C. Roberts Director
Interests:	Supports community development, social services, and the arts. In the arts, support is provided for: museums, music, theater, dance, and historic preservation. Types of support include: building funds, special projects, endowment funds, employee matching gifts, capital campaign funds, and technical assistance. Giving primarily in Boston, Cincinnati, Dallas, and in communities where BRI employees live and work.
Financial Data:	Assets: $42 million YE 12/94
	Gifts Received: $500,000—BRI Corporation
Grant Data:	Grants Paid: $2,295,004 Number of Grants: 280
	High Grant: $175,000—Narrow Victory Memorial Hospital
	Typical Range: $5,000–$20,000
Sample Grants:	Dallas Museum of Art $50,000
	Portland Museum of Art 25,000
	American Repertory Theater 15,000
	Arts and Business Council of NYC 15,000
	National Arts Stabilization Fund 15,000
	Wang Center for the Performing Arts 15,000
	Boston Chamber Music Society 10,000
	Boston Ballet 10,000
	Dallas Symphony Association 5,000
Gifts:	6/95 $7,500 Creative Dance, Corp. Underwriter
	9/94 $250 Symphony Orchestra, Matching Gift
	4/94 $5,000 French Opera, Corporate Sponsor
Contacts:	Trustee Richard A. Doe might know John M. Thornton (President and CEO, Woodbridge Lane Industries, Inc.), since both serve on the board of the New York Stock Exchange.
Sources:	Donor records system and file; BRI Corporation 1994 Annual Report, 10K and 1995 Proxy; The Foundation Directory 1995; Corporate Giving Directory 1995; Dun & Bradstreet Corp. Ref. Book 1995; *Wall Street Journal* Abstracts 3/14/95—Nexis; Standard & Poor's Directory 1994; Reuters 3/4/94—Nexis; Directory of Directors 1995; The Foundation Center Phone Ref.

HYPOTHETICAL CORPORATE RESEARCH PROFILE

CHART 3.4   (CONTINUED)

RESEARCH DATE: 11/96

JOHN M. THORNTON

Address:	**Home:**
	1234 Owls Head Court
	Los Angeles, CA 87654
	(310) 555-1212

567 25th Avenue
New York, NY 34567
(212) 555-1212

Office:
Woodbridge Lane Industries, Inc
1 Woodbridge Lane Center
Los Angeles, CA 23456
(310) 555-1212

Employment: Chair, President and CEO, Woodbridge Lane Industries, Inc., 1993–; Business: diversified public company involved in financial services, chemical manufacturing, aircraft leasing; Revenues: $575 million YE 12/93

Career: Rowland & Thornton Home Corp.: Chair, 1986–93
Thornton, Inc.: Pres., and CEO, 1989–93
Rowland & Thornton, Inc.: Chair, President, and
CEO, 1986–89
Chair and CEO, 1976–86
Chair and President, 1957–75
Co-founded company, 1957
Hamilton Institute of Technology: Asst.
Professor, 1956–57
Accountant, 1954–56
Note: Rowland & Thornton Home Corp. was spun off from Rowland & Thornton, Inc. in 1989, with the remaining company renamed Thornton, Inc. In 1993 Thornton, Inc. was renamed Woodbridge Lane Industries, Inc.

Professional Chair: Keithley National Life Insurance Co.
Affiliations: (subs., Woodbridge Lane Industries, Inc.)
Coast Life Insurance Co. of America (subs.,
Woodbridge Lane)
Director: New York Stock Exchange
Rowland & Thornton Home Corp. (Exec.
Committee Chair)

HYPOTHETICAL INDIVIDUAL RESEARCH PROFILE

CHART 3.5.

	BRI Corporation
	Federal National Mortgage Association
	Chase Manhattan Bank Corporation
	Greenpoint Aircraft, Inc. (subs., Woodbridge
	Lane Industries, Inc.)
	Member: California Business Roundtable
Charitable	President: John M. Thornton Family Foundation
Affiliations:	(see **Philanthropy**)
	Chair: Metropolitan Opera
	Trustee: Brooklyn College Foundation
	California Institute of Technology
	Archives of American Art, Smithsonian Instit.
	Manhattan Theater Club
	American Federation of the Arts
Personal:	Born: April 1, 1933; New York, NY
	Education: BA, cum laude, Bus. Admin., Poly-
	technic University, 1954
	Mother: Rebecca (Jacobson) Thornton (dec.)
	Father: Richard S. Thornton
	Spouse: Jane Lawson Thornton (m. 12/19/54; VP: John
	M. Thornton Family Foundation)
	Children: Barbara Thornton-Smith; Fenella
	Thornton; Hugh Thornton
	Siblings: David Thornton
	Clubs: Regency; Hillcrest Country (Los Angeles)
Awards:	Man of Year Award, Los Angeles, CA, 1970
	Golden Plate Award, American Academy of
	Achievement, 1974
	Humanitarian Award, N.C.C.J., 1978
	Housing Man of the Year, National Housing
	Conference, 1980
	American Heritage Award, American League, 1983
	Public Affairs Award, Smith Foundation, 1984
	Honors Award in Visual Arts, L.A. Arts Council, 1987
Interests:	Art collector of museum-quality works from
	approximately 1910 to the present, with a concentration
	on American art of the 70s, 80s, and 90s.
Wealth:	Compensation: As President and CEO of Woodbridge
	Lane Industries, Inc., 1993
	$2.4 million (cash salary and bonus)
	$8.2 million (cash realized on exercise of stock options)
	$1.8 million (value of restricted stock awarded)
	$12.4 million (total value of 1993 compensation)

Hypothetical Individual Research Profile

CHART 3.5 (CONTINUED)

	Stock Holdings: Woodbridge Lane Industries, Inc.
	Common stock: 587,366 shares (12/93)
	Fair market value of common: $22.3 million (11/94)
	Restricted stock: 95,314 shares (12/93)
	Fair market value of restricted: $3.6 million (11/94)
	Class B stock: 3,734,523 shares (12/93)
	Fair market value of class B: $92.4 million (11/94)
	Unexercised exercisable options: 110,900 shares (12/93)
	In-the-money value of options: $3.8 million (12/93)
	Unexercised unexcercisable opt.: 217,000 shares (12/93)
	In-the-money value of options: $5.9 million (12/93)
	Rowland & Thornton Home Corp.
	Common stock: 1,284,000 shares (1/92)
	Fair market value of common: $16.7 million (11/94)
Philanthropy:	John M. Thornton Family Foundation
	9876 Neptune Avenue, 38th Floor
	Los Angeles, CA 12345
	(310) 555-1212
Donor:	Established in 1980 in CA with funds donated by John M. Thornton.
Officers:	John M. Thornton President
	Jane L. Thornton Vice President
	Peter Q. Doe Secretary
	Cindy S. Smith Treasurer
	The Thornton Family Foundation is a private operating foundation with a collection of contemporary art available for loan to accredited museums and university galleries. The foundation provides support primarily for organizations that support the exhibition of contemporary American art. Giving primarily in CA. Applications not accepted.
Financial Data:	Assets: $31.9 million YE 6/93
	Gift Received: $2 Million—John M. Thornton
Grant Data:	Grants Paid: $27,000 Number of Grants: 8
	Foundation-administered programs: $1,577,477
Grants List:	National Gallery of Art $10,000
	Archives of American Art 5,000
	Lehman College Art Gallery 5,000
	American Friends of Israel Museum 2,000
	UCLA Art Council 2,000
	DIA Center for the Arts 1,000
	San Francisco Museum of Art 1,000
	Whitney Museum of Art 1,000

HYPOTHETICAL INDIVIDUAL RESEARCH PROFILE

CHART 3.5 (CONTINUED)

Foundation	Art Acquisition Program	$1,258,108
Programs:	Art Exhibition Program	$183,903
	Art Study Center	135,466
Other Philanthropy:	Brooklyn College, 1993	3 million
	Museum of Contemporary Art, 1985	1 million +
	California Institute of the Arts, 1992	$500,000
Gifts:	None	
Contacts:	Trustee Richard A. Doe knows John Thornton through the board of Polytechnic University.	
Sources:	Donor records system; Who's Who in American Art 1993–94; Woodbridge Lane Industries, Inc. 1993 Proxy; Guide to U.S. Foundations 1994; *Los Angeles Times* 11/12/93, 10/5/85—Nexis.	

HYPOTHETICAL INDIVIDUAL RESEARCH PROFILE

CHART 3.5 (CONTINUED)

The list of new prospects should include promising sources as well as past donors who have not contributed recently. Soliciting those that have not contributed for several years may prove fruitful, because circumstances that prevented them from contributing may have changed. However, if a reason has been given for denying support, and if there is evidence that the reason still holds, no request should be made.

A likely new prospect is a source that has demonstrated an interest in the organization, such as through a subscription purchase or through attendance at a single performance or special event. Equally promising are personal friends and business colleagues of board members. Other likely new prospects may be those that support similar organizations in the community or region.

The best way to identify these prospects is to regularly peruse the organization's subscriber, membership, and ticket-buyer lists and to examine the programs and annual reports of similar organizations in the area. Short lists of new prospects should be circulated among board members on a regular basis for their reactions.

Culture is only one of many philanthropic causes for which 'charitable support is solicited. Most businesses, foundations, and individuals contribute to those causes in which they have a special interest. It is a waste of time to pursue prospects that have demonstrated no interest in the organization's particular area of activity unless there are exceptional circumstances, such as close personal contacts at the board level.

Donors often prefer to support organizations within specific geographic areas. Some corporations, for instance, support organizations in communities where they have plants or branch offices. Therefore, it is important to research all appropriate funding sources local to the organization. Only organizations with a national scope will be successful in raising funds outside their own regions unless, of course, key individuals have close personal contacts at funding sources in other regions. Exceptions to this rule may also be made by organizations that regularly tour or travel—sending their exhibitions or performers to other locations.

The inclination of prospective donors to give is also dependent on their financial ability to make contributions. During economic downturns, for example, many businesses will cut back giving in all but a few primary areas; in extreme cases, they may cut out giving entirely. When analyzing funding prospects in the business community, it is important to determine the financial condition of each business, as well as the economic condition of the industry and related industries. In general, in researching a prospect's inclination to give, organizations should look at the history of contributions by that prospect. If it hasn't given elsewhere, it probably does not tend to be philanthropic.

Research should also reveal the type of support a particular donor gives and the usual amount of the contribution. There are five basic types of financial support: general, project, capital, endowment, and matching or challenge. Capital support and endowment support are not considered part of an annual campaign to raise funds for current operations.

- *General support.* This type of funding is unrestricted as to its use. General support typically covers operating expenses such as telephones, salaries, administration, and general program costs. It can be requested on an annual basis.
- *Project support.* This type of funding is restricted to the support of a specific project for which the institution has requested funds. Project grants are often awarded on a one-time-only basis and are not renewable.
- *Capital support.* This type of funding is given for building, renovation, or construction projects, as well as for the purchase of equipment. Capital support is usually given on a one-time-only basis. Grants for construction projects are frequently referred to as "bricks-and-mortar" grants.
- *Endowment support.* This type of funding is given to an organization to begin or to add to its endowment fund. An endowment is a reserve of funds that the organization invests in a variety of ways to yield the maximum interest and dividends. The income from these investments is used by the organization to pay its expenses. If the principal is properly invested, it will provide long-term financial security for the organization. An organization is ready to embark on an endowment campaign only if it has a long-range plan and is financially stable. It should have an operating cash reserve as well as solid support from a substantial number of donors and no accumulated debt (see Chapter

9 for more information). An operating cash reserve is set aside by the institution for special opportunities or emergencies; it can also be used to ease cash-flow problems by borrowing from it rather than from a bank (thus avoiding interest payments). A cash reserve should be replenished at the end of each fiscal year and increased in accordance with budgetary growth.

- *Matching grants or challenge grants.* These types of grants are awarded on the condition that the dollar amount of the grant is equaled, or matched, by dollars contributed from other sources. The match can be a direct one-to-one ratio or a multiple of as much as three-to-one. Many grants from the National Endowment for the Arts, for example, have been of this type. The "challenge" is made by a funding source to an organization, requiring that it raise a certain amount of funds from other contributors before the source will match the funds offered in the challenge grant. Funds provided through matching or challenge grants can be earmarked for general, project, capital, or endowment support.

Other types of support, such as bequests and deferred or planned gifts through trusts, annuities, and pooled-income funds, are not, in most cases, part of an annual campaign to fund current operations. Rather, they are usually associated with endowment and capital campaigns. To secure these types of gifts, specialized legal and financial expertise is often required (see Chapter 9).

The size of gifts to an annual campaign varies widely, depending on the funding source; contribution levels usually relate to the total amount of money set aside for contributions. For example, if a business has a total annual-contribution budget of $80,000, it would not under normal circumstances approve a request for a grant of $20,000. A request for $1,000 to $5,000 would be more appropriate.

Organizations need to evaluate renewal candidates and new prospects in terms of all the above-mentioned criteria. It is not unusual for the giving policies of businesses to vary from year to year due to changes in personnel, financial performance, or perception of community needs. Individuals' philanthropic interests also change. Therefore, it is wise to do regular research and to keep records and contacts current.

Prospect Research Information Sources

This section gives a general introduction to the types of information sources that can aid organizations in researching donors and prospects. Lists of specific research sources can be found in Appendixes B–I.

Directories

Concise information on thousands of individuals, corporations, foundations, government agencies, and associations can be found in numerous annual directories. When using directories, researchers should be aware that some individuals, corporations, and other philanthropists might not be prominent enough outside the local community to be included in a national or international directory. In such cases, a regional or state directory would be of more use. Also of use in such cases are specialized directories that provide information about individuals or corporations in particular professions or industries. Depending on the publisher, directories are available in print, CD-ROM, or on-line form.

Periodicals

Newspapers, magazines, and newsletters can greatly expand the amount of information available about a prospect. For example, a magazine article might shed light on the source or extent of a prospect's wealth or on his or her interest in the arts and in philanthropic activities. Newspaper and newsletter stories can provide recent information about corporate earnings, management changes, or philanthropic and sponsorship interests. A useful tool for locating newspaper or magazine stories is a newspaper or periodical index in either print or computer form. In addition, on-line services can provide abstracts or full-text articles from thousands of newspapers and periodicals. Another method for locating news articles is contacting the newspaper or magazine directly. Some newspapers and magazines make research services available to the public for a fee. One other method is to contact the local library or historical society in the prospect's town. The local library might maintain a clippings file on locally prominent individuals and corporations, and a check of that material might turn up articles of interest about the prospect.

Annual Reports

In the United States, a publicly held company is one that issues stock traded on an exchange or in the over-the-counter market. Publicly held companies will almost always provide annual reports to nonshareholders upon request. Private companies, with some exceptions such as banks and insurance companies, very rarely provide annual reports to the public. The financial reports (annual report, 10-K, proxy, and so on) of a publicly held company contain a great deal of information about both the company's operations and its officers and directors. The proxy statement is of particular interest, because it provides compensation and stock-ownership information for the top five officers of a company. In addition, it lists the stock ownership and affiliations of the company's directors. Large foundations, both private and corporate, usually publish annual reports, grant application guidelines, and information on areas of programmatic interest. Typically, a foundation's annual report lists its directors, its assets, and recent grants paid. In most cases, small to mid-sized foundations and corporate giving programs provide only grant guidelines. Also of interest to prospect researchers are the annual reports of other non-profit organizations, because they usually list trustees and contributors.

Federal Government

Various federal regulatory agencies require that individuals, corporations, and foundations file public disclosure documents. The most familiar federal agency among prospect researchers is the Securities and Exchange Commission (SEC). Among the many filings required of public companies by the SEC are: 10-K (comprehensive annual report), 10-Q (quarterly financial report), proxy statement (annual meeting notification), and 20-F (10-K for certain foreign companies with registered securities in the United States). The SEC also requires certain individuals to file disclosure documents such as: Form 3 (initial disclosure of stock owned by directors, officers, and 10-percent share-holders of a company), Form 4 (amendment to Form 3, reporting a sale or purchase of stock), Form 5 (annual statement of beneficial ownership of stock), Form 144 (notice of the proposed sale of restricted stock), and Schedule 13D (disclosure of the beneficial owners of more than 5 percent of a stock). The financial documents of public companies are available from private vendors in print, CD-ROM, or on-line form, as well as from the SEC. Another well-known government agency, the Internal Revenue Service (IRS), requires nonprofit public charities and private foundations to file annual financial reports. IRS annual reports are filed on Form 990 for a public charity and on Form 990PF for a private foundation. The Federal Election Commission requires all federal candidates to file financial disclosure reports listing net worth, sources of income, investments, liabilities, and positions held outside the U.S. government. It should be noted that other government agencies, such as the Office of Thrift Supervision, the Federal Deposit Insurance Corporation, the Comptroller of the Currency, and the Federal Reserve Board, require annual filings for thrifts, state-chartered banks, commercial banks, federally chartered national banks, and bank holding companies. In addition, the Federal Energy Regulatory Commission requires that electric, natural gas, and oil pipeline companies file annual reports with their agency. Overall, there are more than 30 federal government agencies that require filing of disclosure documents of one form or another.

State Government

Like the federal government, state governments are a source of information on those corporations, foundations, and individuals within the state's jurisdiction. The type, location, and public availability of this information varies from state to state. A brief overview of several state government offices will provide an understanding of where to locate information of interest in prospect research. In the office of the secretary of state, corporations file articles of incorporation and amendments, annual reports, and limited partnership agreements. The State Banking Office requires similar filings for the state-chartered banks it oversees. The State Insurance Commission is responsible for regulating insurance companies doing business within a state and requires them to file annual reports containing financial information. The annual reports of nonprofit public charities, private foundations, and tax-exempt charitable trusts can be found at the office of the attorney general in the state where the organization is registered. The State Health Department maintains birth and death records and sometimes marriage and divorce records. The licensing of professional occupations is carried out by several state offices, including the Accountancy Board, the Securities Commission, the Education Department, and the Medical Board.

County Government

Local government offices offer the prospect researcher information on real estate ownership, estates, fictitious business names, and marriage and divorce records. Information on real estate ownership is available at the office of the county assessor, which is usually located at the county seat. It should be noted that large cities typically have a city assessor separate from the county and also that in some states all real estate assessment is done locally by the town assessor. Most assessors will provide real estate information over the phone, with the exception of some city assessors who handle requests by mail only. Depending on the assessor, real estate information can be located using either the property address or the name of the owner. The researcher should keep in mind that the property address might be different from the mailing address of the owner. This difference might be an indicator of additional real estate holdings or of business interests in another county or state. In addition to the assessed value of a property, the "assessment to fair market value" ratio should also be requested to obtain a more accurate valuation for the property. Local governments are also a good source of information regarding a deceased person's estate, which can be found in the Surrogate or Probate Court Office in the county or city were the deceased maintained primary residence. Typically, an estate file will contain a copy of the will, codicils to the will, the estate inventory, and the estate distribution. Information regarding a trust that was not established by the will of the deceased will not be found in the estate file, however. Another local government entity that can provide the researcher with information is the office of the county clerk. An individual or corporation doing business in the county using a fictitious name, or d.b.a., is required to register the name with the County Clerk's Office. Depending on the county, a fictitious name statement may list the owner of the business, the type of business, and other names under which the business has operated. Marriage certificates and divorce records can also be found at the County Clerk's Office. Divorce records may include financial information and, in the case of a contested divorce, may include an IRS tax return.

Associations

Professional associations have membership rosters, specialized libraries, and detailed knowledge of particular professions or industries that can be of enormous help in the research process. The membership roster of a local chamber of commerce is a typical example. The chamber of commerce can provide information regarding the nature, contact person, and address of a local business. Consider the case of a prospect researcher who is trying to determine the name and address of a tugboat company that is the source of a family's wealth. By contacting an association of tugboat and barge operators, the researcher would be able to obtain both the name and the address of the company with one phone call. Two organizations of special interest in the field of prospect research are the Foundation Center and the Association of Professional Researchers for Advancement. The Foundation Center is a nonprofit organization that publishes directories and operates five libraries providing information about private foundations and philanthropy. The Foundation Center is best known for its microfiche collection of private foundation tax returns (IRS Form 990PF). In addition to the libraries, the Foundation Center also operates cooperating collections in all 50 states. The core holdings of a cooperating collection consist of the various foundation directories published by the center. At least one cooperating collection in each state includes tax returns for foundations located within the state and possibly neighboring states. The Association of Professional Researchers for Advancement (APRA) is a professional association of researchers, development officers, and consultants involved in the field of prospect research at nonprofit organizations. APRA publishes a quarterly newsletter and holds an annual conference dealing with research techniques and sources as well as issues of interest to prospect researchers. In addition, APRA has more than 20 local chapters in the United States, which enables members to meet and discuss issues of interest in the field between annual meetings.

On-line Services

On-line databases increase not only the speed at which information can be retrieved but also the scope of sources that can be searched. For example, locating an obituary that appeared in the *New York Times* 10 or 12 years ago can be done in a few minutes using a full-text on-line information service. Locating the obituary without the use of a computer would require a search through several newspaper indexes at the library to find the correct date and page number, after which the correct microfilm would have to be found and the obituary photocopied. If the obituary had appeared in a newspaper without an index, the task of locating it would be even more time consuming. For prospect researchers, easy access to thousands of English and foreign-language newspapers and periodicals is the major advantage provided by on-line databases. In addition, on-line services provide access to corporate directories, biographical directories, stock quotes, news wire stories, radio and television transcripts, and demographic and marketing information. Government documents such as SEC filings, real estate assessments, deed transfers, local and state judgments and liens, federal tax liens, state corporation filings, and state limited partnership filings are also available on-line. By using on-line services, researchers can get depth of coverage as well as scope. *Business Week,* for example, is available on-line from several information providers. Depending on the provider, however, access to back issues can vary from the last few years to the last two decades. (See Appendixes C and D for information on research sources.)

Internet Research

The Internet provides an additional tool with which to locate information about prospects. Finding information on the Internet in an efficient manner can be a challenge because there are so many Internet sites. However, there are several ways in which the Internet can be of use to prospect researchers. First, as more corporations and foundations establish a presence on the Internet, information regarding officers, directors, financial data, application guidelines, and grant listings can often be found on their sites. The type of information that can be found will, of course, vary from site to site. Second, the Internet can be use to access public documents held by government agencies. For example, the Securities and Exchange Commission maintains an Internet site with a database of corporate filings such as 10Ks, 10Qs, and proxy statements. In addition, many state and local governments maintain a presence on the Internet and the information they provide can be of use in the research process. Third, many nonprofit organizations and for-profit information providers such as newspaper, magazine, book, and electronic publishing companies have established Internet sites on which they offer a variety of information. The information at these sites can be available free of charge or for a fee. In addition, some sites offer free samples but require a fee to access additional information. Appendix C includes a brief listing of Internet sites that prospect researchers will find useful. The majority of sites listed in Appendix C have links to other Internet sites. These links will quickly multiply the number of prospect research related Internet sites that can be explored. See also Appendix D.

DEVELOPING CULTIVATION PLANS

After compiling lists of renewal candidates and new prospects, it must be determined who will share with the development director the responsibility of approaching, or "cultivating," prospective donors. The individuals designated to help approach prospective donors on behalf of the cultural organization are called referees. The cultivation plan identifies the methods leading to the actual request or solicitation.

The list of renewal candidates should be circulated to all board members to determine who among them might know individual donors or key people associated with institutional funding sources; such board members would appropriately act as referees. This is particularly helpful in cases where the organization is asking a funding source for an increased level of support. Even when relationships are already established with renewal candidates, it makes sense to follow this process, because it may uncover stronger contacts and new information. The membership of the organization's board of trustees, and the decision makers of the institutional funding sources, may have changed during the year. It is always important to identify new contacts.

The list of new prospects, which includes the names of funding sources—and, in the case of businesses, foundations, and government agencies, their top officials—should also be circulated to board members in advance of the campaign and throughout the year as additional prospects are identified, and again, trustees should identify the individuals they know. The development director then arranges to meet with each board member to discuss how each funding source should be approached—in a personal meeting with a representative of the funding source, through a letter written on personal or business stationery, or through a telephone call—and what the development director's role should be. When appropriate, the managing director and program director should be asked to participate in solicitations.

Once the referees and cultivation plans have been determined, the development director should make the solicitation process easy for them by drafting all appeal letters for their approval and by preparing accompanying materials and setting up appointments. The development director must make certain that all referees receive the proper information and backup materials and that all carry out their responsibilities.

SOLICITING THE FUNDING SOURCE

After the development director has determined the cultivation plan, the actual solicitation of the gift can take place. The solicitation process usually involves the following steps: a telephone call is made, an introductory letter is sent (see Appendix K) or a proposal package is submitted, and a face-to-face meeting takes place. The process is not necessarily this formal when individuals are being solicited.

Introductory Telephone Call or Letter

To initiate the solicitation process, the development director usually makes a telephone call directly to the funding source. This call, often made to an assistant or secretary, informs the funding source that a request for funds will be submitted. The call also allows the development director to verify basic information about the individual or agency, such as the correct spelling of names and the appropriate person to address. This call should be kept brief—it is not a substitute for in-depth research. If for some reason the funding source cannot be reached on the telephone, it is appropriate to write a letter. In the case of individuals, the solicitation process is often initiated by the referee rather than by the development director.

Proposal Package

The proposal package is made up of a cover letter, the proposal, and accompanying materials. The letter should be written to the individual prospect, to the grants officer, to the president, or to whomever has been identified as the appropriate contact person at the business or foundation. This letter should briefly mention the nature of the particular request and describe the accompanying materials. If the grant request is to a past contributor, there should be a statement of thanks for past support. In a request for general operating support, all the items normally included in the proposal and the covering letter are often incorporated into one appeal letter. The proposal should

- Introduce the organization and state its purpose and mission.
- Indicate why the organization is unique and worthy of support from the particular funding source.
- Briefly describe the project or general program of the organization for which funds are being requested.
- Cite some of the organization's program highlights; the audience, attendance, or participation figures; positive critical reviews; and associations with notable people.
- Mention a few of the organization's major current donors. This serves as an endorsement of the organization and may enhance its credibility with the particular funding source. Small and new organizations that may not be widely known need to pay special attention to this area of their proposal. The mention of current donors may not be as necessary when dealing with a source familiar with the institution as it is with new prospects. A complete list of donors is typically included as an attachment to the proposal.

- Make the request for funds. Ask for an appropriate amount of money, which has been determined through prior research. Indicate as specifically as possible the benefit of the potential contribution to the organization; if applicable, mention public relations advantages or employee benefits that the contributing business would accrue, such as credits on promotional materials, free admissions, discount tickets, special events, or a ticket hotline service.
- Indicate that a follow-up call will be made in about a week by the development director to make sure the proposal has been received and to set up a meeting or to offer an invitation to attend a performance or tour the facilities.

REVENUE
  Ticket Sales $
  Parking Lot Concession
  Hall Rentals
  Concessions and Other Income
  Advertising Sales
  Touring Fees
                                    Subtotal $_____

PUBLIC AND PRIVATE SUPPORT
  Private $
    Foundations
    Businesses
    Individuals
    • Patrons
    • Lower Level
  Public
    Federal
    State
    Municipal
                                    Subtotal $_____
                              Total All Income $_____

EXPENSES
  Program $
  Administration
  Interest
  Parking Lot
  Equipment Rental
  Rent
  Utilities
                                    Subtotal $_____
                            Total All Expenses $_____

ORGANIZATIONAL BUDGET

CHART 3.6

Generally, the proposal should be concise—no longer than two or three pages. A lengthy proposal will most likely not be read. When a major project is being developed in conjunction with a funding source, a more lenghty, in-depth proposal may be needed. The proposal should present the organization in the most professional and organized manner possible. It should be accu-

---

New Theatrical Production

EXPENSES

Commissioning Fees	$
Performers' Fees	
Stagehands	
Wardrobe	
Advertising and Promotion	
Legal and Insurance	
Box Office	
Ushers	
Maintenance and Security	
Mail-Order House	
Postage	
Instrument Tuning	
Administrative and Benefits*	
Printing	
Total All Expenses	$_____

INCOME

Earned $
   Ticket Sales

Private and Public Support
(List actual sources if known)
  Private
    Businesses
    Foundations
    Individuals
  Public
    Federal
    State
    Municipal

Total All Income	$_____
Amount remaining to be raised	$
Amount requested from (name of source)	$

PROGRAM BUDGET

CHART 3.7

*Percentage of total administrative costs allocated to this program.

rately typeset and easy to read. (For examples of some proposals, see Appendix K: Corporate General-Support Proposal, Corporate Special Project Proposals I and II, and Foundation Special Project Proposal.)

The materials accompanying the proposal should be those specific pieces of background information most necessary to funding sources in making their funding decisions. The following items should accompany requests:

- Overall organizational budget and, if requesting special-project support, individual project budgets. (Clear, comprehensive budgets are essential to the proposal package; see Charts 3.6 and 3.7 for examples of budget formats.)
- Brief history of the institution and statement of future plans.
- List of donors from the previous fiscal year.
- IRS 501(c)(3) tax exempt identification letter.
- List of board members and their professional affiliations.
- Schedule of programs taking place during the year.
- Most recent audited financial statement.
- Most recent annual report.
- Illustrative materials, such as brochures, newspaper clippings, and magazine reprints.

These documents should accompany most requests made during the campaign. The history and plans, donor list, board list, and program schedule should be accurately typed on the organization's letterhead and reproduced in quantity by offset printing. If information in these documents changes significantly, they should be updated and reprinted. The funding source should not be inundated with reviews, brochures, and other publicity materials. Instead, it is best to send only the most significant documents.

The Meeting

The meeting is of primary importance to the success of the funding request. Because of the enormous number of requests that funding sources receive and the even greater number of persons trying to contact them, it can be difficult to schedule an appointment. It is important, however, to establish a working relationship with the funding-source contact and to pursue an appointment. A personal encounter with the contact is more effective than a proposal alone. Relationship building can often be the key to a successful fundraising effort.

Making the call to request an appointment is one of the hardest parts of a fundraiser's job. The referee can be helpful in securing the appointment either by making the call directly or by allowing the development director to mention his or her name. When making a cold call, the development director should refer to the introductory letter or proposal and explain that a meeting is the best way to convey the impact of the project and its compatibility with the funding source's grant-making objectives.

Once an appointment has been made, the development director must be prepared to present the organization as programmatically significant and administratively sound. The following points should be kept in mind when meeting with the funding source:

- Be on time for the appointment.
- Begin the discussion by reiterating the goals of the organization and then explain the administrative structure that backs up the programmatic aims. Establish the credibility of the institution. This is particularly important for small and mid-sized organizations, which may not be as well known in their communities as larger institutions. A quick review of the organization's mission and history, as well as the mention of prominent board members, will help generate credibility.
- It may make sense to include other appropriate representatives of the organization at this meeting—perhaps the program director or managing director or a board member. Usually no more than three persons from the organization should attend. These representatives must be well informed and articulate and must contribute to the meeting.
- After providing a general description of the institution, explain the project, the reason for requesting funds, and how the donor will benefit by lending support. For example, if the donor is concerned about reaching teenagers from low-income neighborhoods and the project addresses that issue, then it is critical to make the connection in a manner that will be obvious to the potential funder.
- Explain how the project will be managed. Include a brief description of the marketing campaign (articulating how the target audience will be reached) and the fundraising effort. Donors like to know who else is participating and if the other donors are good partners for their grantmaking goals. If a donor demands exclusivity, it is important to assure the funder that its condition will be honored by the institution.
- Review the package of benefits the donor will receive if it chooses to support the project, including credits on all related press and promotional material, tickets, participation in special events, and product sampling (if requested). (See Chapter 9 for a complete description of corporate sponsor benefits.) Give the donor an opportunity to help shape the sponsor benefit package and to describe not only its requirements from the institutions it supports, but how it would like to participate.

- Be prepared to answer questions about the composition of the audience, the budget, and the uniqueness of the proposed project. Present the institution as administratively sound, well organized, and artistically viable.
- Always dress in a manner that will make the donor comfortable. If the meeting is taking place in a formal corporate setting, it is wise for the representatives of the institution to appear at the meeting formally dressed. Be positive and clear, and keep the meeting concise. Take time to listen; this is a chance to hear directly from the source how its funding decisions are made and what its interests and policies are. Don't waste time trying to influence the donor to fund something in which it has no interest. Either look for a way to connect its goals to the institution and its request or accept the fact that this prospect is unlikely to fund. In the latter case, thank the contact for his or her time and leave graciously.
- As soon as possible after the meeting, the development director should write to thank the potential funder for taking the time to meet.
- If the request for funds results in a grant, send a thank-you letter and official receipt shortly after the funds are received; if funds are denied, send a note of appreciation for considering the proposal. Good manners always count in the fundraising process.

BUILDING A SENSE OF OWNERSHIP

Successful fundraising requires that the organization's leaders build a sense of shared ownership among the staff, board of trustees, audience, donors, and community at large. By instilling a sense of ownership in actual and prospective donors, the organization enhances the likelihood of receiving contributions and grants and of having them renewed in subsequent years. A sense of ownership can be developed through such thoughtful donor services as newsletters, priority ticket services, and receptions. Certainly, all donors should be included on the organization's general mailing list, and information about performances, programs, exhibitions, and special events should be sent to them on a regular basis.

Keeping donors informed is one of the most important, though often neglected, activities in a fundraising campaign. To sustain their interest and encourage their involvement, donors should be kept aware of new activities and programs, new appointments to the board, staff changes, and grants received. Newsletters, donor magazines, and press releases are excellent vehicles for conveying this information.

Donors should also be invited to performances, exhibitions, screenings, and lectures/demonstrations. There is no more effective way for a donor or prospective donor to become involved in the organization than by experiencing its activities firsthand. Complimentary tickets, VIP seating, and priority subscriptions are extra benefits that can be made available to donors.

Special premium packages can be developed for donors at various contribution levels. Premiums may include use of a patron lounge at performances; invitations to special receptions; discounts on tickets and boutique items; offers of merchandise such as tote bags, books, or records; or subscriptions to a newsletter or magazine.

Special premiums can also be developed for employees of corporations contributing at a specified level. These premiums may include discounts on merchandise and tickets or free parking and admission passes for the employees' families. On the other hand, it is important that merchandise and services not be given away too cheaply and that delivering them efficiently not require an excessive amount of staff time.

Organizations should attempt to communicate with donors in ways other than requesting funds. The organization should express appreciation to donors for their generosity at every opportunity—by sending them holiday greeting cards, for example, or by giving them souvenir booklets and anniversary programs that list their names.

An annual report should be produced at the end of each fiscal year and should be made available to both donors and the general public. The annual report is the organization's external statement of its financial and programmatic performance during the preceding year. The report should summarize the organization's activities and management practices and should state the amount of funds raised, the donors, and the manner in which the funds were spent. The organization's audited financial statements should also be included. Every organization, no matter how small, should produce an annual report. The annual report need not be a glossy four-color book to give an effective presentation of the organization's achievements. (See Appendix K, "Annual Report," for an example.)

CHAPTER 4

Businesses

Businesses, recognizing the important work done by not-for-profit organizations in the United States, have supported health, education, and welfare causes to varying degrees since the 1940s. It was not until the 1970s, however, that businesses began to contribute to arts and culture in a sizable way. The Business Committee for the Arts (see Appendix I) reported that in 1967 businesses contributed $22 million to the arts and that by 1994 the figure had risen to $875 million.

While philanthropy from the business sector has increased over the years, it still represents only 4.7 percent of total charitable contributions. Contributions from businesses to all causes totaled $6.1 billion in 1994. Culture receives approximately 11 cents of every corporate contribution dollar, with education receiving 38 cents; health and welfare, 26 cents; civic activities, 11 cents; and all other causes, 14 cents.

According to the Business Committee for the Arts, 47 percent of all businesses in the United States with annual revenues of $1 million or more are supporting the arts in some way, and only 3 percent were responsible for over 25 percent of all corporate support for the arts. This latter group includes most of the nation's largest corporations—those most affected by the recent wave of mergers, acquisitions, and general corporate downsizing.

In the nonprofit sector, arts and cultural groups must compete with health, education, and welfare organizations for a share of corporate largess. Support given to cultural programs can often provide a business far greater visibility and prestige than support given to other charitable causes. In order to secure corporate grants, cultural organizations must educate businesses in their communities about the benefits they gain in doing so. To involve businesses in supporting arts and cultural organizations, an organization's development personnel must understand

- Why businesses support arts and culture
- The facts that determine the giving policy of businesses
- How businesses make funding decisions
- The types of support available
- How to approach businesses for support

WHY DOES BUSINESS SUPPORT ARTS AND CULTURE?

Businesses support arts and culture for sound business reasons as well as altruistic ones. A firm's operations and its ability to earn a profit are often improved through involvement in and support of the community in which it does business. An arts and cultural organization offers services that directly benefit a corporation's customers, clients, and employees. A thriving cultural community can be an asset to a business trying to recruit and retain highly educated and talented personnel; it can also stimulate economic development by attracting people to theaters, galleries, museums, restaurants, and shops. Arts and culture are generally viewed as positive forces that promote goodwill within a community.

For all of these reasons, businesses tend to contribute to cultural organizations in the communities in which they have headquarters, major markets, plants, or branch offices. A recent survey of 1,000 corporations conducted by the Business Committee for the Arts showed that 93 percent of them allocated a majority of their resources to arts projects at the local level.

Corporate managers recognize the public-relations value of supporting culture (see Appendix J). By underwriting such programs, a business identifies itself with artistic and cultural excellence and adds a human element to its corporate image. Additionally, businesses benefit enormously from supporting popular productions, exhibitions, and national television programs. The rationale is simple: The greater the number of people who see these programs, the more there will be who think positively of the program's corporate sponsor.

WHAT ARE THE FACTORS THAT DETERMINE A BUSINESS'S GIVING POLICY?

A business's giving policy—how much money it gives to which types of charitable causes—is a reflection of its markets, products, image, earnings, and, in general, its way of doing business. Industries such as commercial banks and utilities, which are dependent on large consumer markets, tend to support a broad range of highly visible organizations. In contrast, a manufacturing firm selling to a wholesale market may give little support, if any, to arts and culture.

Many businesses like to target support directly to their major or developing markets. For instance, a local fast-food chain whose primary market is children would likely consider supporting a series of children's concerts performed by local symphony orchestras in the communities it serves.

A business's product line can often influence its choices regarding philanthropic support. Pharmaceutical firms, for example, may direct their funds entirely to programs in the health field. A high-technology corporation, on the other hand, may allot its charitable budget to educational programs in engineering and the sciences. During the latter half of the 1970s and the early 1980s, the large oil companies as a group spent millions of dollars annually to sponsor nationally televised programs that promoted favorable public opinion.

A company's giving policy is also affected by its earnings profile. The size of a business's philanthropic contribution budget is generally based on profits earned during the previous year. If earnings are below expected levels, contributions are unlikely to be increased; they may be cut back or even withheld.

Cultural organizations must analyze each corporate prospect in terms of its markets, products, desired image, and earnings. By approaching businesses with this knowledgeable stance—as equals rather than as supplicants—arts and cultural organizations can establish business partnerships with corporations. In exchange for funding support, an organization can provide a business with valuable public relations opportunities, improved market or product identification, and, in some cases, increased revenue.

HOW DO BUSINESSES MAKE FUNDING DECISIONS?

A business's decision to fund a cultural organization is based on many criteria and is often several years in the making. Support awarded beyond the token level is typically the result of judgments made by the business about its own interests and needs.

A business makes a grant to an organization only after researching it thoroughly. The business's first requirement is that the organization be a not-for-profit, tax-exempt corporation. Other important factors are the level of referee contacts, the professional qualifications of the board members and management staff, the makeup of the audience or client group, the financial condition, and the participation figures.

Ultimately, businesses give to those organizations that are the most credible, the most relevant to its interests, and of the highest quality.

WHAT TYPES OF SUPPORT ARE AVAILABLE?

Business support to arts and culture is generally of five types:

- General support
- Special-project support/sponsorship

- Service-in-kind support
- Employee matching gift programs
- Special-event support

General Support

Grants from businesses to help cover the operating expenses of an organization usually range from $500 to $10,000, depending on the size and resources of the donor. This money is typically paid out of an annual contribution budget. It can take three years of repeated appeals to a likely prospect before a general support grant is received. Once a business has given a grant, it becomes easier for an organization to win support in subsequent years. A request for support must be made every year, whether or not the business has incorporated the organization as a line item in its annual contribution budget.

Special-Project Support/Sponsorship

Special-project funding, such as sponsorship of a play or art exhibition, tends to be larger—$10,000 to $50,000 or more—than general-support grants and may come, in part or in total, from a business's marketing, advertising, or public affairs budget. As government grants decrease, business sponsorships represent for arts organizations the greatest opportunity to leverage large sums of money. The tax implications of giving and receiving these types of grants need to be examined by both the sponsor and the institution to determine the appropriate deductibility. UBIT (unrelated business income tax) regulations recently have been revised and amended and are in a state of flux with regard to arts sponsorships, and therefore they should be checked carefully before commitments are made.

Sponsorships are becoming increasingly popular in the corporate sector and are viewed by businesses not only as philanthropy but as a way to enhance their image or income. As the sponsor of a special project, the business or its product can acquire public relations benefits because its name is directly attached to the project and publicized through brochures, television, and print advertising. The essence of the sponsorship concept is to give the corporation or product maximum visibility and identification. Sometimes referred to as cause-related marketing, or CRM, associating a brand or business with a cause or an institution has become increasingly popular, as both a fundraising tool for institutions and a promotional and sales strategy for businesses.

When seeking a sponsor for a special project, the cultural organization should attempt to match the project's expected audience with a business that has a similar customer profile and demographics. A bank dealing with an upscale clientele may be an appropriate sponsor for a chamber music series. A corporation with international business interests may wish to sponsor a project featuring arts and culture from areas of the world where it has a corporate presence. (For example, a cosmetic product designed for African American women might be an ideal sponsor for an African dance festival, or a department store chain might tie a complete store promotion of Asian-inspired linens, fashion, and jewelry to an Asian music series.)

Many organizations survey their audiences for relevant demographic "lifestyle" information that may be helpful in identifying sponsors. For example, an institution may profile its audience to determine the kinds of cars they drive, brand affiliations they have, magazines they purchase, and so on. This information allows the organization to confidently claim to a sponsor that its audience is a good match with the sponsor's particular product. Companies launching new products may be interested in testing markets with a specific demographic composition. This is an ideal opportunity for an arts organization to design a sponsorship that gives the sponsor access to a demographically appropriate sample audience.

The arts organization and the corporation must work together to design a sponsorship package that is mutually beneficial. Because of the nature of sponsorships, the business will want to be involved in publicity and marketing decisions associated with the project. The more creative the partnership between the nonprofit organization and the sponsor, the more impact the sponsorship will have on the intended audience.

A comprehensive sponsorship benefits package for a performance series or festival, for example, might include the following:

- *Credits package.* A written credit line, such as "The ABC play series has been sponsored by a grant from the XYZ Corporation," should appear on all printed material developed for the project, including brochures, newspaper ads of a reasonable size, and the in-house program. The credit should be large enough to be noticed and may include the corporate logo. Many sponsors require that their name (and sometimes logo) be part of the title of a program. This can be useful in generating increased funds for other projects with the institution (by attracting other "title sponsors"), but it could also potentially affect how the program is identified to the public—overemphasizing the sponsor may make the institution seem too commercial.

  Credits can be extended to include an article about the sponsorship or an ad recognizing the sponsor in the program or institution's newsletter. If media ads are purchased on radio or television, sponsor credits should also be included, provided enough time is available. Sponsors also like to be mentioned in print press coverage. The manner in which the sponsor logo, credit, or image is connected to the press and marketing campaign is essential. The sponsor should be included in the headline of press releases about the event, and it would be appropriate to include a quote from the sponsor's chief executive officer in the first paragraph. Corporate sponsors often want to include their own separate release in the institution's press kit.

- *Events.* The sponsor should be given a prenegotiated number of complimentary tickets, including tickets to the opening night. If the sponsor wishes a large number of tickets, they should be sold to the company at a discount. For example, a performing arts organization may offer 20 complimentary seats to the opening for the sponsor's chief executive officer and the corporation's top clients, 4 free tickets to each additional night, and all other tickets at a 20 percent discount. Naturally, the sponsor should be given good seat locations.

  Alternatively (or additionally), the cultural organization could offer to host an event for the sponsor's employees, for which tickets would be discounted and complimentary refreshments provided. Sometimes a sponsoring corporation wishes to host a small, private dinner for its guests with the artistic director of the institution after a performance. The development director should work with a staff person from the corporation on all plans for the event and be as helpful as possible. The corporation would typically pay for the dinner in this situation. If an opening-night party takes place, the sponsor should be publicly acknowledged and thanked at the event; sometimes top corporate officials can be designated as guests of honor and as speakers.

It is important to be flexible and creative when developing the sponsor benefits package. A sponsor may wish to put a small exhibition of its products in the lobby, insert information in the program, offer a special coupon or premium to members of the audience, do a special mailing to all of the members of the institution, or add a "stuffer" to their monthly bills to customers. Sponsors may create merchandise such as T-shirts and mugs related to the program. They may even be interested in selling such items in their gift shops (if they have that kind of space) or through direct mail. Ideally the institution could negotiate a royalty from such sales, which would increase their sponsorship dollars. Sponsors may also opt to host "meet the artist" events at their own site if they are a store or restaurant wishing to increase traffic and introduce more people to their products. The arts organization should be cooperative but careful not to become too involved in commercial ventures that might overstep the boundaries of good taste, thereby undoing the goodwill that is the basis of the sponsorship.

In some cases, a business may develop a cause-related marketing effort with an organization; that is, a sponsorship concept designed to tie corporate income to a designated project—for example, an arrangement in which every time an individual uses a certain kind of credit card to buy a ticket, that credit card company would donate a specific amount of money to the institution.

Affinity credit cards, cards that are tied to a specific institution or theme (see Appendix K), are another example of this kind of *quid pro quo* relationship between a sponsor and an institution. The affinity card concept works in the following way: A financial institution works with an organization to design a credit card that features the logo or message of the arts organization. The bank then writes a letter over the signature of the organization's head to its members or ticket buyers to let them know that every time the card is used, a certain percentage of the bank's fee will be donated to the institution. In this way, individuals who believe in the institution have yet another opportunity to offer support at no additional cost to themselves. The institution is the recipient of additional funds, and the bank has many new customers. This relationship can be of potential benefit to everyone, but the arts organization must also be aware that it is obligated to one bank exclusively and cannot run similar programs with competitive credit card companies. It also must be made clear to the organization's members that this is an additional way to help the organization and not a replacement for an annual donation.

Affinity sponsorships are not limited to credit cards. Redemption programs such as mailing in box tops, bottle caps, or other items that demonstrate product usage can help support institutions (by giving the institution some financial benefit from the consumer's purchase of the designated item), stimulate product sales, and in some cases be offered to customers as a means of receiving discounts on tickets. Relationships that create brand identification with certain programs will bring in sponsorship dollars and create fundraising opportunities. A wine might become the "official wine" of a festival, or there might be an official limousine service or soft drink. Arts organizations, following the lead of sports events, have done very well with these kinds of tie-ins, particularly for a once-in-a-lifetime type of event such as the opening of a new museum. Arts organizations must accept responsibility for promoting and servicing these relationships.

Because sponsorship is a way to both generate larger grants and develop higher visibility, the development director should focus on how to take program plans and develop them into special projects. For example, an institution could seek a sponsor for a series of plays or a sponsor for each production. A membership drive could be sponsored, as well as a series of institutional ads.

If a project is large and too expensive to be sponsored by a single business, the development director could develop a consortium sponsorship and seek out compatible corporations to sponsor a project collectively. Consortium sponsorship is a growth area for institutions. It can take the form of a number of unrelated corporations or products each sponsoring the same series as "partners" for their own reasons. Partners can also be identified because of a similar connection to an event. For example, a real-estate developer and a bank might agree to be partners, whereas two banks—which are competitors—might not.

Sometimes the possibility of an effective partnership is more attractive to a potential donor than an exclusive sponsorship. A Swedish film and theater festival might be sponsored by a group of Swedish multinational companies based in the festival's host city; and the partnership might also include the Swedish Travel Bureau, a Scandinavian airline sponsor (for travel), a Swedish-made alcoholic beverage, and government support from the consulate. In this situation, each partner is related to the "content or theme" of the event, and it makes good business sense for them to work together as a consortium. This layering process of fundraising allows the organization to capitalize on several sponsorship opportunities for special projects and to raise more money than they could through a single sponsor. In dealing with so many important sponsors, however, the development director must carefully track their individual needs and respond accordingly.

Recently, groups of performing arts institutions have joined forces on programs, a strategy that can increase chances for finding major sponsorship. For example, a number of institutions that focus on Native American culture might organize a touring dance festival (with outreach, education programs, and so on) to six cities across the country. Together, the institutions could seek sponsorship from product sponsors looking to support events that are national or regional rather than local. In this manner, the sponsor can underwrite one program and receive maximum impact because of the event's extended geographical reach. Museum tours have been funded nationally for many years and appear to be quite successful.

Consortium sponsorship can induce peer pressure among sponsors; development directors can often leverage participation of one sponsor through another's commitment. If a supermarket chain sponsors an event, for example, it may also be able to bring its vendors into the program by offering them more shelf or display space in return for their participation. Special displays not only enhance product sales, but it is hoped that they will also draw increased traffic into stores where the artistic program and its sponsors are promoted.

In almost every case, corporate sponsors will allow the institution to supplement their donations with foundation and government funds.

Service-in-Kind Support

In-kind support is a donation of business services, as opposed to money, often at little actual cost to the business. The value of donated services to organizations can often be far greater than the amount of a cash grant. The development director should review the organization's annual expense budget with an eye to items that could be contributed in kind, thereby saving the organization the expense of purchasing them.

Donations may include used furniture and equipment; office, rehearsal, or exhibit space; and printing and design, word processing, or other professional services. A business may offer its lobby space to a visual arts organization for use as an exhibition area, for example. This expands the gallery space of the organization and brings in a wider audience, serving the interests of both the business and the arts organization.

In-kind donations from airline and shipping sponsors, which help offset travel and freight costs, are extremely popular, especially when the arts organization is seeking such assistance off season. In exchange for "official airline" status, an airline might be persuaded to provide an agreed-upon number of free seats per year or to provide freight-shipping services. They might also donate free tickets to supplement those tickets purchased at a discount. In-kind sponsors are interested in credit packages and other sponsor benefits—such as being given an opportunity for their "preferred" customers to purchase house seats or have a private viewing of an exhibition.

Some businesses have policies prohibiting donations of their products, while others gladly provide samples of goods such as perfume or liquor to large gatherings of people at special events. Product sampling generally supplements a cash contribution. Small local businesses are good prospects for in-kind service donations and will often participate in special events such as street fairs. It is often easier for them to provide in-kind support than to make cash grants, although they should certainly be encouraged to do both. Because they are neighbors and have a vested interest in their neighborhood's vitality, small businesses can be an excellent source of funds.

Employee Matching Gift Programs

An employee matching gift program provides a way for businesses to contribute to the arts while also giving their employees an incentive to contribute. It works this way: A business makes a gift to an organization to "match" the contribution already donated by one of its employees. The business's donation can equal the employee's, or the matching ratio can be even greater, depending on the policy of the individual business. If an employee contributes $100 to a local museum and registers the gift with the matching gift program of his or her employing firm, and the firm has a policy of matching employee gifts on a two-to-one basis, the museum receives a total of $300. Most businesses set restrictions on the type of not-for-profit organizations to which it will contribute and on the size of gifts that are eligible for matching funds.

Because employees sometimes fail to report their contributions to the firm's matching gift program, arts organizations should try to follow up on gifts that might be eligible for matching contributions. Requesting the individual's business affiliation on the donor pledge card helps in the follow-up process. Also, the organization can include a small brochure listing the names of businesses known to have matching gift programs with the thank-you note mailed to donors. This brochure reminds donors to register their gifts with their employers. The Business Committee for the Arts in New York City publishes a list of matching gift programs, as does the Council on the Advancement and Support of Education in Washington, D.C.

Special-Event Support

Many businesses have funds earmarked for the support of special events in the community such as benefit dinners, opening nights, parties, testimonials, and balls. Businesses may purchase blocks of tickets, underwrite the event's expenses, or donate goods. Special events are another way to involve businesses in the activities of arts and cultural organizations. (See Chapter 8 for more information on special events.)

HOW DO ORGANIZATIONS APPROACH BUSINESSES FOR FUNDS?

Many businesses and products have no formalized giving policies or structures for disbursing funds for philanthropic purposes. Often the special interests and commitment to social responsibility of the chief executive officer are decisive in the giving policies of a firm. In businesses where the philanthropic function is well established, such contributions are often within the purview of a specific department in the firm, such as public affairs, community relations, personnel, or corporate communications.

The surest entree into a business is to approach the chief executive officer or another top executive through a personal friend or business colleague. Board members of cultural organizations are key intermediaries ("referees") in approaching top-level executives. The development director should have information about business and personal contacts of each board member and senior manager of the organization and be able to determine if any of them knows a top official in the firm in question (see the section on cultivation plans in Chapter 3). After being contacted, the top official, if interested, will make the appropriate staff person in his or her firm aware of the request. The staff person will then handle the details relating to the request. It is important that the development director establish a relationship with this staff person and include him or her in the solicitation process.

If no personal contacts exist between the board members or senior managers of the organization and the executives of the targeted firm, the development director should determine the staff person responsible for contributions by researching the firm thoroughly; then he or she should make a telephone call to the firm to determine if and when a request for funds is appropriate.

A grant request should be tailored to the firm being approached. The request should be short and concise; it should contain an appropriate request for funds based on research and on information received at the exploratory meeting with the firm's representative. As discussed in Chapter 3, some funding sources prefer to receive a request for funds before agreeing to a meeting. The request should clearly explain why the business and the institution are a good match, and it should include a persuasive presentation of the benefits the business will receive for providing support. These benefits can be stated broadly or specifically. Corporate proposals should be efficient and practical. Generally, these proposals focus more on promoting the relationship between the institution and the business, rather than on problem solving. They should be mailed with appropriate background materials (see Appendix K).

Businesses in which philanthropic giving is an established practice use several different grant-making structures to disburse funds. The most common are

- Corporate contribution programs
- Corporate foundations
- Advertising and/or public relations departments
- Special markets

Some businesses use all of these structures, sometimes combining them. An understanding of these structures and their interrelationships within a business aids the development director in identifying the individual in charge of charitable giving and the correct way to approach that person.

Corporate Contribution Programs

The corporate contribution program is, in most cases, under the auspices of the public affairs, public relations, or community service department. It may also be administered out of the chief executive's office. Large businesses with national operations often allow branch offices to manage their own contribution budgets under general guidelines determined at corporate headquarters.

Contribution programs typically are managed by one or two persons responsible for dealing with requests from all types of not-for-profit groups, including arts and cultural organizations. In some businesses, administration of the contribution program is just part of one person's job. Contribution program officers are often overworked and have inadequate staff. They may have only a rudimentary knowledge of the arts and culture field. Most of these officers work closely with a contribution committee made up of executives of the firm. This committee formulates the giving policy, establishes the total annual contribution budget, and determines specific grants.

Corporate Foundations

A corporate foundation is a legal entity established by a corporation as separate from the business. The funds that the foundation disburses annually, however, come from the corporation and are dependent on its earnings. The corporation often influences the foundation's giving policies. As is the case with corporate contribution programs, corporate foundations are usually managed by small staffs that work with a board of trustees—similar to the committee overseeing the corporate contribution program—to determine policies and grantees.

Advertising and/or Public Relations Departments

The advertising and/or public relations department may also disburse funds to not-for-profit organizations. However, funds disbursed by these departments are often treated as business expenses and are used to cover advertising, public relations, promotions, and costs associated with sponsorships of special projects and events. The funds in these departmental budgets tend to be more discretionary than those in corporate contribution or corporate foundation budgets. A cultural organization may receive general-support funds from a corporation contribution program or a corporate foundation and also receive special-project funds from the corporation's public relations or advertising budget. Potential sponsors often want to compare the return from advertising dollars spent versus the return from sponsorship funding, since both are primarily a marketing tool. The advantages of each are described in Appendix J. Some product sponsorships are approved and run by outside advertising and public relations agencies serving as consultants to brands. Arts institutions often work directly with a representative from the brand and with their ad agency on details of credits, sampling, and so on. These funds, as previously stated, are more consumer oriented and less concerned with philanthropy.

Special Markets

Many large businesses have special divisions to deal with certain consumer constituencies—such as the Latino market, the teenage market, or the women's market. These departments have budgets for sponsoring and supporting programs they believe will increase customer awareness within these special interest groups. Special markets can also be determined by geography; a product could be launching one type of campaign in urban areas and another in rural communities, for example. All of these markets represent opportunites that can be explored by development staff to consistently match the right prospect with the right product.

CHAPTER 5

Foundations

A foundation is a not-for-profit organization established to enrich the public welfare primarily by making grants to social welfare, educational, and health organizations, and to the arts and culture, as well as to other charitable causes. The modern American foundation has been in existence since the early part of this century. The Carnegie Corporation and the Rockefeller Foundation were established in 1911 and 1913, respectively. Today, there are nearly 38,000 foundations operating in the United States, many of them established after World War II.

Through the years, foundation support has overwhelmingly gone to educational organizations and health and social welfare causes. The first foundation support of the arts and culture occurred because of the specific interests of wealthy families. The Andrew Mellon Foundation, established in 1930 as the Mellon Trust, has through the years made grants totaling over $70 million to the National Gallery of Art in Washington, D.C. The Mellon Foundation continues to be a leading donor to many arts organizations throughout the United States. The Rockefeller family also was a major early supporter of the arts, and the Rockefeller Foundation remains a very visible presence in arts and culture philanthropy today.

It was not until 1957 that the arts began to attract broad-based foundation support. In that year, the Ford Foundation, through the initiative of the late W. McNeil Lowry, began an extensive program of support to performing arts organizations, which served as a catalyst for other foundations to do the same. During the 1960s and 1970s, the Ford Foundation disbursed more than $250 million to the arts and humanities alone, helping theater, dance, music, and opera groups throughout the country to flourish.

Contributions from foundations to all causes totaled $9.91 billion in 1994, which represents only 7.6 percent of all philanthropic contributions. Education and health still receive the greatest share, with arts programs receiving 15 percent of foundation funding.

The number of not-for-profit organizations seeking foundation support has increased steadily. As reported in *Foundation Fundamentals,* one million requests for funds are made annually to foundations. Of these requests, no more than 7 percent are successful. However, many of the programs for which foundation support is denied are clearly outside the defined interest areas of the foundations. Appendixes D, E, and K offer useful supplementary materials for institutions seeking foundation support.

Arts organizations can increase their chances of receiving funding from foundations by researching prospects carefully and by understanding the following:

- How foundations operate
- What determines the giving policies of foundations
- What types of support are available
- How to approach foundations for support
- How foundations make funding decisions

HOW DO FOUNDATIONS OPERATE?

A foundation is established by an initial gift of money from a principal donor or donors. The money is then invested—in stocks, bonds, or real estate, for example—and generates income. Foundation fund distribution is regulated by the Internal Revenue Service, which requires that a minimum amount of funds be paid out annually in grants. The minimum payout is 5 percent of a foundation's assets in each taxable fiscal year.

According to *Giving USA,* of the approximately 37,571 grant-making foundations operating in the United States, 457 have assets over $50 million and award 48 percent of the grants. There are six major types of foundations. The first four types listed below are generally grouped as independent foundations:

- *Proprietary foundations.* In this type of foundation, the actual donor—or donor's spouse—is active in the foundation's activities. A proprietary foundation distributes funds according to the interests of the donor, who determines whether there is a specific program focus.
- *Family foundations.* In a family foundation, policy is determined by family members—usually siblings, children, or grandchildren of the original donor. Grants from this type of foundation follow the original donor's interests, but the family may broaden the interpretation of those interests. A variation on this type of foundation is the "hybrid

family foundation," in which nonfamily trustees play an integral role in determining grant-making policies.

- *Trusts.* A trust is a foundation or fund in which the responsibility for operations has passed into the hands of friends, partners, or business associates of the original donor. In many cases, trusts are administered by law firms or banks.
- *Professional foundations.* This category consists of foundations, such as the Ford Foundation, in which control of assets and activities has passed entirely into the hands of a nonfamily board of trustees, which defines policies and programs administered by a professional staff.
- *Community foundations.* This type of foundation is established in a specific community with funds derived from a variety of individuals rather than from one individual. It is governed by a board of community representatives. Usually only one community foundation serves a particular area. Community foundations, such as the New York Community Trust, the San Francisco Foundation, and the Cleveland Foundation, respond to the special concerns and interests of the people in their communities. Individuals contributing to a community foundation have the option of restricting the types of gifts made from their funds or allowing the staff and board of the foundation to make all grant-making decisions. Often, many of the grants made by community foundations result from the wishes of the foundation's donors rather than from decisions by its board of trustees.

  Of all the various types of foundations, community foundations grow the fastest. Many have professional full-time staff to publish information on foundation activities, meet with prospective grantees, and carry out carefully planned contribution programs.
- *Corporate foundations.* This type of foundation is established by a corporation to maintain a regular philanthropic program (see Chapter 4). The giving policies of a corporate foundation are usually consistent with the goals and interests of the corporation. Not all corporations have a corporate foundation; some may instead make donations through corporate contribution programs. Other corporations operate both a corporate foundation and a corporate giving program.

It is also important to be aware of the term *operating foundation.* An operating foundation is a not-for-profit organization that uses its endowed funds for its own programs. It is not a grant-making entity.

Most foundations are managed by a board of directors made up of the donor and the donor's family members, friends, or colleagues. These individuals usually serve in a voluntary capacity. The vast majority of foundations do not employ a staff, hold regular office hours, or publish information describing their activities.

Usually only the larger community, corporate, and professional foundations employ full-time staff members and operate under well-developed grant-making guidelines. Foundation program staff members thoroughly investigate project areas and carefully screen applications. They are also equipped to handle requests for information and to deal with the public.

WHAT DETERMINES A FOUNDATION'S GIVING POLICY?

A foundation's giving policy is designed to provide either general purpose funds or funds for a clearly defined program. A foundation with a giving policy of providing general purpose funds usually offers grants to a wide range of organizations or individuals in the fields of health, education, social welfare, and culture. The giving policy of a particular foundation will often reflect the interests of the foundation's original donor, the donor's family, or the foundation's board of trustees. Many foundations determine the focus of their philanthropy by identifying problems in a particular discipline. The needs of the local community or problems of national or international concern may also affect a foundation's giving policies. Awards are granted to institutions that have projects designed to solve those problems. For example, a foundation may be interested in U.S. relations with the People's Republic of China. An arts organization's plan to present a major ballet company from China may be of special interest to such a foundation.

Some foundations are endowed for a special purpose and support only programs related to that purpose. Professional foundations, in particular, will limit their grants to a few specific program areas that are perceived as important to society. As social conditions change, these foundations adjust the focus of their giving programs accordingly. It is important to note that because there are so many different types of foundation grant-making models, some foundations have a mission that is extremely focused and proactive (having guidelines aimed solely at addressing certain specific societal issues), whereas others are reactive (supporting any request the donor or his representative may choose).

WHAT TYPES OF SUPPORT ARE AVAILABLE?

In addition to general purpose and special-project grants, certain foundations make grants for capital projects and endowments. Foundations are usually more willing than businesses to consider providing seed money for experimental projects, and foundations do not usually require the same kind of public relations benefits from their grant-making activities as businesses do.

Foundation grants are awarded for varying lengths of time—annual or multiyear—depending on the policies of the foundation. Small foundations are more apt to give annual support, whereas large foundations often prefer to fund special projects over several years. Furthermore, some foundations will discontinue support to an organization after two or three years of involvement. Foundations with giving polices designed to solve problems tend to focus on new projects and areas of interest when the problem currently being funded has been or is near to being solved. Many foundations also have a dollar limitation on grants awarded to a single organization in a given year.

HOW DO ORGANIZATIONS APPROACH FOUNDATIONS FOR SUPPORT?

Many of the larger foundations include in their annual reports or publish separately information on funding policies, areas of interest, and application requirements. It is important to review these guidelines carefully so that the grant proposal addresses areas of concern to the foundation. In cases where no publications are available, information can be gleaned from entries in a number of reference books on foundations and through research profiles compiled in the manner described in Chapter 3.

Proposals to foundations concerned with addressing specific problems can often be detailed and lengthy (see "Foundation Special Project Proposal" in Appendix K). It is best to write proposals of this type using a problem-solving approach in which the organization describes how its project will meet needs or solve problems already defined as areas of special interest to the foundation.

As in all areas of fundraising, personal contact with foundation trustees and staff members is enormously helpful in the grant-seeking process.

HOW DO FOUNDATIONS MAKE FUNDING DECISIONS?

Funding decisions are typically made by the foundation's board of trustees after a presentation by a staff member (if any) or by a board member. The board meets periodically during the year to make its funding decisions.

Prior to each meeting, the foundation staff person or designated board member examines the proposals received, chooses the most interesting and appropriate projects to bring to the board's attention, and then prepares a short summary of each project. It is this summary, rather than the original proposal in most cases, that is initially reviewed by the board. Since the staff member or designated board member is key in determining which proposals the board will see, it is important to develop a good working relationship with this individual.

The first part of the foundation's board meeting is usually devoted to a discussion of the foundation's investments and other business matters. During the second part of the meeting, grant proposals are presented and discussed.

The board is most often concerned with the following questions when reviewing proposals:

- Does the project address foundation program areas creatively?
- Is the organization qualified to implement the project?
- Does the organization have a solid reputation in its field?
- Is the organization's board of trustees capable of providing leadership?
- How long will the organization require support from the foundation?
- Will the project be self-supporting, or will it develop other means of grant support after a reasonable amount of time?
- How will the organization evaluate the success of the project?
- Is the plan well thought out?

Following this inquiry, the foundation's board makes its funding decisions. Award letters are then sent to the successful applicants; in most cases, letters are also sent to those organizations not awarded funds.

An organization that receives a foundation grant should keep the foundation formally apprised of the progress of the project. Progress reports update the foundation on the status of the project and highlight major new developments. Reports should be accompanied by appropriate budgets and selected supplementary materials. Often, foundations request from the organization interim and final reports evaluating the success of the project against the initial project goals. These reports should be as well prepared as the original proposal. The best way to build a continuing relationship with a foundation is to manage the project successfully and to keep the foundation informed throughout the process.

CHAPTER

•••••••••

Individuals

I ndividuals are by far the most significant source of support for America's not-for-profit organizations. In 1994, individuals contributed $113.86 billion—87.7 percent of all philanthropic support. This compares with $4.5 billion from corporations and $5.17 billion from foundations.

Arts and cultural organizations have traditionally been great beneficiaries of individual generosity. In 1994, according to the American Association of Fund-Raising Counsel, Inc., arts and cultural organizations raised over $7.14 billion dollars from individuals—nearly 10 percent of all individual giving.

Individual support can be generally divided into two categories: major-donor support and membership support.

MAJOR DONORS

Major donors are individuals who make sizable personal contributions. The minimum contribution necessary for a major-donor designation varies from organization to organization; the figure can be in the thousands or the hundreds of thousands of dollars. There are several reasons why these donors are among the most desirable sources of support for arts and cultural organizations.

First, major donors tend to be a reliable source of annual funding, with financial commitments frequently extending over a number of years. Second, unlike corporations or foundations, major donors are not regulated by time frames, restrictive giving policies, or committee judgments; they can give as much as they want to whomever they wish, with few or no bureaucratic strings attached. For this reason, many development departments turn to these donors to support particularly risky projects from which other kinds of funders may shy away. Third, because many major donors have extensive contacts in business, political, and social circles, they can be vital sources of connection to additional funding sources, including other individuals, corporations, and foundations.

Virtually all major donors have a substantial interest in the life and mission of the organization(s) they support. Beyond personal interest, their reasons for giving can vary greatly. Some enjoy the glamour and prestige that come with supporting a major cultural organization, such as a world-renowned museum or opera company. Others may prefer to support smaller or more experimental organizations, in which their contribution may play a critical survival role and their voice will be particularly influential. Still others may wish to fund one or more projects, like a concert with a favorite conductor or a special art exhibition. Donors may in fact have a number of these objectives in mind.

Occasionally, however, major-donor support can have drawbacks. For example, an individual making a large gift may want to influence programming decisions in ways that would compromise the mission of the organization. A major donor who is also a member of the board of directors may exert excessive influence, thereby inhibiting the board's governing process. In addition, although donors may develop an allegiance to a new organization, there is also the possibility that they may abruptly withdraw their support without warning, leaving the organization without expected support. Despite these possible pitfalls, the importance of major donors cannot be overstated.

Identifying Prospective Major Donors

The process of identifying prospective major donors is ongoing, requiring the continuous attention of both the board of directors and the development staff. Fortunately, arts and cultural organizations have a lot of resources at their fingertips. Board members, for example, as well as being major donors themselves, are some of the best sources for identifying new donors. Relying on their often extensive networks of personal connections, they can identify and solicit friends and colleagues who might be good candidates for support. Board members should be encouraged to make such cultivation an important part of their service.

Current major donors to the organization are another excellent resource in identifying prospects. Their help can range from simply providing lists of contacts to throwing parties to introduce friends to the organization's director.

Development staff should also be attentive to donors who are giving lower-level gifts to the organization. While many of these donors do not have the means to donate at a higher level, a significant number do; they may simply require further cultivation to become major supporters.

There are some tell-tale clues as to who these potential higher-level donors may be. Existing donors who express a particularly strong interest in the organization, whether in a letter or through personal contact with a staff member, are good candidates, as are donors who have recently increased their support to the next higher level or who live in neighborhoods known to be wealthy. Subscribers who have purchased a substantial number of tickets are also possibilities for higher-level support. These individuals have already confirmed their interest in the organization; the next step is to develop a stronger relationship with them.

Beyond the organization's existing base of support, it can be helpful to scan the lists of supporters of other local arts and cultural organizations. Often, a donor's particular interests are revealed in the kind of organizations he or she chooses to support. Donors to a French-American cultural exchange organization, for example, may be especially receptive to funding an exhibit of French painting at a local museum.

In all of these cases, research plays a vital role. By using *Who's Who in America*, the *Directory of Directors*, and other sources, the development staff can discover potential donors' occupations, places of business, social standing, and overall potential for giving (see Chart 3.5, Hypothetical Individual Research Profile). This information can then be used to develop the courses of action for contacting the individuals to seek their support. Appendixes C and D also suggest avenues for researching prospective donors.

Overall, the development director and staff must constantly be on the lookout for information about future prospects. Every opening-night party, every contact with existing donors, and every meeting of the board of directors, for example, can yield crucial tidbits of information that, when acted upon in the proper way, can help win significant new support for an organization.

How to Approach Prospective Major Donors for Support

Approaching major donors requires discretion and an understanding of their individual likes and dislikes. One patron' may prefer simply to send a check to the organization every year without receiving a solicitation, whereas another may request a detailed proposal in writing. Some donors may have a close relationship with the president or artistic director and need only a quick phone call; others expect to be brought up-to-date on the organization's activities at a luncheon meeting before making their annual contribution. In all cases, major donors should be made to feel comfortable and should be rewarded for their support with frequent acknowledgment and special privileges.

Some major donors wish to make their gifts anonymously, whereas others desire public recognition. Historically, the latter have had a building, theater, rehearsal room, study center, cafeteria, or garden named in honor of them or a loved one of theirs, often as part of an endowment campaign. Smaller-scale forms of recognition include naming seats in a theater after major donors or listing their names in a program.

How to Ensure Long-Term Support

An organization must never rest on its laurels after receiving a major gift from a new donor. Only through further cultivation will this donor become a reliable, annual source of funding for the organization's programs—and possibly more.

This cultivation process begins immediately upon the receipt of a new donor's first check, with a thank-you note and a phone call from the president or artistic director. The donor should receive "top-of-the-line" inside treatment, including advance notice of productions or exhibits, copies of favorable reviews, and invitations to the most prestigious events. The goal here is to build in the donor a sense of shared ownership in the organization, a sense that will strengthen over time.

The time spent cultivating donors pays off in a number of ways, the most important of which is that their support may well increase over time. There are other benefits, too: Once invested in the organization, new donors may bring in support from other individuals, or they may offer service or advice in their areas of expertise. Some donors may even be excellent prospects for the organization's board of directors.

DESIGNING A MEMBERSHIP OR ANNUAL FUND PROGRAM

The vast majority of donors to an organization share the same interest and enthusiasm for its programs that major donors do, but they may not have the same financial resources. Other donors have the ability to give more than they donate initially, but they may prefer to begin giving at a lower level.

It is important that arts and cultural organizations build a broad base of lower-level contributors. Added together, the contributions of lower-level contributors can have an important financial impact; they often surpass the total of major-donor contributions. A broad base of support also helps build the major donor program, since, through cultivation over many years, donors may increase their contributions to a much higher level. Long-term donors also tend to be among the most passionate of the organization's supporters, and can be counted on to increase attendance, ticket sales, and store and restaurant sales.

A membership or annual fund program is the best way to bring lower-level contributors into the organization. These programs generally offer donors the choice of a range of different contribution levels, each of which is accompanied by an appropriate package of benefits. With a gift of $75, for example, a contributor might become a "Friend" of the Hometown Art Museum and be entitled to free admission for an entire year, as well as discounts at the museum restaurant and shop. At higher levels of giving, a contributor might be offered premiums of a more exclusive and unique nature, such as an invitation to a luncheon with the director of the organization.

Membership or annual fund programs should be a key component of an organization's overall development strategy because they help ensure that customers follow a path of increased involvement in the life of the organization. Chart 6.1 is an example of a customer track for a performing arts institution.

Single-Ticket Buyer Subscriber Friend (lower-level donor) Patron (higher-level donor) Major Donor Endowment Gift Planned/Deferred Gift Board Member
SAMPLE CUSTOMER TRACK
CHART 6.1

Why Individuals Become Members or Annual Fund Contributors

Devotees of arts and cultural organizations have various reasons for contributing. The best-designed fundraising programs create giving and benefit options with all of these reasons in mind. For some individuals, being a member or annual donor is about staying connected to an institution. An infrequent attendee of a nonprofit theater, for example, may become a member to ensure that he or she receives all the announcements and mailings about future programs and events. In a more intangible version of this idea, an out-of-towner visiting New York's Metropolitan Museum of Art may desire to "bring the museum home" by becoming a member. Donors with this motivation would most likely respond to premiums like a free poster or an exhibition guide.

Some donors contribute out of a desire for a deeper connection. Hearing of an upcoming sculpture exhibition at a favorite museum, a person might wish to take advantage of special "insider benefits" like a members-only preview of the exhibit or a lecture by the curator. These donors might also appreciate the opportunity to meet a visiting choreographer or the organization's director at a reception.

Other potential contributors want to take advantage of the special service provided by an institution to its members or donors. Someone who enjoys excellent seats would surely appreciate a patron ticket service guaranteeing access to the best seats in the house for all performances. Still others appreciate the "social benefits" of membership, including invitations to galas and opening night receptions.

It is important to match appropriately giving levels with benefits. A discount at a museum shop, for example, is of general interest and is appropriate for the lowest giving level. On the other hand, a patron ticket service that reserves the best seats is a more exclusive privilege and is a suitable reward for someone at a higher level. When building a membership program, benefits and giving levels should be structured so that moving up the ladder of giving is an attractive and enticing option that brings the individual in closer contact with the mission of the organization. The greater an individual's involvement with an institution, the greater his or her largess tends to be.

Developing a Persuasive Message for Giving

Whether at a lobby table, in a brochure or letter, or over the phone, all communication with potential donors must deliver a strong and persuasive case for support. This is no time for modesty; donors must understand exactly why the organization needs their support and why their support will make an important difference.

In designing a persuasive message, the development staff should begin by stressing the unique aspects of the organization in a clear and powerful manner. The local performing arts institution, for example, can highlight the innovative and dynamic programming it brings to sold-out houses year after year. The city art museum can describe its classes that serve 50,000 young people each year. Shakespeare in the Park can emphasize its decades-long history of providing theater absolutely free to the public every summer.

It is incorrect to assume that an organization's potential donors know all of its special qualities. Someone who enjoys the town symphony, for example, may have no idea that donors' gifts help support musical education for young people. Even those patrons who understand the unique qualities of the institution benefit from hearing them repeated in a strong and clear manner; this can only reinforce their interest and increase their commitment to giving.

Stressing the unique aspects of the organization is only the first step; potential donors must also understand exactly how their support will be used and what it will help accomplish. It is useful to be very concrete; a membership table set up at an opera performance, for example, can be a venue for informing attendees that their support will go directly toward funding several exciting new projects next season. Some organizations even point out that membership dollars help pay for basics such as lighting and musical equipment.

Patrons should also be given a clear rationale for why their support is needed *now*. In a telefundraising call, for example, a potential donor could learn that his support is needed *now* to help the organization determine how extensive its future programming will be. It can also be helpful to be honest about aspects of the organization's financial situation. If cutbacks in government support are having a serious effect, for instance, potential donors can be told that their support has never been more necessary or urgent.

Finally, communication with potential donors must always stress the fact that contributing is more than a simple exchange of money for benefits. This is not to downplay the usefulness of benefits in signing up and keeping new members or donors. In seeking membership or annual fund support, however, an organization is asking their patrons to deepen their connection and become part of the future of the institution. In return, the organization is promising not just privileges, but a lifetime of treasured programming and service to the community. And from a practical point of view, an organization takes a risk if it overemphasizes donor benefits in its campaign; if those potential benefits are not valued or are underutilized, an individual will be left with no motivation for contributing.

ACQUISITION OF NEW MEMBERS

In developing a strategy for a membership or annual fund acquisition campaign, the fundraising staff must clearly identify their target audience and maximize the opportunities for reaching this audience.

Identifying the Target Audience

Visit a local art museum, theater, or concert hall on a busy day, and you'll have no trouble finding potential candidates for the target audience. Everywhere you look, visitors to the institution are enjoying a variety of programs and deepening their involvement. This is an ideal group of people to reach with information about contributing. Having spent time getting to know the organization (and presumably building good feelings for it), these patrons tend to be uniquely receptive to hearing about the importance of their support for the organization's future. It's also a good bet that these individuals would be interested in learning about various membership or annual fund benefits that would increase their enjoyment.

Potential donors and members can also be found throughout the local area. They may not be regular visitors to the institution—some may have never even stepped foot inside—but they may appreciate the value of the organization to the community enough to support it even though they are less likely to become involved than those who have attended events. With the help of a list broker, the organization can reach these less easily identified prospects.

Reaching the Target Audience

Arts and cultural organizations have several ways of reaching potential members and annual fund donors.

Lobby Opportunities

There is an excellent opportunity to connect with potential members or annual fund donors while they are actually attending and enjoying the institution's programs. Staffing a lobby membership table with a knowledge-able volunteer, for example, is a very effective means of promoting contact. Membership information should be contained in all written material patrons receive during their visit, including all programs and journals. Membership brochures should be readily available, and there should be obvious opportunities for making on-the-spot contributions.

These techniques are useful not only for signing up new donors, but also in raising patrons' consciousness about the organization's fundraising needs and activities. In the future, when these patrons receive a direct-mail solicitation or a call from a telefundraiser, they will already have some knowledge of the membership or annual fund program and may be more likely to respond.

Program Brochures

Program brochures should include information about the membership program and provide an easy way to make a donation. Many patrons find it convenient to make a contribution while ordering tickets or planning future events, because they can then handle all their financial transactions with the organization at once. Others may not have intended to donate, but will do so because they are excited about the programming or because of special ticket or admission privileges associated with membership or annual fund involvement.

Direct Mail

Around the December holidays, and to an increasing extent throughout the year as well, a wide range of nonprofit organizations barrage mailboxes with direct-mail fundraising solicitations. And with good reason. According to the Direct Marketing Association, Inc., direct-mail appeals in 1995 brought in over $61.3 billion in revenue for nonprofit institutions. By 2000, the annual total is estimated to be $80.1 billion.

Most nonprofits, including arts and cultural institutions, use direct mail for two different types of campaigns: renewal and acquisition. Renewal campaigns seek donations from those who are already giving to the organization. Acquisition campaigns target people who have never donated money to the organization or whose support has lapsed.

Direct-Mail Acquisition Campaign

Perhaps the most daunting aspect of acquisition appeals is their cost. Before even a dollar is raised, an organization must pay for the design and printing of the package, the folding and insertion services of a mailhouse, and postage. Also daunting is the fact that an organization will rarely recoup its investment in an initial acquisition mailing. Therefore, an organization must decide if there are a sufficient number of potential new prospects to warrant the time and expense required for a direct-mail campaign. If the circumstances are indeed right, these campaigns can pay off handsomely in the long run, because a significant percentage of new donors will renew and increase their support year after year at a much lower solicitation cost. To ensure that costs remain manageable, it is vital to maintain a strict budget that takes into account all expected costs of the appeal.

Organizations that include direct mail as part of their annual acquisition campaign must build in a significant amount of time—often two or three months—for the preparation of all necessary materials. It is highly advisable to use a reverse timetable with deadlines for all stages of writing, designing, printing, and assembly; there can be a significant loss in contributions if the mailing goes out later than expected.

The Mailing Audience

Certainly the "warmest" group of potential donors for an acquisition direct-mail campaign are those who have recently participated in the organization's programs. Another warm list consists of lapsed donors who have not contributed in the last 24–36 months. Many of these past donors may have left the fold due to a change in giving priorities or simple inertia; an acquisition appeal is an excellent vehicle for bringing them back.

There are also a variety of "cold" prospect lists to which an organization can send a direct mail piece. They include donor lists from similar organizations; common-denominator lists giving names of individuals in a particular income bracket, occupation, or zip-code area (for example); and magazine subscriber lists. Many of these can be purchased from a list broker, often at significant cost; an exchange of lists with other organizations can be a less expensive alternative.

Because the cost of obtaining lists is often high, it is important to choose lists that are narrowly tailored, with similar profiles in one or more aspects to the organization's list of current donors. A list that is too broad (for instance, all residents in one zip code) tends to yield an inadequate return relative to cost, except in the case of a raffle-type appeal designed for a mass audience.

It can be helpful to test lists by mailing sample request packages to a small number of names on each list and comparing the rate of return. Someone knowledgeable about testing, such as a direct mail consultant, should determine the numerical base necessary to produce an accurate sample response. Generally, it is advisable that only one variable of a direct mail package be tested at a time.

Choosing the Theme

In developing the theme of their direct mail campaigns, arts and cultural organizations are confronted with a number of conceptual possibilities. Some choose a "high-concept" theme: an entreaty to "Enter the World of the Contemporary Arts Museum" on the outside envelope, for example, will lead to a brochure inside in the shape of the museum's building. Upon "opening the doors" of the brochure, recipients discover the world of pleasures that awaits new members.

Other organizations choose what may be termed an "anti-concept" theme, adopting a generic design that presents a simple, straightforward appeal for funds. Sometimes "anti-concept" mailings make a virtue out of *not* offering their new donors a special premium (one such mailing stressed that the organization would not "waste your valuable support on another totebag or mug"). The idea of this type of message is to convince the potential donor that their money is going directly to support the organization's programming and not to pay for its fundraising activities or premiums.

Yet other organizations entice their potential donors with one or more special benefits, such as an advance preview of an upcoming exhibit or the opportunity to order tickets before they are generally available. Additional possibilities include a raffle appeal, in which a contribution to the organization buys the chance to win expensive prizes, or an appeal based on more "emotional" themes, like the value of the arts to young people in the community. Quotes from favorable press reviews can be helpful in lending credibility to an emotion-based appeal.

As these different options make clear, there is no one right way to approach potential donors through direct mail. In general, the theme of the appeal should be succinct, easily grasped, and of interest and value to the potential donor. It should strive to highlight the virtues of the organization in a way that makes the reader feel a personal connection. When deciding on a theme, it is often helpful to test different ideas on focus groups of potential donors to see which elicit the most resonance.

Writing the Appeal Letter

The appeal letter, usually signed by the president or the chairman of the board, is the organization's opportunity to speak directly to the prospective donor in a highly personal and persuasive manner. In the letter, the theme of the appeal is developed and expanded upon in a way that makes the most convincing possible case for giving. Once again, testing different approaches and different lengths or versions of letters with focus groups can be very helpful in deciding which is the most effective.

There are several important stylistic guidelines that contribute to powerful and effective letters:

- Speak directly to the reader. A fundraising letter is not an abstract communication with a general audience. It is a direct form of address from a leader of the organization and to a specific person—the reader. Frequent use of the word *you* is an effective way of establishing a personal connection with the reader.

- Quickly capture the reader's attention in the lead. The opening of the letter should always provide a "hook" to quickly capture the reader's interest. The letter might start out with an arresting anecdote or exciting news about future programming, written in a pithy and engaging style.
- Treat the reader as a valuable participant. A potential donor is more likely to consider an increased donation if he or she feels a sense of ownership in the organization. Therefore, the letter should make very clear that giving is more than simply writing a check; it is, instead, a valuable means of participating in the life of the organization and contributing *directly* to its future success.
- Directly ask the reader for a contribution several times. The request for a donation should never be hidden within the letter. The best appeal letters spell out the request early, and mention it at least twice again during the appeal. The reader should understand exactly what the organization wants them to do, including making a contribution at a specific level.
- Be specific about what the contribution will help accomplish. General statements about the importance of a donor's support rarely convince the reader to contribute. Readers are more responsive to information about the anticipated results of their support, such as more of their favorite opera programming or scholarships for 10 additional dancers.
- Do not list the benefits of membership; describe them. Lists of membership premiums rarely convey their exciting nature. Instead of simply including "passes to six working rehearsals" as an entry in a list, tell the reader that "you'll have the unique experience of watching the Royal Shakespeare Company in an intimate rehearsal."
- Use bold, italics, and underline, within reason. Text highlighters such as these can be helpful for drawing the reader's attention to certain key phrases or sentences. Overuse of these devises, though, can make the letter overly cluttered and difficult to read.
- End with a P.S. The P.S. tends to be the second-most-commonly read section of a letter after the opening paragraph. It is, therefore, a valuable tool for special emphasis.

Choosing the Design

The design of the direct mail appeal should complement and help convey its theme in the most appealing and straightforward manner possible. A package that is colorful, easy to read, and (if possible) includes pictures and interesting visual material helps make the theme resonate more strongly.

Sometimes the design can even be an integral part of the message. In the "Enter the World of the Contemporary Arts Museum" piece, for example, the design can help convince the potential donor of the excitement and beauty that lie inside the doors—something that words alone cannot convey. In the case of the "anti-concept" appeal, the generic character of the design can highlight the theme of simplicity and directness.

In most cases, it is advisable to be frugal when designing a direct-mail piece. It is hard to convince a potential donor of the organization's need for funds with a package composed of extravagant color designs and custom-made envelopes and paper. At the same time, bold strokes such as large-sized lettering on the outside envelope or a uniquely shaped brochure can make the piece fun and intriguing.

Choosing the Components

In addition to the appeal letter, most fundraising packages also include a descriptive brochure about the organization and information about membership premiums and giving levels. Other possible enclosures include a short, personal note from a member of the board of trustees, a small gift such as a decal, and an insert highlighting one or more special premiums. These enclosures can be very effective in reinforcing the theme of the package, providing more detailed information, and highlighting certain key aspects of the appeal. When coordinated in message and design with the appeal letter, enclosures such as these can help make a more persuasive case to the potential donor.

The remaining components of the appeal, including a reply device, a reply envelope, and an outside envelope, should be relatively simple and straightforward.

The reply device usually includes a brief restatement of the theme of the letter ("YES! I'd like to enter the world of the Contemporary Arts Museum as a member!"), as well as sections for choosing a gift level, selecting special premiums, recording credit card information, and any additional information. An extra thank you on the reply card is a nice touch. The reply device is usually stamped with an address label that shows through the window of the outside envelope; this allows for easy mailing as well as quick identification when the donation is received. It is also helpful to add a code to the reply device or address label to help distinguish and track responses from various lists.

Donors use the reply envelope to mail their reply devices and contributions. Many organizations supply postage-paid reply envelopes (otherwise known as business reply mail—BRE). The organization pays the postage only for those envelopes that are mailed back.

For the outside envelope of the direct mailing, it can be useful to experiment with an arresting pitch designed to entice the potential donor to discover what's inside. A recent appeal from the Brooklyn Academy of Music, for example, engaged the reader with an outside envelope that exclaimed in big, colorful letters "The Best of BAM Is Inside." (See Appendix K.)

Additional Practical Details

Once the senior staff of the organization have approved the components, format, copy, and final design of the package, production can begin. At this stage, the graphic designer works closely with the printer to ensure that all components are printed to exact specifications. It is important to see a blueprint of the package to confirm all details before it goes to press.

Unless the mailing is on a small scale (under 2,000 pieces) and unless volunteers are available, it is advisable to hire a mailing service to assemble the package—that is, to affix labels to the reply device, fold and insert all the components of the appeal into the outside envelope, and add the postage. The mailing service should put together a sample to be approved by the organization before beginning the large job.

Organizations sending out large mail appeals should use third-class bulk mail when possible. The advantage of third-class mail is its cost; at current postal rates, the savings per piece is more than 60 percent over first-class mail. Knowledgeable mailing services can increase the savings even further with special presorting. The downside to these cost-saving measures is longer delivery time; bulk mail can take anywhere from a few days to several weeks to arrive. That's why it is best to plan ahead and ensure that there is enough time to make bulk mail a reasonable option. It is also advisable to work with a mailing service when sending out an appeal at the bulk-mail rate, because it requires much arduous sorting and bundling.

First-class mail should be used only when letters need to reach people quickly, or when there are not enough pieces to secure a bulk-mail rate. Many organizations use bulk mail for their large appeals and use first-class postage for their smaller, more personal renewal mailings.

Evaluation

Evaluation is the final step of a direct-mail campaign. Only by analyzing the campaign for both positive and negative outcomes can the organization ensure that future campaigns will build upon its success (or avoid its points of failure).

Important variables to be tracked include the number of packages mailed to each mailing list, the date the packages were mailed, the number of positive responses received from each list, the amount of income generated from each list, the percentage of gifts received from each list, the average individual gift, and the amount of income generated per thousand pieces mailed. It is also useful to compare the total number of responses to the total number of packages mailed to determine the percentage of return, or response rate, for the entire campaign (see Chart 6.2 for a form that tabulates telefundraising results). With this information, the organization can discover which lists were "hotter" than others, whether attempts at securing gifts at higher levels were successful, and whether income is in line with projections.

RENEWING EXISTING MEMBERS AND ANNUAL CONTRIBUTORS

While always being on the lookout for new members, the development staff must also have an effective renewal strategy for maintaining the support of its current members and donors. A renewal strategy does not begin and end with a renewal letter once a year. An effective strategy lasts all year round and includes the components listed below.

A Prompt Response after the Initial Gift Is Made

New members and donors are often anxious to receive their package of benefits and their membership card. A long delay in the mailing of these materials starts the relationship off on the wrong foot and can anger a new member—or at least dampen their excitement. New-member packages should be sent out no more than two weeks after receipt of the contribution (and preferably earlier), along with a warm letter thanking them for their support.

Excellent Customer Service

Most members and donors join with the reasonable expectation that their gift will earn them a sympathetic ear and a prompt resolution when they have a problem. Individuals also join in part because of the special treatment they are promised, whether it be access to the best seats, free lecture tickets, or direct phone ticket ordering. If the organization does not fulfill its end of the bargain, it is a prescription for hostility this year and unrenewed support the next.

Providing excellent customer service must be the central mission not only of the membership and development office, but of the entire institution. If members and donors are treated in a respectful and courteous way and receive everything they are promised, their willingness to renew will be much greater.

Continual Recognition

The development office should recognize the support of its contributors whenever possible throughout the year. All opportunities for recognition should be utilized, including listing by name in the program for higher level donors or as a group for lower level donors, special advance notice of upcoming events, or a telemarketing call for ticket sales that begins with a thank you. All of these techniques can be of great value in building a strong relationship with the contributor.

The Mail Renewal Process

Generally, for annual membership programs, the process of renewing memberships begins with a renewal letter mailed approximately two months ahead of the expiration date. After a month, if the donor doesn't respond, most organizations send out a second, more urgent letter. If this letter doesn't bring a response, it is appropriate to call the donor as part of a telefundraising campaign, because additional mailings tend to be of little effectiveness.

In some membership programs, the donor makes a gift at a point within the calendar or fiscal year that is not tied to a specific giving month. In these programs, the organization may send out more than two letters, with the goal of securing a higher cumulative contribution from each donor within the year. Additional letters may also be sent to donors who prefer to give at a specific time during the year.

Renewal letters should be personal and friendly; they should address the donor as a true partner in the life and future of the organization. Most letters begin with a strong statement of thanks for the donor's support and an accounting of the successes and accomplishments of the past year that were made possible by the donor's help.

In the body of the letter, it is helpful to remind the donor of the organization's most appealing qualities, such as the unique exhibitions it mounts year after year. This is also a good opportunity to highlight programs that may be less familiar to the donor, such as arts education or programs for seniors.

It is also important to point out to donors that renewal will bring them another year of membership privileges. Benefits should be not be the only focal point of the solicitation, however, because the member may not have taken advantage of them and may not see them as a motivation to renew. It is better to position benefits as the special appreciation offered to the donor in return for his or her continued, generous support of the institution.

In almost all cases, the renewal letter should ask the donor for renewed support at a higher level. It is particularly effective to tie a request for increased support to a special circumstance, such as a decrease in government support, or to an exciting new development, such as expanded programming during the upcoming season. It is also effective to offer the donor special premiums in return for an increased gift. Organizations should never be shy about making this request, for it is often possible to secure higher contributions from 50 percent or more of those who renew.

In the follow-up letter(s) to those donors who do not renew initially, the tone can be slightly more imploring, with a more urgent message of need. A follow-up letter from a public television station might picture a blank television screen to portray dramatically the potential negative outcome of insufficient continued support from donors. Donors who still do not respond should receive a phone call as part of a special phonathon or though the telemarketing office. In general, organizations should strive for a renewal rate of about 60–70 percent, with an even better rate for donors at higher giving levels (see Appendix K for an example of the donor renewal letter).

WAYS OF GIVING

Arts and cultural organizations can offer their donors a number of ways to give that are beneficial to both the organization and the donor. Charitable gifts can be deducted from donors' taxes, and through certain planned giving options (usually in conjunction with an endowment campaign), donors can increase their own income while playing an important role in the organization's current programs and future development. All such options should be developed in close consultation with professionals specifically knowledgeable about these areas and should be presented to potential donors in a clear, easy-to-understand manner.

Outright Gifts

Outright gifts of cash, securities, or real estate are especially welcome, as they can be used immediately for the purpose designated by the donor. The donor can also realize substantial tax savings and, through certain planned giving options, can even increase his or her own income.

Donors making cash gifts (by credit card, check, and so on) can deduct the gift from their taxable income to a level of up to 50 percent of their adjusted gross income in the year the gift is made. In the succeeding five years, the donor can claim any deductions exceeding the maximum deduction permitted in the initial tax year. Thus, for a donor in the 30 percent tax bracket, the net cost of a $5,000 cash gift is only $3,500, because taxes are reduced by $1,500. Yet the full $5,000 benefits the organization.

In the case of appreciated property such as securities, the donor can avoid paying capital gains tax (on the difference between the original price and the current market value) for all property owned for more than a year. Further, the individual can deduct the current market value of an appreciated property gift, to a level of up to 30 percent of the donor's adjusted gross income. For example, take the case of a donor who would like to make a gift of 300 shares of stock. When purchased, the securities cost $75 per share, or $22,500. If the current market value is now $200 per share, or $60,000, the donor receives a $60,000 charitable deduction *and* bypasses the capital gains tax on the appreciation of $37,500.

Additional options for outright gifts include gifts of closely held stock, real estate, and taxable personal property (e.g., artwork or jewelry), each of which offers the donor different advantages.

Deferred/Planned Gifts

A donor may choose to make a gift that will benefit an organization in the future. Deferred gifts can be tailored to the donor's personal circumstances to achieve reductions in current personal income taxes and estate taxes while maintaining or even increasing income from the donated assets. Deferred gifts are extremely important features of endowment campaigns. Often the endowment donor who has already made an outright gift is also approached for a deferred (or planned) gift that will benefit the institution beyond the lifetime of the donor. Planned gift giving options are described in detail in Chapter 9.

TELEFUNDRAISING

Many arts and cultural organizations include telefundraising to individuals as an integral part of their annual giving campaign. Using telefundraising to secure donations is usually more personal and effective than direct-mail appeals, although it is often more expensive. In general, the cost of phone solicitation is between 40 and 50 cents of each dollar raised, and the cost of acquisition calls is even higher.

Telefundraising encompasses more than simply conducting an end-of-the-year phonathon during which the organization's staff and volunteers call the donors who have not yet renewed. Sophisticated telefundraising often requires the help of a consultant, who develops the phone schedule and budgets, creates the telephone script, hires and trains the callers, and records and tabulates the results. Consultants to larger firms often map out a campaign and then assign an on-site captain or staff manager to run the campaign on a day-to-day basis. If the campaign is ambitious and ongoing, it may be useful to hire a consultant for a full year to alternate between telefundraising and telemarketing (e.g., phoning for the purpose of selling ticket subscriptions), with expenses divided between the development and the marketing departments.

Telefundraising generally includes three distinct types of calls. *Renewal calls* are to current donors (individuals who contributed the previous year) who are reaching the end of their membership term. *Calls to lapsed donors* target those individuals who last contributed more than one year ago. Both of these calls are follow-up measures aimed at those who have been sent letters, but have not yet responded. *Acquisition calls* are made to prospective donors who have not yet responded to an advance mailing.

Leads for acquisition calls are garnered from the organization's database or from direct-mail lists and are then segmented according to their different levels of involvement with the organization. Acquisition call groups include *subscribers*, individuals who have made multiple purchases of the primary product or service of the organization, but who have not yet contributed; *single buyers*, who have made one purchase, but have not made a contribution; *general interest*, those who have signed up to be on the mailing list but have not participated in the institution as either a purchaser or a donor; and *cold calls*, individuals whose names were acquired through outside lists.

There are other types of calls that can be made depending on the length, scheduling, and budget of the campaign. Special-appeal calls, such as an extra-gift campaign six months prior to donor's renewal dates, help generate twice-yearly contributions. Reminder calls to individuals with outstanding pledges, made two to four weeks after a second mailing, increase the rate of pledge fulfillment and the amount of net campaign revenue. Also, a separate phone campaign can be created as part of a capital fund or endowment campaign, if appropriate.

Scheduling and Budgeting

Scheduling is a crucial part of the phone campaign. The telefundraising schedule should be integrated into the schedule of the overall development campaign and complement rather than compete with direct-mail efforts, galas, and subscription drives.

When scheduling calls to various groups of potential donors, it is important to hit the "hot lists" first. In other words, renewing donors should be called soon after their donations are due, and subscribers or single-ticket buyers should be contacted soon (generally two weeks) after they have attended events. If calls are not timely, it is difficult to capitalize on a person's interest in the organization.

Budgeting is usually based on the consultant's fee, the staff manager or site captain's fee, and the number of callers needed. Sometimes there are additional costs incurred in tabulating the results of large campaigns. Callers are usually paid by the hour. It is often wise to give callers an incentive by offering them commissions or bonuses based on their success rate.

Hiring and Training Callers

The number of callers an organization needs for a telefundraising campaign is based on the number of calls that need to be made and the anticipated timetable. Callers should be interviewed by the staff manager to assure that their phone personalities reflect the image the institution wishes to project. There should be regular training sessions for new callers to familiarize them with the work of the organization and to demonstrate effective telephone techniques. One of the phone captain's responsibilities should be to monitor each caller's progress every night, to help develop the caller's efficiency and effectiveness. The captain must have the authority to remove callers who cannot maintain minimum quotas.

Creating and Using the Phone Script

First and foremost, telefundraising callers must be sincere, courteous, and enthusiastic about "selling" the institution. In most cases, the phone captain develops a script ahead of time and, during the training session, gives the callers an opportunity to familiarize themselves with the script and to practice by making simulated calls.

The script for renewal calls is usually quite simple, because the donor is already knowledgeable about the organization and is generally receptive to being approached. The script should solicit the donor's response to the institution's recent programs and should verify address information.

The acquisition call seeks to reorient the individual's relationship with the institution to being one of a donor. Different approaches are required for different calling groups, so the script is often more complex and requires the presentation of more detailed information. At the same time, it must be general enough so that the listener is not confused by a barrage of details. The script must provide the essential facts about the institution, including its mission, a summary of its most successful programs, important new developments, and the reasons contributions are important.

The script for acquisition calls also provides answers to common questions and listener responses, as well as instructions on how to record credit card information and other important facts about the new donor. (See Appendix K, "Telefundraising Renewal Script and Telefundraising Acquisition Script," for examples.)

Telefundraising staff should be trained to deal with objections from those being solicited. Predetermined responses to frequently raised objections can accompany the script (see Appendix K, "Telefundraising Objection Responses").

Recording and Tabulating Results

Telefundraising campaign results should be tabulated in the following ways:

- Weekly results
- Comparative weekly results, evaluating each week against the others
- Total results

All reports should document the number and percentage of donations paid by credit card and pledges. The revenues generated by calling should be compared against expenses to determine the cost per gift, the overall net revenue of the campaign, and the cost as a percentage of net revenue (cents spent to raise a dollar). The report should also state the amount of the average gift, the number of calling hours used, the average dollar amount raised per calling hour, the number of leads used, the number of contacts per calling hour, the number of positive and negative responses, and the percentage of positive responses in relation to the total number of calls. Responses should be categorized by acquisition calls and renewal calls to provide the clearest, most specific information about the success of the campaign (see Chart 6.2).

		Campaign Total	
	Total	Acquisition	Renewal
REVENUE			
Credit Cards Paid	number $		
Pledges Mailed	number $		
Total	number $		
LEADS USED—Description and Number			
Campaign Length	number		
Total Calling Hours	number		
Total Calls Dialed	number		
Percent Leads Contacted	number		
Contacts per Hour	number		
Yes Response	number		
No Response	number		
Credit Card Rate	number		
Avg $ per Call Hour	$		
Average Gift $ Amount	$		
EXPENSES			
Staff Manager Salary			
Callers, Clerical Payroll			
Total	$		
Cost per Gift	$		
Exp/Rev (cents on the $)	$		
Received Pledges	# $		
Unpaid Pledges	# $		
NET REVENUE (Actual)	$		

(Net Revenue = Credit Card $ + Received Pledge $ − Expenses $)

PROJECTED NET REVENUE*$

TELEFUNDRAISING RESULTS REPORT

CHART 6.2

*Assumes 75–80 percent average fulfillment on pledged contributions for renewal, less for acquisition. This chart provided by Richard Larter, Brooklyn Academy of Music.

CHAPTER

Government

Government support to arts and cultural organizations is available at the federal and state levels, and in some cases through municipal governments and community agencies. An organization's ability to secure public funds at each level depends to a large degree on the quality of its programs and whether it reaches the audiences targeted by the granting agency. As with corporate, foundation, and individual funding sources, an organization is most likely to receive support from the government sources closest to home—local and state agencies.

As a group, state agencies historically have provided support to many more organizations than the National Endowment for the Arts or the National Endowment for the Humanities, the primary sources of arts and cultural funding at the federal level. For this reason alone, arts and cultural organizations should establish ties with state agencies early in their fundraising efforts.

Identifying and approaching support programs at the community level should also be one of the first steps in an organization's search for funding, especially as the federal government continues to phase out its support for the arts. Depending on the locality, community support programs can provide significant funds. The community support programs in Houston and in Dallas-Fort Worth, for example, are major sources of support for local arts and cultural organizations. Some local agencies provide technical and management assistance but offer no funds.

This chapter discusses the major federal funding agencies and offers a general discussion of state agencies and community support programs.

FEDERAL GOVERNMENT SUPPORT

The first commitment made by the U.S. government to support a cultural activity took place in 1836, when a skeptical and reluctant Congress enacted legislation that pledged the faith of the United States to the execution of the terms of James Smithson's bequest. This resulted in the establishment of the Smithsonian Institution in 1846, as a privately endowed institution with the United States government as trustee. Nonetheless, broad government support for artistic endeavors was still many years away.

During the Depression of the 1930s, the Works Progress Administration (WPA) provided jobs for unemployed artists through several programs. The Federal Theatre Project, for instance, employed over 10,000 artists and helped launch the careers of many important actors and playwrights. These programs were primarily designed to cope with unemployment rather than to support the arts, however.

During the next three decades, several events increased awareness of the arts in the United States: World War II, one result of which was to bring Americans closer to Europe and its artistic traditions; the advent of television, which brought art and entertainment directly into the home; and the development of national tours for performing companies and art exhibits, which brought art and culture to communities throughout the United States. During the same period, many community-based arts organizations were established across the country.

The government's role in fostering the growth of the arts was not clearly defined until 1965, when the National Foundation on the Arts and Humanities Act was passed. This act established the Federal Council on the Arts and Humanities and its operating agencies, the National Endowment for the Arts and the National Endowment for the Humanities.

The events leading to the passage of the law dated back to the early 1950s, when Senator Hubert Humphrey first called for federal support of the arts. President John F. Kennedy also advocated support for culture and the arts, but he did not live long enough to bring about a formal procedure for providing funds. It was not until President Lyndon Johnson's administration that a mechanism was set up to disburse funds to the arts and humanities. In fact, the federal arts and cultural policy was in keeping with Johnson's Great Society legislation, and he became the primary advocate of a national cultural policy.

The National Endowment for the Arts

The National Endowment for the Arts (NEA) was established in 1965, under the leadership of Roger Stevens, with a modest appropriation of $3 million and the mission of encouraging and supporting American arts and artists. Following the election of Richard Nixon as president in 1968, Nancy Hanks was appointed to succeed Stevens and oversee a budget of $8.2 million. By late 1977, when Livingston L. Biddle, Jr., became chairman, the budget had increased to $114.6 million. Francis Hodsoll, who became chairman in November 1981, managed total appropriations for 1982 of $143 million, down from $159 million in fiscal year 1981. This represented the first reduction in government support of the arts since the Endowment was established in 1965. By 1988, however, the appropriation was $167 million, representing the highest amount to that date.

When the NEA was up for funding reauthorization by Congress at the end of the 1980s, the agency's support of exhibits by two visual artists, Andres Serrano and the late photographer Robert Mapplethorpe, spurred a dispute about the role the government should play in supporting the arts. In response to the controversial paintings and photographs, Senator Jesse Helms (R-NC) proposed restrictions that would prohibit federal funds from being used to "promote, disseminate or produce obscene or indecent materials, including but not limited to depictions of sadomasochism, homoeroticism, the exploitation of children or individuals engaged in sex acts; or material which denigrates the objects or beliefs of the adherents of a particular religion or nonreligion; or material that denigrates, debases or reviles a person, group or class of citizens on the basis of race, creed, sex, handicap, age or national origin."

The Senate approved Helms's restrictions, and the House, in an effort to avoid a total cutoff of NEA funds, voted to reduce the NEA's $171 million budget by $45,000, the amount granted to support the two exhibitions. So came a turning point in federal support of the arts. A heated controversy ensued, and by late 1995 a Senate-House conference committee agreed to cut 40 percent from the National Endowment for the Arts budget for 1996. At that time, NEA Chair Jane Alexander, appointed by President Bill Clinton in 1994, announced a 47 percent cut in staff (from 279 to 148) and a reduction in budget from $167 million to $99.4 million.

Until 1996, the NEA provided financial support in the form of grants to individual artists and to not-for-profit organizations to promote awareness of the arts among the general public. As a result of agency restructuring in January 1996, the NEA revamped its producedures and guidelines, eliminating both seasonal operating support and most grants to individuals (with the exception of Literature Fellowships, American Jazz Masters Awards, and National Heritage Awards).

Purpose and Goals

The purpose of the National Endowment for the Arts, as set forth in its statement of mission dated November 1986, remains as follows:

The mission of the National Endowment for the Arts is to foster the excellence, diversity, and vitality of the arts in the United States, and to help broaden the availability and appreciation of such excellence, diversity, and vitality.

In implementing its mission, the Endowment continues to exercise care to preserve and improve the environment in which the arts have flourished. It must not, under any circumstances, impose a single aesthetic standard or attempt to direct artistic content.

In 1996, as a result of changes in the grantmaking process and structure, the agency, in addition to recognizing excellence at institutions large and small, began to encourage all arts organizations to work more closely together and to share information and resources creatively through partnership agreements.

Structure

The NEA's basic organizational structure consists of

- The National Council on the Arts
- Office of the chair
- Office of the deputy chair for grants and partnership
- Office of the deputy chair for management and budget
- Theme area divisions
- Advisory panels

The National Council on the Arts is composed of 26 individuals who are widely recognized for their knowledge of, expertise in, or profound interest in the arts and who have established records of distinguished service, or have achieved eminence, in the arts. Council members are appointed by the president of the United States and serve six-year terms staggered so that approximately one-third of the members are replaced every two years. The Council advises the chair of the NEA on policy matters and on decisions regarding grants. The Council holds four three-day meetings annually to consider applications, review guidelines, discuss major developments affecting any or all of the disciplines, and debate policy and program matters.

The chair, who is also appointed by the president, is the official head of the NEA and is responsible for running the agency and making final decisions on grants and policies. This individual is, by law, the chair of the National Council on the Arts.

The deputy chair for grants and partnership, under the supervision of the chair, is responsible for the management of the NEA's grants, along with its partnership agreements and leadership initiatives. The deputy chair serves as principal adviser to the chair on program matters and participates in formulating major policies of the agency.

The deputy chair for management and budget, under the supervision of the chair, supervises administration.

Each of the agency's four theme areas (Heritage and Preservation, Creation and Presentation, Education and Access, and Planning and Stabilization) is staffed separately and includes arts policy advisers who specialize in each of the following areas: dance, design arts, education, expansion arts, folk arts, inter-arts, arts programs, literature, local initiatives, media arts, museums, music, theater, opera, opera/musical theater, presenting, and visual arts. The themed departments also include project evaluators, cluster specialists, and cluster assistants. The NEA staff in a particular discipline or field is the primary link between the NEA and arts organizations and artists. The arts policy advisers and their staffs help organizations understand and comply with the NEA's grant-making policies and application processes. They also provide advice, information, and assistance as needed, and respond to questions from arts organizations interested in applying for grants.

Advisory panels, which vary in size depending on the needs of each discipline, are made up of individuals with knowledge and expertise in each grantmaking area. Collectively, these individuals have knowledge and exper-tise in many different areas of a particular arts specialty or discipline. The panelists are selected from all parts of the country to serve on two kinds of panels: policy or overview panels, which develop and review guidelines and consider future plans for the programs; and grant panels, which review grant applications, make funding recommendations, and may also review policy and guidelines. The chair and the deputy chair for grants and partnership agree-ments appoint members of the advisory panels, who generally serve for a minimum of one year and a maximum of three years. Panelists are not full-time employees of the agency; they serve as needed, attending meetings throughout the year.

Grant Programs

The Endowment's current organizational structure for grant making is fairly new—a result of the tremendous budget cuts in 1996. Although the agency is no longer divided into discipline areas, it remains committed to supporting a broad range of artistic activity, including arts edcuation, dance, design, expan-sion arts, folk and traditional arts, international projects, literature, media arts, museums, music, opera-musical theater, presenting, theater, and visual arts. Theme areas have replaced discipline areas; the four theme areas as of January 1996 are:

- *Heritage and Preservation.* The Heritage and Preservation area provides support for projects that honor, assist, and make visible the arts rooted in the traditions that make up our nation or that preserve the most significant artistic accomplishments and works of art.

- *Creation and Presentation.* The Creation and Presentation area provides support for the creation of new works or the presentation of new and existing works of any culture, period, or discipline.
- *Education and Access.* The Education and Access area provides support for projects that broaden and deepen educational experiences for people of all ages, that reach audiences who have not been reached before, or that expand awareness and appreciation of art forms to which exposure has been limited or nonexistent.
- *Planning and Stabilization.* The Planning and Stabilization area supports projects that focus on organizational planning, strengthening capacity internally or within an arts field, sustaining the arts, building partnerships, and developing new resources.

Two additional support programs, Partnership Agreements and Leadership Initiatives, have also been added to assist state and regional programs (not individual institutions).

- *Partnership Agreements.* The Partnership Agreements area was created specifically for state and jurisdictional arts agencies (SAA) and their regional arts organizations (RAO). The Endowment will review a single application from each SAA and its RAOs for funds to carry out plans that serve artists, arts organizations, arts education efforts, underserved communities, and comprehensive statewide development of the arts. SAAs and RAOs also may apply to a theme area for a project to assist underserved communities.

- *Leadership Initiatives.* Leadership Initiatives has been created to sponsor specific initiatives for projects of national significance and impact or that serve as models in one discipline or across the different disciplines.

All 50 states and 6 U.S. special jurisdictions (including Guam and the District of Columbia) have official state arts agencies (see Appendix F). With the exception of the private Vermont Council on the Arts, all are agencies of state government. In addition, the states have formed seven regional groups to administer programs and services most efficiently carried out on a multistate basis. NEA grants go to assist designated state agencies and regional groups in carrying out plans for the support of the arts.

Methods of Funding

The NEA makes most of its grants through its four main theme areas. The grants offered are determined by each particular program office based on the needs of the artistic discipline and the particular grantee. An organization may submit only one application in one of the four theme areas.

Grants are made from both program and treasury funds. All program fund grants (except for Planning and Stabilization, which has more stringent matching requirements) must be matched at least one to one by nonfederal funds. The matching requirement means that the organization must raise at least 50 percent of the costs of a given project, to equal the amount of the NEA grant. For example, if a project costs $15,000, the organization must raise at least $7,500 from other sources; the organization can request no more than one-half, or $7,500 in this case, of the total project costs from the NEA. Permissible sources of matching income are grants from private sources, revenues from ticket sales or other income-producing activities, and the value of project-related in-kind services.

The match required by a Planning and Stabilization grant is determined by the amount of the grant award. In this category, all grants of $100,000 or less require at least a one-to-one match, grants between $100,001 and $250,000 require a match of at least three to one, and grants between $250,001 and $500,000 require a match of five to one.

Treasury fund grants are made at the discretion of each program area, based on a grantee's ability to meet the more stringent matching requirements. These grants must be matched with at least three nonfederal dollars for each federal dollar. The grantee is required to certify to the Endowment that it has secured a portion of the match through pledges, cash and in-kind contributions, and earned income before the treasury funds are released.

Fellowship grants are awarded to individuals of exceptional artistic talent for the purpose of developing their work. Offered only to U.S. citizens and permanent residents, these grants have been all but eliminated. Congressional legislation has limited fellowships to the following: Literature Fellowships, American Jazz Masters Awards, and National Heritage Awards. The Jazz Masters and National Heritage Awards are made on a nomination basis only. Applications are not accepted.

How to Approach the NEA for Funds

Detailed funding guidelines for each NEA program are published annually. These guidelines provide prospective grantees with information on the application process and deadlines, typical grant sizes, eligibility requirements, and the program areas for which funds are available. The first step an organization takes in approaching the NEA for funds is to obtain a copy of the guidelines from the appropriate theme office. It is helpful to meet and establish a working relationship with the director and other staff members of the most relevant NEA program.

It is also a good idea to add the appropriate NEA arts policy advisers and staff members to the organization's mailing list to keep them informed about activities throughout the season. After an organization has applied for an NEA grant, the key staff should update the NEA advisers and staff through a personal visit. Grant recipients should make it a point to visit NEA staff annually.

The NEA has defined a number of eligibility requirements with which all organizations must comply to receive funds. It should be noted that each funding program may have additional funding requirements. The NEA requires that prospective grant recipients be:

- Tax-exempt, that no private stockholder or individual may benefit from the net earnings of the organization, and that charitable donations are allowable as decreed under Section 170(c) of the IRS Code of 1954, as amended
- In compliance with Title VI of the 1964 Civil Rights Act, Title IX of the Education Amendment of 1974, and Section 504 of the Rehabilitation Act of 1974. Generally speaking, these laws prohibit discrimination on the basis of sex, race, religion, personal handicap, or national origin.
- In compliance with parts 3, 5, and 50(s) of Title 29 of the Code of Federal Regulations requiring appropriate compensation for all professional personnel, laborers, and mechanics

In all cases (except for folk art and traditional arts organizations), applicant organizations must have a four-year history of programming prior to the application deadline.

To apply for NEA funds, the development director should become familiar with the four themes, the eligibility requirements, the review criteria, and the application process as outlined in the funding guidelines. The second step is to select the theme area that relates best to the purpose of the project. After this is done, the "intent to apply" card from the guideline booklet should be mailed by the designated deadline. The final step is to complete an official NEA application form and submit it with the specified materials prior to the application deadline. The program guidelines provide step-by-step instructions for completing the form (refer to Chart 7.1 at the end of the chapter). Once the application has been submitted, it passes through various channels before a decision is made:

- The application is reviewed by NEA staff in the appropriate discipline/field for eligibility and completeness and is then passed on to experts in the field for review. Their recommendations and the application go to theme panels for another review. Theme panel recommendations are then presented to the chair and National Council.
- The National Council reviews the panel's decision and presents its recommendations to the chair for approval.
- The chair reviews the National Council's remarks and makes the final decision. If the award is granted, notification is sent to the arts organization.

- The applicant signs and returns a copy of the award letter, indicating acceptance of the grant.
- The applicant requests the funds from the grants office according to the conditions of the grant—that is, as a cash advance or as reimbursement. The request is made by completing the appropriate form and mailing it to the NEA.
- Payments are authorized by the NEA and mailed to the grantee.
- Progress reports are required from grant recipients, as well as a final report describing in narrative form the outcome of the project and accompanying fiscal documentation. These are sent to the grants office by the organization within 90 days of the end of the grant period.
- The final report is approved by the NEA, and the grant is concluded.

The National Endowment for the Humanities

The National Endowment for the Humanities (NEH) was established in 1965, along with the NEA, to support research, education, and public programs in the humanities—including fields such as history, philosophy, linguistics, languages, literature, archaeology, jurisprudence, ethics, education, comparative religion, and the history and criticism of the arts.

In 1996, the NEH, like the NEA, suffered a 40 percent budget reduction, resulting in a budget of $110 million, down from its 1989 appropriation of $140.4 million. The NEH awards funds to both not-for-profit institutions and individuals and expects its support to leverage other nonfederal dollars and to complement existing or planned private and local initiatives. With the reconfiguration that has taken place as a result of its significantly reduced budget, the NEH provides support to the activities that best meet its guiding tenets: activities that are best done at the national level, that have long-term impact, that have few other sources of support, that strengthen the institutional base of the humanities, and that reach broad sectors of the American public.

The Endowment's focus is on the following areas:

- Supporting original scholarship
- Preserving American cultural heritage
- Providing learning opportunities for the nation's teachers
- Engaging the American public in the humanities

Structure

The NEH's basic organizational structure, which parallels closely that of the NEA, consists of

- The National Council on the Humanities
- The office of the chair, which includes the deputy chair, the senior humanities adviser, and special assistants
- Grant-making divisions
- Administrative and information offices
- Peer-review panels

The actual awarding of grants occurs through the major program divisions; the staff members of those divisions are the primary links to humanities organizations. A division's staff recommends projects for funding after guiding applications through a peer-review process. The final decision about awards rests with the chair of the Endowment. The chair is advised by a board of 24 private citizens who make up the National Council on the Humanities. These individuals serve six-year terms. The chair, who is appointed by the president of the United States, serves for four years.

The peer-review process is carried out by nearly 1,000 private scholars and professionals in the humanities, who serve on 150 panels annually. These individuals make judgments on each application, and their reviews are assembled by the NEH staff and then presented to the National Council. The Council meets four times a year to advise the chair on the funding of applications. The chair makes the final decisions.

Grant Programs

The NEH awards grants in the humanities through three program divisions (containing a total of seven divisions within the areas) and one program office. The three main program divisions and the program office are as follows:

- *Division of Preservation and Access.* This program has one set of guidelines and one funding cycle. It encompasses preservation and access projects (such as education and training initiatives, regional field service programs, and research and demonstration projects), the stabilization and documentation of material culture collections, and the U.S. newspaper program.
- *Division of Public Programs and Enterprise.* This division has two programs with one set of guidelines and two funding cycles. The programs are as follows: (1) Public Programs: planning and implementation of public humanities activities, including museum exhibitions, library exhibitions and programs, and radio and television programs; and (2) Enterprise: special initiatives, partnerships with other agencies and the private sector, transdivisional projects, and other activities.
- *Division of Research and Education.* This division administers four programs, each with a set of guidelines and a funding cycle,

encompassing the following: (1) Seminars and Institutes: summer seminars and institutes for higher-education faculty and school teachers; (2) Education Development and Demonstration: materials and model curricula with related professional development and trial implementation (e.g., teaching with technology); (3) Fellowships and Stipends: fellowships for university and college teachers and independent scholars, summer stipends, and faculty graduate study for members of historically black colleges or universities; and (4) Research: editions, translations, basic research, archaeology, humanities study of science and technology, centers, international programs, and conferences.

• *Office of Challenge Grants.* Through this program office, humanities institutions seeking new sources of long-term support can apply for a challenge grant. Funds received, which must be matched on at least a three-to-one basis, must be used to establish or increase institutional endowments, to purchase capital equipment, or to retire debt.

The NEH also supports 56 state councils for the humanities (see Appendix G). These agencies, which provide project grants to foster public events on humanities topics for audiences throughout a state, are independent from the NEH and solicit grant funds from other private sources. These state agencies print and administer their own guidelines.

How to Approach the NEH for Funds

As with the NEA, the first step in approaching the NEH for funds is to obtain the guidelines and application forms for the most suitable program area. The guidelines are fairly detailed, providing deadline dates, eligibility requirements, examples of successful grants, and instructions on how to apply. It is strongly recommended that a working relationship with an appropriate NEH staff member be established.

The United States Information Agency

The United States Information Agency (USIA) sponsors—with an extremely limited budget—international cultural-exchange programs with foreign countries to promote greater understanding between U.S. citizens and other peoples of the world. The USIA's exchanges and visitors programs enable U.S. artists to participate in major international visual arts exhibits and performing arts festivals. This office also provides funds for American cultural specialists to provide artistic and administrative and technical advice to foreign institutions. Historically, additional grantmaking areas of USIA have included: the Creative Arts Exchanges Program, which allows for cooperative exchange between Americans and foreign citizens in the areas of art, culture, and traditions, and the Artistic Ambassador Program, which allows talented musicians to perform and work with musicians overseas. The USIA administers the Fulbright scholarships for student and teacher exchanges and the Grant-in-Aid Program, which offers financial grants to the international programs of private organizations. Through the United States Information Service, the USIA also maintains cultural centers with extensive libraries in more than 95 countries to help foreign citizens learn more about the United States. Due to budget reductions, USIA is evaluating all of its arts programs to determine which should be eliminated and which will continue. It would be wise to check with the agency's office before seriously considering seeking funding.

The Institute of Museum Services

The Institute of Museum Services (IMS) provides support to a broad range of museums, including botanical gardens, aquariums, planetariums, zoos, and arboretums, as well as art, natural history, and science museums. Grants are awarded to such organizations for operating expenses, conservation, professional program assessment, facilities, and education programs. In fiscal year 1995 the IMS received appropriations totaling $28.7 million. However, in fiscal year 1996 its budget was cut by 27 percent to $21 million, roughly $1 million less than in 1988.

Other Federal Agencies

There are a number of other federal government agencies that have in the past supported programs or projects in the arts. Among the agencies that have provided grants to arts organizations are the departments of Health, Education, and Welfare; Commerce; Housing and Urban Development; Defense; Interior; Labor; and Agriculture. Grants have also been given by the General Services Administration, the Corporation for Public Broadcasting, the Community Services Administration, and the National Trust for Historic Preservation.

The availability of funds from these agencies varies depending on the presidential administration in office. Interested development directors should verify the existence of grant programs in these agencies and investigate the application requirements and regulations before entering into a formal application procedure. Officials in congressional offices can be helpful in this process.

STATE SUPPORT PROGRAMS

Support to the arts and humanities at the state level existed long before the federal government began to provide funding through the NEA and NEH. The federal agencies, however, were a major catalyst in the creation of official arts and culture funding agencies in almost every state.

State Arts Councils

According to the NEA guidelines for state programs, "By law, no less than 20 percent of the Endowment's program funds must be made available for grants to designated state arts agencies and regional groups of state arts agencies." These funds are awarded to state arts agencies and regional groups in the form of basic state grants and regional arts programming grants. See Appendix F for a listing of state and regional arts organizations.

These NEA block grants have provided a powerful incentive for local support and have inspired state legislatures to appropriate amounts that at least match the NEA allocation. The New York State Council on the Arts operated with state appropriations of $35.2 million in fiscal year 1995 (down from $54 million in fiscal year 1988), making it the largest state arts agency in terms of total dollars awarded in grants. Michigan was second, with total appropriations of $30.8 million, and Florida was third, with $25.2 million. It is interesting to note that despite drastic reductions in federal funding to the arts, the aggregate appropriations to state arts agencies have held steady or increased over the four-year period beginning in fiscal year 1991. Each state, however, as a result of its own specific political and economic factors, will determine levels of funding for the arts.

The overriding purpose of most state agencies is the development and support of artists, community arts activities, and arts organizations statewide. There are many similarities in the grant-making procedures of state agencies. For example, most state agencies have some kind of matching-fund requirement. However, each state agency is run by an executive director and overseen by a council or board that develops grant-making policies, programs, and application guidelines.

Most state agencies act as information resources for arts organizations and artists in the state. These agencies provide information on arts activities, publish annual lists of arts fairs and festivals, and disseminate information relating to the various kinds of technical and management assistance available.

Development personnel and other top managers in arts organizations should develop a comfortable working relationship with the grants officer of their state arts agency. Most state agencies have clearly defined application procedures, deadlines, and eligibility requirements for prospective grantees. An arts organization that serves a local community has a much stronger case for support at the state level than it does at the federal level because the state agency has tailored its programs to the unique cultural makeup of the state. The state agency also has a more intimate understanding of those organizations located within its boundaries. A local arts group appealing directly to the NEA, for instance, may have a difficult time justifying the need for federal funds because federal funding programs are developed to meet nationwide priorities.

State Humanities Councils

The founding legislation of the National Endowment for the Humanities provided for the distribution of a portion of its funds through state humanities councils. There are humanities councils in all 50 states, the District of Columbia, Puerto Rico, and the U.S. Virgin Islands; see Appendix G. These councils differ from their counterparts, the state arts councils, in that in many cases they are not agencies of state governments but rather committees of private citizens. Each state humanities council establishes its own grant-making guidelines and application deadlines. A wide variety of humanities projects are funded through state councils, including conferences, lectures, workshops, exhibits, media presentations, and scholars-in-residence programs.

COMMUNITY SUPPORT PROGRAMS

There are approximately 2,000 community arts and culture agencies in the United States. The idea of establishing local councils for arts and culture first emerged in the 1950s. It is generally believed that the first community arts group in the United States was in Winston-Salem, North Carolina. Many community agencies are private, not-for-profit organizations, not branches of city or county governments.

The goals, programs, and organization of community groups reflect the unique makeup of their particular localities. The primary functions of most agencies include providing a local clearinghouse for cultural information, acting as cultural advocates in their home communities, and offering administrative and technical services in such areas as bookkeeping, fundraising, and publicity. In some cases—most typically, in small towns—the local arts and culture agency produces or presents all the cultural activities in the community by sponsoring performing-arts series, art exhibits, and film series, and by organizing festivals and competitions.

Some community arts and culture agencies make grants to local organizations and artists/scholars. Others conduct annual united-fund drives among community businesses in behalf of local cultural organizations. Because they represent the larger interests of the community and tend to be more financially stable, community cultural agencies are often more effective than an individual organization in securing state and federal support.

Since the mission of community cultural agencies is to provide services to the cultural organizations in their localities, leaders of arts and cultural organizations should develop a personal relationship with the management of the local agency.

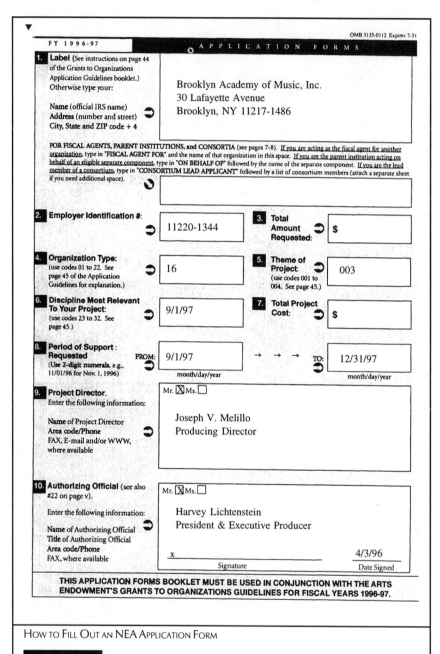

▼

OMB 3135-0112 Expires 7-31

FY 1996-97

APPLICATION FORMS

1. Label (See instructions on page 44 of the Grants to Organizations Application Guidelines booklet.)
Otherwise type your:

Name (official IRS name)
Address (number and street)
City, State and ZIP code + 4

Brooklyn Academy of Music, Inc.
30 Lafayette Avenue
Brooklyn, NY 11217-1486

FOR FISCAL AGENTS, PARENT INSTITUTIONS, and CONSORTIA (see pages 7-8). If you are acting as the fiscal agent for another organization, type in "FISCAL AGENT FOR" and the name of that organization in this space. If you are the parent institution acting on behalf of an eligible separate component, type in "ON BEHALF OF" followed by the name of the separate component. If you are the lead member of a consortium, type in "CONSORTIUM LEAD APPLICANT" followed by a list of consortium members (attach a separate sheet if you need additional space).

2. Employer Identification #:

11220-1344

3. Total Amount Requested: $

4. Organization Type:
(use codes 01 to 22. See page 45 of the Application Guidelines for explanation.)

16

5. Theme of Project:
(use codes 001 to 004. See page 45.)

003

6. Discipline Most Relevant To Your Project:
(use codes 23 to 32. See page 45.)

9/1/97

7. Total Project Cost: $

8. Period of Support: Requested
(Use 2-digit numerals, e.g., 11/01/96 for Nov. 1, 1996)

FROM: 9/1/97
month/day/year

→ → → TO: 12/31/97
month/day/year

9. Project Director.
Enter the following information:

Name of Project Director
Area code/Phone
FAX, E-mail and/or WWW, where available

Mr. ☒ Ms. ☐

Joseph V. Melillo
Producing Director

10. Authorizing Official (see also #22 on page v).

Enter the following information:

Name of Authorizing Official
Title of Authorizing Official
Area code/Phone
FAX, where available

Mr. ☒ Ms. ☐

Harvey Lichtenstein
President & Executive Producer

x _____ 4/3/96
Signature   Date Signed

THIS APPLICATION FORMS BOOKLET MUST BE USED IN CONJUNCTION WITH THE ARTS ENDOWMENT'S GRANTS TO ORGANIZATIONS GUIDELINES FOR FISCAL YEARS 1996-97.

HOW TO FILL OUT AN NEA APPLICATION FORM

CHART 7.1

11. **Project Description.** Describe clearly and concisely how the requested and matching funds will be spent. In the first sentence, identify the specific project for which support is requested; provide more detail in subsequent sentences. Please limit your project description to the space provided; continuation sheets are not permitted and will not be reviewed.

(list of Next Wave 1997 productions with a brief description).

12. **Summary of estimated costs** is a recap of #s 13 through 18 on pages iii and iv of this form.

Direct costs

Salaries and wages (#13)	$	Reminder:		
Fringe benefits (#13)	$	Amount requested		
Supplies and materials (#14)	$	(#3 on page i)	$	
Travel (#15)	$	Plus "Total match		
Permanent equipment (#16)	$	for this project"		
Fees and other expenses (#17)	$	(#19 on page iv		
Total direct costs	$	of this form)	+ $	
Indirect costs (#18)	$	Must equal		
Total project costs	$	⇔ "Total project costs"	= $	

▲

How to Fill Out an NEA Application Form

CHART 7.1 (CONTINUED)

FY 1996-97

A P P L I C A T I O N F O R M S

Items # 13-18 Breakdown of "Summary of estimated costs" #12 on previous page.

13. Direct costs: Salaries and wages (Include artists' compensation if paid on a salary basis. Do not include salaries and wages associated with fundraising.)

Title and/or type of personnel	Number of personnel	Annual or average salary range	% of time devoted to this project	Amount
Administrative:		$		$
General Mgmt.		$		$
Programming		$		$
Marketing		$		$
Press		$		$
Community Relations		$		$
Technical Personnel		$		$

Total salaries and wages a. $
Fringe benefits   Total fringe benefits b. $
Total Salaries and wages (a. + b.) $

14. Direct costs: Supplies and materials (List each major type separately.)   Amount

Total supplies and materials $

15. Direct costs: Travel (Any foreign travel must be in conformance with government regulations)
Is foreign travel included?   Yes ☐   No ☒

TRANSPORTATION OF TRAVELERS

Number of travelers	From	To	Amount
Next Wave Festival	local travel		

Total transportation of travelers a. $

SUBSISTENCE

Number of travelers	No. of days	Daily rate	Amount

Total subsistence b. $
Total travel (a. + b.) $

How to Fill Out an NEA Application Form

CHART 7.1 (CONTINUED)

Items # 13-18 Breakdown of "Summary of estimated costs" #12 on page ii.

16. **Direct costs: Permanent equipment** (Equipment costing $5,000 or more per unit with an estimated useful life of more than one year. Written justification is required.)   Amount

Total permanent equipment	$

17. **Direct costs: Fees for services and other expenses** (List each item separately; include artists' compensation if paid on a fee basis. Do not include entertainment, fines and penalties, bad debt costs, miscellaneous, contingencies, or costs incurred before the start of the official grant period.)   Amount

Company Fees	$
Contractual Services	$
Orchestra	$
Equipment Rental	$
Freight	$
Hauling	$
Patron Bus/Promotion	$
Insurance	$
Total fees for services and other expenses	$

18. **Indirect costs:** (Attach rate negotiation agreement with the National Endowment for the Arts or another Federal agency)

	Rate	%	Base	Amount
				$

19. **Total match for this project** (must equal "total match for this project" in #12 on page ii)

A. Cash match	Amount
Total cash match a.	$

B. In-kind contributions (identify sources; items must also be shown as direct costs)	Amount
Total in-kind contributions b.	$

C. Grants (identify sources; do not list any Arts Endowment or other Federal grants)	Amount
Corporate	$
Foundation	$
Individuals	$
City and State Total grants c.	$

D. Revenues (identify sources)	Amount
Box Office	$
Benefits	$
Total revenues d.	$
Total match for this project (a. + b. + c. + d.)	$

▲

HOW TO FILL OUT AN NEA APPLICATION FORM

CHART 7.1 (CONTINUED)

▼

FY 1996-97 °   A P P L I C A T I O N   F O R M S

20. Financial Information

	Most Recently Completed Fiscal Year	Current Fiscal Year	Next Fiscal Year (Projected)
1. Fund balance (net assets) at beginning of fiscal year	$	$	$
2. Total income	$	$	$
3. Total expenses	$	$	$
4. Surplus (deficit) at year end*	$	$	$
5. Accumulated surplus (deficit)	$	$	$
6. Other net adjustments**	$	$	$
7. Balance at year end	$	$	$
8. Identify any support from the following:			
a. Arts Endowment	$	$	$
b. Other Federal agency	$	$	$
c. Regional arts organization	$	$	$
d. State arts agency	$	$	$
e. Local government sources	$	$	$

Attach a separate sheet to explain:
*Plans for reducing a deficit or utilizing a surplus
**Other net adjustments
*appropriation for capital acquisitions

Most Recently Completed
Fiscal Year (month/year)

    7 / 94 – 6 / 95

21. Delinquent debt

Are you delinquent on repayment of any Federal debt?

☐ Yes   ☒ No   *If yes,* please explain on a separate sheet.

22. Additional Authorizing Official (do not duplicate Authorizing Official listed on page i). The Authorizing Official listed on page i of this application form, and any additional Authorizing Official listed below, certify that the information contained in this application, including all attachments and supporting materials, is true and correct to the best of our knowledge. The Authorizing Official(s) also certify that the applicant will comply with the Federal requirements specified under "Assurance of Compliance" on pages 50-51 in the Grants to Organizations, FY 96-97 guideline booklet. If this application is on behalf of a separate component, the Authorizing Official(s) also certify that this unit meets the eligibility criteria for independent components on page 7 of the guideline booklet.

Name: Mr. ☒ Ms. ☐   Arthur Shaw

Title: Vice President, Finance & Administration

Area code/Phone and FAX: _____

X _____

Signature   Date Signed

▼

HOW TO FILL OUT AN NEA APPLICATION FORM

CHART 7.1 (CONTINUED)

▼ ▼

Applicant Name:

OMB 3135-0112 Expires 7-31-97

23. APPLICATION SELF-IDENTIFICATION FORM. Using the codes on page vii, choose the most appropriate item in each of the categories and place that code (either numeric or alphabetic) in the corresponding space (see page viii for explanations and definitions).

The data requested on the Application Self-Identification Form (pages vi-viii) is important for the development of a statistical profile on the organizations supported by Federal grants. The information is solicited in response to Public Law 99-383 and 42 U.S.C. 1885C. All information provided will be subject to the provisions of the Freedom of Information Act and the Privacy Act of 1974. NOTE: All information requested in #23 A-F is optional, will not be used in the application review process, and is not a precondition of award.

A. Organization Status -- Using the codes on the opposite page, identify the ONE item which best describes your legal status, e.g., if a not-for-profit theater company, use 020.

➦ 020

B. Organization Institution -- Using the codes on the opposite page, identify the ONE item which best describes your organization. Please be as specific as possible.

➦ 15

C. Organization Discipline -- Using the codes on the opposite page, identify the ONE item which best describes your area of work in the arts, e.g., if FOLK ARTS/DANCE best describes your area of work, use 120; if DANCE best describes it, use 010.

➦ 140

D. Organization Race/Ethnicity -- Using the letter designations on the opposite page, identify the predominant racial/ethnic identity of your board, administrative staff, and audience. If at least half of your board, half of your staff, or half of your audience belong to one of the listed racial/ethnic groups, then use that designation. If there is not a predominant racial/ethnic identify, use "General." Please identify only ONE item under each of the three headings.

➦ G

Board

➦ G

Administrative Staff

➦ G

Audience

E. Accessibility/Individuals with Disabilities -- Put a "Y" for Yes in each of the boxes that includes an Individual with a Disability; otherwise leave blank.

➦ | Y | Y | Y |

Board   **Staff**   **Artists**

F. Accessibility/Older Adults -- Put a "Y" for Yes in each of the boxes that includes an Older Adult (65 years of age or older); otherwise leave blank.

➦ | Y | Y | Y |

▼

HOW TO FILL OUT AN NEA APPLICATION FORM

CHART 7.1 (CONTINUED)

▼

APPLICATION FORMS

The following code designations are **only** for use with the Self-Identification Form on page vi:

A. Organization Status

020	Organization -- Nonprofit	060	Government -- Regional	099	None of the above
030	Organization -- Profit	070	Government -- County		
040	Government -- Federal	080	Government -- Municipal		
050	Government -- State	090	Government -- Tribal*		

*Includes Tribal Councils and governing authorities of bands, reservations, or sovereign nations of American Indians/Alaska Natives.

B. Organization Institution

03	Performing Group	19	School District	33	Correctional Institution
04	Perf. Group--College/Univ.	20	School--P.T.A.	34	Health Care Facility
05	Perf. Group--Community	21	School--Elementary	35	Religious Organization
06	Perf. Group--Youth	22	School--Middle	36	Senior (Older Adults) Center
07	Performance Facility	23	School--Secondary	37	Parks and Recreation
08	Museum--Art	24	School--Vocational/Tech.	38	Government--Executive
09	Museum--Other	48	School of the Arts	39	Government--Judicial
10	Gallery/Exhibition Space	25	Other School	40	Govt.--Legislative (House)
11	Cinema	26	College/University	41	Govt.--Legislative (Senate)
12	Independent Press	27	Library	42	Media--Periodical
13	Literary Magazine	28	Historical Society/	43	Media--Daily Newspaper
14	Fair/Festival		Commission	44	Media--Weekly Newspaper
15	Arts Center	29	Humanities Council/Agency	45	Media--Radio
16	Arts Council/Agency	30	Foundation	46	Media--Television
17	Arts Service Organization	31	Corporation/Business	47	Cultural Series Organization
18	Union/Professional Assoc.	32	Community Service Organ.	49	Arts Camp/Institute
		50	Social Service Organization	51	Child Care Provider
				99	None of the above

C. Organization Discipline

010	Dance	060	Design Arts	110	Interdisciplinary
020	Music	070	Crafts	120	Folk & Traditional Arts
030	Opera-Musical Theater	080	Photography	130	Humanities
040	Theater	090	Media Arts	140	Multidisciplinary
050	Visual Arts	100	Literature	150	Non-Arts or Non-Humanities

D. Organization Race/Ethnicity for Board, Administrative Staff, and Audience

N	American Indian/Alaska Native
A	Asian/Pacific Islander
B	Black, not Hispanic
H	Hispanic
W	White, not Hispanic
M	Multi-Ethnic*
G	General
01	Do not choose to answer

*Any combination of two or more racial groups if the combination comprises more than 50% of the total. However, if any one racial group makes up 50% or more of the total, you must use the code for that racial group.

▼

How to Fill Out an NEA Application Form

CHART 7.1 (CONTINUED)

Explanations and Definitions:

A. Organization Status -- Self-explanatory

B. Organization Institution -- Self-explanatory

C. Organization Discipline -- Please select the one code that best describes your primary area of work in the arts.

If you routinely integrate several disciplines into one artform, select Code "110", **Interdisciplinary.**

Folk and traditional arts are those that pertain to oral, customary, material and performance traditions informally learned and transmitted within cultural contexts.

If your area of work fits this description, please select code "120", **Folk & Traditional Arts.**

If your work involves the interpretation of authentic folk and traditional arts (and you fall outside the particular ethnic/folk tradition), please select the appropriate Discipline Code, e.g., "010", **Dance;** "020", **Music;** "070", **Crafts,** etc.

If you routinely undertake a variety of activities in different discipline areas, select the one code that best characterizes your overall work in the arts. If a majority of your work cannot be represented by a single discipline code, please select Code "140", **Multidisciplinary.**

If your work involves technical assistance or services, choose the artform that usually benefits.

D. Organization Race/Ethnicity:

American Indian or Alaskan Native. A person having origins in any of the original peoples of North America, and who maintains cultural identification through tribal affiliation or community recognition.
Asian or Pacific Islander. A person having origins in any of the original peoples of the Far East, Southeast Asia, the Indian subcontinent, or the Pacific Islands. This area includes, for example, China, India, Japan, Korea, the Philippine Islands, and Samoa.
Black. A person having origins in any of the black racial groups of Africa.
Hispanic. A person of Mexican, Puerto Rican, Cuban, Central or South American or other Spanish culture or origin, regardless of race.
White. A person having origins in any of the original peoples of Europe, North Africa, or the Middle East.
Multi-Ethnic. For organizations only. Any combination of two or more racial groups if the combination comprises more than 50% of the total. However, if any one racial group makes up 50% or more of the total, you **must** use that code for that racial group.

E. & F. Accessibility -- An individual with a disability is a person who: has a physical or mental impairment that substantially limits one or more "major life activities," or; has a record of such an impairment, or; is regarded as having such an impairment.

Examples of physical or mental impairments include, but are not limited to, such contagious and noncontagious diseases and conditions as orthopedic, visual, speech, and hearing impairments; cerebral palsy, epilepsy, muscular dystrophy, multiple sclerosis, cancer, heart disease, diabetes, mental retardation, emotional illness, specific learning disabilities, HIV disease (whether symptomatic or asymptomatic), tuberculosis, drug addiction, and alcoholism.

"Major life activities" include functions such as caring for oneself, performing manual tasks, walking, seeing, hearing, speaking, breathing, learning, and working.

An older adult is a person who is 65 years or older.

▼

HOW TO FILL OUT AN NEA APPLICATION FORM

CHART 7.1 (CONTINUED)

Work Sample Index

OMB 3135-0112 Expires 7-31-97

Applicant Organization: _____

Work Samples: Refer to "How to Submit Work Samples" on pages 42-43. List the work(s) submitted as part of your application package in the order in which you want them reviewed.

Work Sample A
1. Format (e.g., video, audiotape, compact disc, slides): _____
2. Name of artist(s): _____
3. Title of work sample, site, date: _____

4. Length of sample: _____
5. Cue information (where applicable): _____

6. Special instructions (if any): _____
_____
_____
_____
_____

Work Sample B
1. Format (e.g., video, audiotape, compact disc, slides): _____
2. Name of artist(s): _____
3. Title of work sample, site, date: _____

4. Length of sample: _____
5. Cue information (where applicable): _____

6. Special instructions (if any): _____
_____
_____
_____
_____

Work Sample C
1. Format (e.g., video, audiotape, compact disc, slides): _____
2. Name of artist(s): _____
3. Title of work sample, site, date: _____

4. Length of sample: _____
5. Cue information (where applicable): _____

6. Special instructions (if any): _____
_____
_____
_____

(If necessary, attach an additional copy of this form and label samples D, E, F, . . .)
FOR STAFF USE ONLY:

How to Fill Out an NEA Application Form

CHART 7.1 (CONTINUED)

Application Checklist

OMB 3135-0112 Expires 7-31-97

Complete this checklist and enclose it as the **first** item in your application package. The Endowment will make every effort to review your application and mail this form back to you if any items are missing. However, we cannot guarantee the return of this form and urge you to double check your application before mailing it. Remember: Late applications and applications that are determined to be incomplete will be rejected.

Applicant: _____

Address: _____

Project Director: _____

Area code/Phone: _____

Area code/FAX: _____

E-mail, if available: _____

WWW, if available: _____

All applicants must submit:

Application Checklist (1 copy)
Application Acknowledgment Card (1 copy)
IRS Determination Letter (1 copy)
Application Forms (Original and copies)
Project Narrative, see pages 32-33 (2 copies)
Biographies of key staff and key project-related personnel (2 copies)
Evidence of commitment by all partners, where relevant (2 copies)
    If a consortium project, signed agreement between partners (2 copies)
If project is based on copyrighted material, assignment of rights documentation (1 copy)
Work Sample Index, if relevant (1 copy)
If you are applying on behalf of an eligible component, documentation of eligibility (1 copy)

All applicants must also submit relevant materials specific to the theme under which they are applying. Please see the following sections for more detail.

Special Application Requirements for Heritage & Preservation, see pages 35-36,
    numbers 1 through 7.
Special Application Requirements for Education & Access, see pages 36-37,
    numbers 1 through 11.
Special Application Requirements for Creation & Presentation, see pages 38-41,
    numbers 1 through 2h.
Special Application Requirements for Planning & Stabilization, see page 41,
    numbers 1 through 4.

**The following materials are missing and must be received no later than
_____for your application to be considered.**

    These materials should be mailed to:

NATIONAL ENDOWMENT FOR THE ARTS
NANCY HANKS CENTER
1100 PENNSYLVANIA AVENUE, N.W.
WASHINGTON, DC 20506-0001

How to Fill Out an NEA Application Form

CHART 7.1 (CONTINUED)

CHAPTER 8

Special Events

Special events are activities undertaken for the purpose of raising money and generating public awareness of an arts or cultural organization. The types and number of special events should enhance the overall fundraising campaign rather than compete with it. Special events have the potential, if undertaken properly, to generate substantial funds and to cultivate prospects. Special events increase an organization's visibility, producing greater public awareness of its programs. Special events often attract people who become new board members and individual donors, and they can serve to thank those who have already given.

Special events include business or community award dinners, luncheons, celebrity benefit performances, marathons, auctions, and even bake sales. Events aimed at cultivation may include a private showing of an exhibition followed by a reception to which members of the state legislature and city council and their families are invited. Cultivation events to get to know current donors in person can be as simple as having a board member host a cocktail party for all of the existing supporters in her zipcode area. Special events might also be tailored to attract new donor prospects within certain business sectors and industries, such as real estate, banking, or fashion. A trustee who is a lawyer or partner in an investment firm might host a breakfast for his partners to introduce them to an institution or an artist.

An organization may choose to have several different special events throughout the year or one major annual function.

More than any other type of fundraising, special events require the participation of the organization's entire staff as well as many volunteers. In most cases, undertaking a special event also means planning a press and advertising campaign to generate visibility for the organization and publicity for the event itself (see examples in Appendix K). In addition, special events carry a great deal of risk because they usually require a large outlay of money before the event occurs, with no guarantee of a return. Special events require the same dedication to planning and research and the same commitment to participation by board members as do other types of fundraising.

Organizations of any size can undertake special events. Newly formed organizations will find special events a particularly helpful vehicle for raising funds before an overall annual campaign has been established. The organization should resist the temptation to overspend; special events exist for the purpose of *raising* money. A detailed budget that has been carefully thought out and closely monitored by the development director will help keep expenses for special events at a reasonable level. In-kind donations can significantly decrease the cost of mounting an event. A donation from a local merchant of wine for a gala is as good as a donation of cash. Companies launching new food and beverage products are ideal in-kind donors, because they are looking for venues that encourage patrons to sample their products. Donations of space, items for a gift bag, and subsidized printing for events all represent worthwhile savings. Undertaking a special event entails

- Choosing the special event
- Developing a leadership base
- Compiling the invitation list
- Designing the invitation package
- Making the sale to invitees
- Implementing the press campaign
- Working with caterers, designers, florists, and photographers
- Using consultants and volunteers
- Following up

CHOOSING THE SPECIAL EVENT

Special events should reflect and enhance the image of the organization and should be appropriate to the community. An event produced by a small avant-garde music group, for example, will most likely be very different from one undertaken by a large opera company.

The nature of the community must also be factored into the choice of event the organization will produce. Talent shows starring political personalities are popular in Washington, D.C., where politics plays a major role in daily life. Auctions can be successful in areas where local businesses and celebrities are willing to donate goods and services and where attendees are willing to spend money spontaneously. A rummage sale near Halloween featuring a theater company's old costumes can be very effective, particularly in a community where there are a limited number of commercial costume outlets.

Large media events, such as television auctions, marathons, and award dinners featuring celebrities and business leaders, can generate a great deal of money but require months of planning, a substantial amount of staff time, and a broad leadership base. In selecting an appropriate special event, the organization must realistically assess the amount of money and staff time it is able to commit to the event.

Fundraising events do not have to be complicated, however. Bake sales, family picnics, and parties in the homes of supporters are examples of simple but effective events that may be particularly suited to small and new organizations.

Once the event has been selected, the date must be fixed. The date should be determined well in advance and should not conflict with other events in the community. The choice between a weekend or a weekday evening will depend on the nature of the community and the type of event chosen. Also, if a celebrity or a community leader is to be honored, the date should be one on which the person is available.

THE LEADERSHIP BASE

Developing a leadership base is the most important step in producing a successful event. The leadership structure for a special event is a pyramid of prominent individuals with wide influence who will help generate funds through their prestige and their encouragement of friends and colleagues to participate in the event. The selection of a chair of the special event is critical; the position requires an individual who has the clout to sell large numbers of tickets and who is willing to enlist colleagues to serve as vice-chairs.

Business executives and socially prominent individuals usually make ideal chairs. Since most businesses and corporations have public-relations budgets with funds allocated for community fundraising events, it is important to have a chair with prestige in the corporate sector. However, the potential chair should not have worked on behalf of too many other organizations, in the process using up all "favors" owed by colleagues. Sometimes it is appropriate to have both a corporate chair, who will generate sales from the corporate world, and a gala chair, who will generate support from social contacts.

Sometimes a chair will have a list of contacts so large and prestigious that only that person is needed to serve in a leadership capacity. In many cases, however, a committee of vice-chairs is named to expand the base of support. To enlist vice-chairs for a special event, the organization usually taps board members, friends of the organization, or other prominent individuals in the community. In addition, the chair of the event, writing on personal stationery, invites as many business and civic colleagues as possible to participate. Celebrities and political leaders should be asked to serve as either honorary chairs or as members of a special-event committee. These individuals add prestige to the event.

THE INVITATION LIST

Once the leadership base for the event has been recruited, invitation lists should be compiled. These consist of the names of the persons that the chair and vice-chairs of the event would most likely know. For example, a vice-chair who is in the real estate business should be asked to provide a personal list of invitees, as well as to review a list of individuals in the realty community and related industries, such as construction.

Lists can be compiled by consulting the membership rolls of the local chamber of commerce and business trade associations. The organization's donors and selected subscribers, friends of board members, and board members of other arts and humanities organizations should be considered as potential invitees. The research process can be bypassed by hiring a consultant who already has accurate and up-to-date lists prepared. This service may be costly, but the quality of the lists may prove to be worth the expense. Organizations should be aware of the power and loyalty of their own members and ticket buyers and should not underestimate them as event supporters.

Once the lists have been compiled, the chair and vice-chairs are asked to peruse the lists, deleting inappropriate names and adding others to whom invitations should be sent. They should also identify individuals on the list whom they know on a first-name basis and suggest an appropriate salutation. The more personal the contact, the greater the possibility of an affirmative response. A business is most likely to purchase tickets when its top executive is asked to return a favor by a top executive at another business. Sometimes, however, key executives of a business purchase tickets because of a keen interest in the event itself, out of civic responsibility, or due to the familiarity of the cultural organization. After the lists have been reviewed, any names left unmarked for personal solicitation should be added to the chair's list and given a formal salutation.

Members of the leadership committee are extremely busy individuals who have graciously accepted the responsibility of fundraising for the organization; their time should be used efficiently and wisely. It is essential that the organization provide its chair and vice-chairs with accurate, well-researched, easy-to-read lists. A poorly prepared list will not be read.

The lists should be scrupulously checked to avoid duplication. An easy way to avoid this problem is to prepare a computer record with the name, address, and place of business of each person invited. Note on the prospect's record the initials of the member of the leadership committee who is sending the invitation. Maintain the information alphabetically by business affiliation, or by name when appropriate. This system also avoids inviting several officials in the same business. Because many corporations purchase blocks of tickets, it can be confusing for a company to receive more than one invitation. The invitation should be sent to the chair of the company or to the leadership committee member's primary contact. (In some cases, it may be appropriate to invite more than one individual affiliated with a particular business, but each invitee should be informed of others being invited from the company and of who is doing the inviting.)

THE INVITATION PACKAGE

The invitation package should be mailed no less than six to eight weeks before the event occurs. The package should include a carrier envelope, the invitation, a reply card and reply envelope, and a letter addressed either formally or informally. (See Appendix K, "Special Event Invitation," for an example.)

The chair and vice-chairs' letters should be written on their own stationery to individuals they know personally; special stationary designed for the event is used to invite both those individuals who are not known personally and for the chair and vice-chairs' personal prospects, if they prefer. The content of the invitation letter must be approved before it is printed on personal stationery. The letter should mention the writer's role as chair or vice-chair of the event and should include a description of the event, reasons the event and the organization should be supported, and general instructions on how to pledge support. The letter should close with a paragraph stating the writer's hope that the recipient will join him or her on the night of the event. The letter should be a concise but stirring appeal, making the reader feel it is his or her responsibility to accept. See Appendix K for an example of such a letter.

The invitation must be simple and easy to comprehend. The date, time, place, and theme of the event should be featured on the cover. The invitation should list the names of the chair, honorary chair, vice-chairs, and celebrity committee members; it should also highlight the name of the honoree, if appropriate, and outline the order of activities for the event. In addition, it should describe how the proceeds will be used to help the organization and, if there is an honoree, indicate why that individual has been selected for an award.

The reply card, which can be designed to resemble the invitation on a smaller scale, restates the theme, time, and place of the event. It should list the ticket prices and the rewards invitees receive in return for purchasing a ticket or block of tickets at a particular price. For example, a business that buys a block of 10 tickets for $1,000 may be called a "patron," with each ticket holder entitled to cocktails, prime seating for the event, and dinner afterward. A "sponsor" may be an organization purchasing 10 tickets for $500, with ticket holders entitled to cocktails and preferred seating. Prices for individual tickets at each level should also be listed.

The reply card should include space for the purchaser to fill in name, address, place of business, and the number and price of tickets purchased. The percentage of the ticket that is tax deductible, as determined by law, should also be indicated, as well as instructions for making out a check or submitting a credit card for payment. An additional line requesting a contribution ("I am unable to attend but enclose a contribution of $_____") should also be printed on the reply form.

The names of the individuals who will be attending the event should also be requested in the reply card. This is done because when blocks of tickets are purchased by businesses or individuals, it may be important for seating protocol to know the names of the guests. Also, it can be embarrassing if empty seats are left at a dinner table or in the theater, and unused tickets can be given to friends of the organization to fill the house.

Once the invitation package has been designed, it must be printed. Carrier envelopes should be printed first so that they can be addressed while the other parts of the invitation package are being printed. In the letter, the typeface used for the personalized salutations must match that used in the body of the letter. This kind of individualized invitation is expensive, but it is more personal and therefore more effective than a "Dear Friend" letter. Invitations without letters can be sent to persons on the list for whom there is no personal affiliation with the chair or a vice-chair.

Attention should be paid to the weight of the papers used in printing so that the package conforms to first-class mailing regulations and does not create an unnecessary expense. First-class postage is recommended for special-event invitations, as are hand-addressed or typed envelopes. Labels or window envelopes should not be used.

MAKING THE SALE

Two weeks after the invitations have been mailed, staff members should telephone invitees who have not responded. The staff members or volunteers should identify themselves as the representative of the chair or vice-chair who sent the invitation, thereby reinforcing the personal nature of the solicitation. "Phone pulls," as they are called, are time consuming and tedious, but they net positive results. More than one call may need to be made before a definite yes or no is given. If so, a reasonable period of time should be left between calls. Of course, if the invitee specifically asks the caller not to call again, no further calls should be made to that person.

THE PRESS CAMPAIGN

The press campaign for a special event is critical to its success. The campaign must be well planned and designed to reach potential ticket buyers; attention must be paid to the demographic profile of the audience of a particular medium to be sure it includes people who can afford a special-event ticket and who might be interested enough to purchase one. Promotion costs, however, should be kept to a minimum.

The organization should carefully weigh the pros and cons of buying newspaper, radio, or television advertising and producing posters and flyers to be circulated in the community. "Free" press, including radio or television interviews and feature stories in arts or society newspaper columns, can be very helpful and should be taken advantage of. It is important to send advance items to society and gossip columns to build "hype" and social interest in an event—especially if a celebrity is attending or if there is a special news angle. As the event draws near, it is a good idea to invite key print and electronic media writers to cover the event.

Perhaps the most valuable press coverage is that of the event itself. Photographs in local newspapers as well as magazine and television coverage of an event will help generate glamor for the institution, thereby enhancing the overall fundraising campaign. Press items from events can be used to reinforce the case for supporting an event with potential future sponsors, since business leaders and product donors are always looking for positive press.

CATERERS, DESIGNERS, FLORISTS, AND PHOTOGRAPHERS

Special events often involve providing food and creating a special atmosphere for guests. Organizing the catering and decorations for an event can be creative and enjoyable. These are costly items, however, so careful planning and budgeting is important. The development director would do well to involve the chair or representatives of the chair in this aspect of the event, as they are probably knowledgeable about party planning.

Caterers should be asked to submit sample menus that are within the organization's budget and to hold a tasting for the principal staff and leadership. It is common for caterers to submit a written proposal including their complete menu and bar setup, a floor plan showing how the room will be arranged (to ensure efficient service), the number of waiters and other service people required, a list of rental items that the organization may need, and the terms for payment. Itemized prices for each component—food, service, rental items—should be included in the proposal.

If a florist or a designer is to be hired, the organization should ask for written plans, or drawings if necessary. Once the caterer's and florist's proposals have been accepted, they should be rewritten in the form of a contract and signed by both the vendor and the organization. Musicians should also submit a contract indicating when and how long they are scheduled to play, the number of musicians and their instruments, and the cost of their services. It is also a good idea to hire a photographer. A photographic record of the evening may be useful in promoting the organization at a later time, particularly if celebrities and corporate, social, civic, and political leaders are present.

Before hiring anyone—florist, caterer, photographer, or designer—the organization should know all of the details regarding the vendor's plans for the event and should not be inhibited from requesting them. The individuals hired form the "production team" for the special event and must work well together to make the event a success. It is important that the development director supervise these individuals and provide them with realistic budget figures and adequate time for setting up, as well as an understanding of the facility and a thorough orientation to the organization and the purpose and nature of the event.

Guests at special events are usually paying a significant amount of money to attend, and they deserve to be treated well. If the event is a success, the organization should be able to sell tickets even more easily in the future.

CONSULTANTS AND VOLUNTEERS

If volunteers are involved in an event, they must have a staff liaison working with them to ensure adequate communication between the development department and the volunteers. Volunteers should have specific assignments and deadlines for completing them. Responsibilities range from making telephone calls and greeting guests to actually planning and carrying out the entire event. Special events can be very rewarding for volunteers, but they must not be taken advantage of by the organization. The development director must be careful to give each volunteer a variety of tasks, depending on his or her interests.

In planning a special event, if the development director determines that the organization's staff and volunteers do not have the time or expertise to carry it out, a good solution might be to hire a consultant. Special-event consultants can be expensive but, under the right circumstances, extremely cost effective. Consultants from reputable firms have excellent invitation lists and their own printers, mailhouses, and phone-solicitation staffs; they are also able to produce and mail the invitations and make the follow-up telephone calls efficiently. Consultants can also help conceptualize the event, develop the budget, and assist in retaining a caterer, florist, or designer. They keep records of ticket purchases, meet with the leadership committee as needed, and help with seating arrangements if required.

Before hiring a consultant, it is a good idea to check his or her references and to attend one of the events the consultant is running. The organization should find out how many clients the consultant has during the time his or her services are needed, to be certain of getting the contracted number of hours.

THE FOLLOW-UP

After the event is over and thank-you letters have been sent, the names of those who attended should be added to the organization's mailing lists and attendees should be researched as potential new board members or donors. Keeping good records of the entire event will ensure that the knowledge gained from this experience will be helpful in the future.

CHAPTER 9

Capital and Endowment Campaigns

More not-for-profit organizations are embarking on capital or endowment campaigns than ever before. Institutions undertake a capital or endowment effort when they have a significant one-time need, such as a major renovation project, the construction of a new wing, a major new program initiative, or a stabilization effort.

This chapter discusses how to conduct large-scale campaigns either for *capital* purposes such as construction or renovation projects or for *endowment* purposes. These campaigns are intense efforts to raise a large amount of money, often millions of dollars, during a finite period of time (typically three to five years). This type of campaign differs from the annual campaign discussed in earlier chapters, which systematically raises funds for annual operations.

The emphasis in capital and endowment campaigns is on face-to-face solicitation of well-qualified prospects by volunteers. Some campaigns involve very large staffs and hundreds of volunteers. The early identification and involvement of key volunteer leaders—who can raise significant gifts from others and make substantial personal gifts—is critical to its success. Because of the complexity of capital and endowment campaigns, outside consultants are typically hired to provide professional advice, extra staff when needed, and an objective voice in the development and implementation of campaign plans.

The impetus for a capital campaign effort is a shared desire among the institution's leaders to make a substantial change. This could be a major expansion into a new building, the launching of a major new program initiative, or an institutional stabilization effort designed to provide predictable annual income. Whatever the reason, it must be shared within the organization and be a felt need among the community's leaders.

A capital campaign, if conducted successfully, produces enormous benefits for the institution. It forces long-range planning because it is an effort that spans many years and shapes the organization's future operations, it develops new leadership within the organization's staff and its board of trustees, it raises the giving of current donors to higher levels, and it identifies many new prospective donors for the institution. And lastly, because it is such a large effort, it focuses the community's attention on the institution and unites all its constituencies in a common cause. Following is a step-by-step discussion of the elements in a capital or endowment campaign effort.

FEASIBILITY STUDY AND CAMPAIGN PLAN

The first step along the journey of a capital or endowment campaign is the feasibility study. Such a study tells the institution what it must know before starting the campaign and, in many cases, if it should start all. For the study to be accurate, it must be conducted by an "outside expert," typically a professional working for a fundraising consulting firm. The consultant interviews key members of the board, senior staff, and leaders in the community confidentially. The confidential nature of these interviews is important to the success of the campaign. Later, the consultant's objective analysis of the results will provide the most reliable possible information for the institution. Any shortcuts in this approach compromise the entire effort.

The organization's leaders must be willing to take this all-important first step and allocate the funds to hire a qualified individual to conduct the study. If the leaders are unwilling, then it is doubtful they will make the other substantial contributions required to achieve a major campaign goal.

The lead staff member for the effort and the consultant begin by drawing up a list of individuals to be interviewed. In addition to board members and senior staff, community leaders such as heads of foundations and key corporations should be put on the list. The consultant develops the interview guide for the confidential discussions. Typical questions include: How would you describe the organization to a prospective donor? What are the strengths and weaknesses of the institution? How do you rate the board, the key staff members, and the program activities? What suggestions do you have for improving performance? What do you think of the plans for capital or program expansion? Who do you think could make the largest gifts to the campaign? Would you consider contributing to and working on the effort yourself?

The consultant then conducts an in-depth audit of the organization's development department to assess the readiness of staff and systems to take on this task. The audit, together with the confidential interviews, provides the consultant with the information he or she needs to write the feasibility study.

A feasibility study typically outlines a campaign plan, proposing an achievable campaign goal and recommending changes to be made in the organization before launching the campaign. It evaluates whether if there are enough willing contributors in the community to make the effort successful. The study assesses the strength of the case for support and the extent to which it is felt by the community and by key institutional leaders. It names leaders among the institution's board of trustees who might be available to head the effort. It states the percentages of the goal that can reasonably be expected from board members, individuals, foundations, corporations, and government sources; and it establishes a timetable of campaign phases and the length of the campaign. It also includes a budget and outlines the scope of consulting services necessary to support the institution in launching and implementing its campaign.

The study should be presented to the board of trustees in a meeting format that allows them ample time to digest the content and to ask questions. The board should vote on whether or not to accept the recommendations of the feasibility study. This step is an important one, to be done deliberately. The majority of the board needs to embrace the plan, or it will fail.

PLANNING PHASE

Once the board has given the green light to the campaign, the next step is a planning phase during which a number of elements in the campaign plan and recommendations for institutional change are implemented. This is what is sometimes referred to as the "quiet" phase of the campaign. There is little publicity about the campaign during this time because the probability of the goal being met and the exact timing of the various campaign phases are still unclear. The goal and the plans should not be announced until approximately 50 percent of the funds have been raised.

During the planning phase, a number of important elements of the campaign are put into place. They are

- Recruitment of the campaign chair
- Formation of a campaign steering committee
- Writing the case for support
- Research and qualification of prospects
- Development of gift tables, naming opportunities, and donor recognition privileges
- Campaign policies
- Campaign materials
- Budget and staffing

Campaign Chair Recruitment

During the feasibility study, the consultant met privately with each member of the board to discuss confidentially the institution's plans for expansion. This experience should enable the consultant to identify one or two board members qualified to be the campaign chair. Qualifying characteristics would include being a widely respected leader (not just on the board but also in the community), being able to give one of the largest gifts to the campaign, having experience personally asking others for funds, and being available to lead the effort over a number of years. The campaign consultant, together with the board chair or the organization's executive director, typically visits the potential campaign chair to attempt to secure his or her commitment.

Formation of the Campaign Steering Committee

The next step of the planning phase is to identify and recruit a steering committee to work with the campaign chair on policy matters and the overall campaign effort. Steering committee members should be other board members (and often non-board members who are involved with the institution and are capable of making substantial gifts) that the institution is counting on to make large donations. They should also be selected for their ability to be the chairs of the various successive campaign phases. Once the committee is formed, the chair and committee members establish a meeting schedule.

The Case for Support

With the campaign chair recruited and the campaign steering committee formed, the case for support needs to be formulated. The case for support is generally a five- to eight-page document that serves as the basis of any subsequent brochures, proposals, or general communications about the campaign. The case states in persuasive language the need behind the institution's large campaign and the means the organization plans to use to carry out its physical or programmatic expansion or its stabilization effort.

Writing of the case for support has the potential to excite the campaign chair and steering committee further about the institution's plans. A useful process for writing the case is, with the help of the consultant, to involve board members in small group discussions. Board members are divided into groups of approximately 12, with one consultant assigned to each group. The board members are asked key questions about the reasons for the campaign. The conversations are taped, enabling the writer of the case to use the board members' own words to describe the importance and urgency of the project. This technique brings the case statement alive and imbues it with greater powers of persuasion.

Research and Qualification of Prospects

The next step in the planning phase is to research and qualify the prospect pool. The typical campaign solicits first those who can make the largest gifts and are closest to the institution, and then approaches individuals and funding sources that are more removed from the institution and who will probably give smaller amounts. The first group that is researched and qualified is the board of trustees. These individuals are the most invested in the organization and are typically able to make the largest gifts. The research and qualification process involves learning as much as possible about the philanthropic habits and resources of prospects in order to answer the question: What size gift can reasonably be expected of these individuals if they were approached in the right way by the right person? To find the answer, it is helpful to research what they have given to other institutions in the community and to their alma mater, and to determine the assets of any foundations with which they are connected. Subsequent research should focus on prospective individual donors who are not on the current board of trustees, and then on corporations and foundations. These research steps follow those outlined in Chapter 3.

Development of Gift Tables, Naming Opportunities, and Donor Recognition Privileges

Gift Tables

In large, multiyear campaigns, usually one-third of the funds comes from the top 10 gifts, the next 100 gifts bring in another third, and the final third comes from the smaller contributions of many donors. A gift table can be constructed that indicates the number of gifts needed at various levels to reach the goal (see Charts 9.1 and 9.2). Together with the campaign phase timetable, the table helps guide the prospect identification process by indicating how many prospects need to be identified, researched, and qualified for each successive phase of the campaign.

Gift Size	Number of Gifts Needed	Number of Prospects Needed	Total	Cumulative
$250,000	1	1	$250,000	$250,000
$150,000	1	2	$150,000	$400,000
$100,000	3	6	$300,000	$700,000
$75,000	4	8	$300,000	$1,000,000
$50,000	8	16	$400,000	$1,400,000
$25,000	15	45	$375,000	$1,775,000
$10,000	30	75	$300,000	$2,075,000
$5,000	40	100	$200,000	$2,275,000
$2,500	50	125	$125,000	$2,400,000
Under $1,000	many	many	$100,000	$2,500,000

GIFT TABLE: GIFTS REQUIRED/PROSPECTS NEEDED FOR A $2,500,000 CAPITAL AND/OR ENDOWMENT CAMPAIGN

CHART 9.1

Gift Size	Number of Gifts Needed	Number of Prospects Needed	Total	Cumulative
$1,000,000+	1	2	$1,000,000	$1,000,000
$500,000+	2	5	$1,200,000	$2,200,000
$100,000+	3	8	$450,000	$2,650,000
$50,000+	5	15	$300,000	$2,950,000
$25,000+	25	75	$750,000	$3,700,000
$10,000+	125	375	$1,400,000	$5,100,000
Under $10,000	250	1,000	$900,000	$6,000,000

GIFT TABLE: GIFTS REQUIRED/PROSPECTS NEEDED FOR A $6,000,000 CAPITAL AND/OR ENDOWMENT CAMPAIGN

CHART 9.2

Naming Opportunities

Naming opportunities are programs, physical spaces, or academic chairs that can be named for a donor giving at a particular level (see Appendix L). For example, the programs being expanded through an endowment campaign can be named after a major donor, as can the new staff positions made necessary by the expanded programs. In a capital campaign, physical spaces can bear the name of a donor. Assigning a price tag to each of the possible naming opportunities is a matter not so much of their actual cost, but of how desirable they are and the amount of recognition and visibility they will offer the potential donor. The pricing also needs to relate to the gift chart. The most visible naming opportunity must have the same price as the largest gift on the gift chart, with other naming opportunities priced proportionally smaller, also according to the gift chart. Typically, no naming possibilities are offered for gifts below a certain amount.

Donor Recognition Privileges

A list of donor recognition privileges also needs to be developed. Donor recognition privileges are a set of benefits given to donors acknowledging their generosity. The larger the gift, the more exclusive the benefits. Examples include special tours, lectures, and dinners with an architect or artist. The set of benefits should be designed around the mission of the institution, so that donors come to understand the institution is a deeper way. These donors become the best prospects for future gifts.

Campaign Policies

There are many details involved in launching a large capital or endowment campaign. The more these details are foreseen and written into policies, the clearer communications will be with prospective donors. An outside consultant's experience is a valuable asset in setting the policies that will guide the institution through the multiphase, multiyear effort.

One of the first policies that needs to be determined is the payout time allowed for pledges. Many organizations allow from three to five years from the time a gift commitment is made to when it is due in full. To make this decision, the organization needs to balance its immediate cash needs against donors' tolerance for paying pledges in full within a shorter period of time. Because it gives them more financial flexibility, donors usually want as long a period as possible to pay pledges, whereas the organization typically wants the pledges as quickly as possible. Once the payout policy is determined, it needs to be clearly communicated in the campaign literature and by the volunteer solicitors. It may be the case, however, that during a negotiation with a donor about his or her gift, a longer payment period may be offered if it results in a larger overall pledge.

Another key decision is how to stage the various phases. How long will the first phase of the campaign (typically called the advanced gift phase) last? During this phase, the largest donor prospects are quietly solicited to raise the funds that assure the institution that the campaign goal will be met. The goal of the advanced gift phase can range from 30 percent to 70 percent of the overall goal, depending on the size and giving potential of the overall constituency. The other phases need to be timed as well. These decisions should be written up and put into the campaign plan for approval of the board of trustees.

The campaign steering committee needs to agree on how to acknowledge gifts once they are made. Acknowledgment entails one or more campaign leaders thanking the donor through a personal letter and the donor signing a pledge form or letter of intent (see Appendix L). The letter of intent is a legally binding document that informs the institution of how much the donor is pledging and when and in how many payments the donor will pay the pledge in full. One donor may pay in equal annual installments in December of every year for five years, whereas another donor may make semiannual payments in increasing amounts so that the pledge is paid in full by the end of year five. Letters of intent should be reviewed by the institution's attorney. A donor to a large campaign may also sign a named gift reservation form. This is simply a form that records the named gift the donor has selected and how the donor would like his or her name listed. The form is retained by the development office as a permanent record. It is used later to ensure that the institution knows the donor's wishes with respect to their named gift.

The development office produces all thank-you letters, oversees the acknowledgment process, and ensures that complete letters of intent are on file in the institution's business office. Using the letters of intent, the development office can build a process that reminds donors their pledges are due. This is a huge tracking job that needs to be systematized. In a large campaign, it is not unusual to have 200 to 1,000 donors in a pledge tracking system, all at different stages of payout on their pledges.

A document spelling out the ways a donor can give to the campaign should be drawn up. Most gifts are paid in cash by personal check or with checks from the donor's personal foundation or trust or through the transfer of securities (stocks and bonds). The finance office should provide clear instructions on transferring stock to the institution and should make them available to the development office for easy communication to donors. Most organizations immediately sell gifts of stock for cash proceeds. In some cases, donors may wish to transfer tangible property such as real estate, jewelry, or art to the institution to be sold in payment of pledges. Because holding such property even for a short time can create other problems and responsibilities, the institution needs to have a stance on the acceptance of these kinds of gifts. Usually the immediate cash needs of the institution require that pledges be paid in cash or in marketable securities. Each particular situation needs to be reviewed, however, because in some cases the value of the donated property is quite large and the liquidation costs quite low, making the transaction worthwhile for the institution.

Lastly, the campaign committee needs to agree on the reports it wishes to receive and how often it needs the information. Typically, a set of reports on the progress of the campaign is prepared and updated on a monthly basis. The information most frequently tracked and reported is the number of gifts and the total dollar value of gifts raised within each phase of the campaign as measured against the predetermined phase goal. Usually reports include name-by-name listing of donors and the amount each gave, a listing by level of gifts received as measured against the campaign's gift table, and a breakdown of gifts raised by each campaign volunteer. As pledges are made and funds are invested, a report detailing the financial performance of the investments should be circulated to appropriate board, staff, and steering committee members.

Campaign Materials

A range of materials—such as case statement brochures, videos, slide shows, portfolios, and artist renderings—are produced for capital and endowment campaigns (see Appendix L). The materials are designed to inspire the reader to give a substantial gift. Different materials are required for the various phases of the campaign, because the prospect pool is different for each. At the beginning of a campaign, when the typical prospect pool is the board of trustees, it is usually not necessary to produce an expensive four-color brochure; if all the advance work was done in the feasibility study and the case-development process, the board should already be convinced to give. No amount of striking visuals will do a better job. A simply produced but persuasively written case statement is all that is needed. As the prospect pool shifts to people or firms less knowledgeable about the institution, the materials carry more weight in convincing potential donors. They need to play those themes that are most effective with each type of prospect. Organizations may produce a case statement just for use in the business sector, for example—one that emphasizes the economic impact of the organization in the community or the institution's positive effect on the quality of life in the city where the corporation does business.

Budget and Staffing

A budget needs to be prepared for the multiyear campaign and approved by the steering committee or another board-designated committee. A key part of the feasibility study prepared by the outside consultant is the pro forma budget showing the expenses anticipated for the campaign effort. There is a general guideline that campaign expenses should total no more than 5 percent of campaign proceeds. This percentage can vary, however, depending on the geographic dispersion of an organization's donor base and other industry-related factors. Other organizations in the same field that have gone through similar campaigns are good sources of information about appropriate spending ratios. Expenses generally include personnel, printing, the cost of events, legal fees, postage, and meeting expenses.

The top staffing priority is the hiring of a campaign manager to be the primary staff contact for campaign leaders and prospective donors. Another key priority is the recruiting of a prospect researcher. It is the job of the prospect researcher to develop the files and research the gift histories for each of the campaign's prospects. This individual helps determine which prospects to solicit for a gift, specifies the amount of each request, and prepares the background materials for the solicitor. Key attributes of these and other staff members hired to work on a campaign are the ability to work with many different types of people, the ability to write easily and clearly, and the stamina to work many hours over several years to achieve the campaign goal.

CAMPAIGN IMPLEMENTATION

The implementation of the campaign should flow directly out of the feasibility study and campaign plan. In the campaign plan, the phases and the time frames for their rollout are outlined. A typical phase order is: lead gifts, major gifts, special gifts, and general gifts. (Solicitations of corporations and foundations are often handled in their own separate phases.) The gift table should be the guide as to what sizes of gifts fall under which phases. In the gift table shown in Chart 9.1 for a $2,500,000 campaign, for example, the lead gifts would be the top 10 or so gifts, the next 20 to 25 would be the major gifts, the next 70 or so would be the special gifts, and the remainder would be the general gifts.

Ideally, it is good practice not to proceed to the next phase until the goal of the current phase goal is reached. Completing phases in order produces higher gifts per donor than accepting gifts in all phases at once. Successfully completing a phase at a higher gift level has the effect of encouraging those being solicited at the next lower level to make the largest possible gifts they can under their present circumstances. Another reason to implement one phase at a time is to ensure that campaign volunteers stay focused on the job at hand and that they do not lower their sights on the size of gifts that can be raised. Also, campaign staff conduct prospect research and provide support more productively if they concentrate on one task at a time.

Each phase of the campaign typically has a chair and a campaign committee of volunteers who have agreed to identify and solicit prospective donors in the gift range for which they are responsible.

As the campaign gets underway, campaign volunteers and staff will be asked many questions by prospective donors. It is a good idea to anticipate these questions and prepare volunteers and staff for them by providing standard answers. In many cases, the organization implements a volunteer training program to ensure that volunteer leaders feel comfortable asking for gifts on behalf of the institution.

Training and Motivating Campaign Volunteers

Effective programs for training campaign workers have several elements: a peer trainer or a consultant together with a peer campaign volunteer, a well-thought-out set of materials, and role-playing sessions.

A typical session often begins with the peer volunteer making a statement about why he or she chose to volunteer time to the campaign effort and why the institution is important to the community. An inspiring talk by someone the campaign volunteers view as a peer can have very positive effects. If a peer leader is not available, another effective technique is to have everyone in the group share why they decided to volunteer. Usually a few people in the group will have very inspiring reasons.

The most important component of the campaign training manual should cover a number of elements. The most important is the job description of the campaign volunteer. Typical expectations are: to personally make a reaching gift to the campaign, to identify prospective donors in the phase gift range, and to ask others to give. A note should be included about the confidentiality of campaign business. In addition to the job description, other essential components of the manual are: the gift table; bulleted list of how to prepare for a successful solicitation visit; information about the ways that donors can make gifts to the campaign—be they stock, cash, or other deferred gift arrangements; a listing of the named gift opportunities and recognition privileges for donors at various levels; and a question-and-answer document that helps volunteers answer questions commonly asked by prospective donors. All materials and brochures prepared for the campaign, as well as any newspaper or magazine articles appearing on the project, should also be given to the campaign volunteers.

Once the training leader has reviewed the information in the manual and answered any questions the campaign volunteers may have, the role-playing part of the training program usually follows. It is helpful to prepare scripts ahead of time, each dealing with a different type of situation. The setting of an appointment with a prospective donor over the telephone could be role played, as could the solicitation meeting itself. Different scenarios, such as dealing with a turndown or closing a gift with a prospective donor, can also be rehearsed.

During a campaign that spans several years, it is important to keep campaign volunteers motivated. Any number of ways can be employed but the basic idea is to celebrate the successes of the group, to deal in an upbeat manner with any questions or issues that come up, and to thank the campaign volunteers as frequently as possible.

Asking for the Gift

The first step in the solicitation process is to identify and qualify the prospective donor. As discussed earlier in the planning phase section of this chapter, the campaign staff typically takes the lead in researching a potential donor. It is a good idea for the designated individual on the development staff to review the research with the volunteer designated to solicit the prospective donor to ensure the information is accurate and complete.

The next step is to plan the gift strategy with the volunteer. Among the questions to be resolved are: Who else, if anyone, should be paired with the lead volunteer? Are there other individuals who could strengthen the institution's ability to receive a generous gift from the prospective donor, if they were involved in the call? Is the recommended "ask" amount correct? Should it be higher or lower? What key aspects about the institution should be stressed in the face-to-face solicitation? Which named gift is best suited to the prospective donor's interests and is therefore the most appropriate to suggest at this gift level? What steps need to be taken by the institution prior to setting the solicitation meeting?

Often a prospective donor has not participated recently in the life of the institution and needs a reintroduction to its work. This is frequently referred to as an "involvement step." Among the things that can be done to increase the individual's involvement is inviting him or her to a performance, an opening, or a special event. The most effective way to accomplish this is to have the key volunteer bring this individual as his or her guest. Reacquainting the individual with the institution's mission through a direct experience of its programs is the best way to ultimately realize a significant gift.

During the course of the campaign, the campaign staff and the campaign committee should collaborate on a series of events and communications designed to create momentum and excitement for the project. This makes those who have made donations feel positive about having done so and those who have not yet contributed increasingly ready to join the effort. Developing a public relations and press component to enhance these events and communications is very important. For a building project, for example, press and media attention could be generated around such events as the announcement of the architect, the unveiling of the building design, the groundbreaking, and so on, until the final dedication of the completed building. All these occasions bring contributors together to mark the historic progress of the project and also to spread the excitement of participating in a community project.

A newsletter series is a useful tool for informing a broad population about consistent progress on the project in a cost-efficient way (see Appendix L). The newsletter could include feature articles on the campaign's major donors and the institution's programs that will be touched by their generosity. A listing of the donors to date should also be included in each issue. This growing list can be an effective motivator to those who have not contributed.

When the volunteer and the staff feel prepared to approach a prospective donor for a gift, the volunteer, depending on his or her relationship with the donor, typically calls to set a meeting. During this meeting, the volunteer, employing the agreed-upon gift strategy, discusses the institution and the role the prospective donor can play in its growth. The volunteer uses the campaign brochure, the gift table, the named gift listing, and any other pertinent campaign material to illustrate the meaningful work the institution does in the community. It is important that the solicitor listen carefully to the prospective donor's responses for clues to his or her interests, issues of concern, or complaints. It is the solicitor's job to handle the concerns as best he or she can. At the appropriate point in the conversation, the solicitor asks for a commitment of funds. This is as simple as stating, "I would like you to consider a gift of $10,000 payable over five years." In the next moments, it's important to let the prospective donor respond rather than to keep talking, and to take the cue from what the individual says next. The solicitor then graciously concludes the discussion and thanks the individual for his or her time. Shortly after the visit, the volunteer should send a thank-you note to the individual and report the details of the visit to the campaign staff.

Once the individual has been asked, the solicitor needs to stay in touch. The gift is final only when the institution receives a signed gift commitment form or letter of intent; this should be kept in a safe place in the institution's offices. The gift can, at this point, be properly counted toward the campaign goal.

While the receipt of a gift commitment is the last step in the gift solicitation, it is really the beginning of a deeper relationship with the donor. It is important to invite donors to involve themselves in the institution's programs. They should be put on the appropriate mailing lists so they receive all information and invitations. Thank-you letters from the institution's board chair, chief executive, and campaign solicitor need to follow shortly after the gift commitment. Frequently, donors like to be asked to serve on committees. By involving them right away, they are likely to stay connected to the life of the institution.

Rollout of the Remaining Phases

The remaining phases of the campaign are launched and concluded according to the campaign timetable. The process described above is repeated by all the campaign volunteers as they work through their list of assigned names. The last phase in the campaign is frequently called a "general gifts phase." This is a broad-based effort designed to raise many small gifts from many people. Fundraising during this phase is done through a direct-mail and telephone follow-up process rather than through face-to-face solicitations. The mail/phone effort is best conducted by an outside firm, as it takes a professional approach to be successful. The object of this phase is not so much to raise a significant amount of money, but to reach as many different people as possible and expand the *number* of gifts to the campaign.

An integral part of endowment fundraising is the solicitation of planned or deferred gifts, which can occur at each stage of the campaign for donors who wish to contribute in this manner. Deferred gifts can be tailored to donors' personal circumstances to achieve for him or her important reductions in personal income taxes and estate taxes while maintaining or even increasing income from the donated assets.

EXAMPLES OF DEFERRED/PLANNED GIVING OPTIONS

The following section is adapted with permission from H. F. Weissenstein and Co., Inc. See also Chart 9.3, which follows. This section briefly summarizes some of the ways a donor can make a charitable gift to an organization. It is not intended to replace the professional services of an attorney, accountant, tax adviser, trust officer, or others who are qualified to advise the donor on individual estate planning and tax situations. Donors are encouraged to consult with tax and financial advisers to determine the most advantageous ways to give to the institution of their choice under current, applicable tax laws.

Bequests

Gifts by will, whether in the form of cash, securities, or other property, may be fully deducted in determining federal and state taxes on a donor's estate. The gift may be a specific designated sum, a percentage of the residuary estate after provisions for survivors or others are fulfilled, or a combination of these alternatives. A simple way to include an organization in a completed will is to add a codicil or addendum.

Life Insurance

A donor receives an income tax deduction when he or she irrevocably assigns a life insurance policy to an organization. A gift of life insurance may be appropriate for a donor when the growth of other assets or the reduced need of dependents decreases the policy's value. A tax deduction—approximately equal to the cash surrender value of the policy given to the organization—can be taken if the donor continues to pay premiums on the policy; he or she can continue to take them in full as deductible contributions. Proceeds of the policy are not subject to estate taxes.

Current Commitment to the Endowment and Current Activities with Principal of Gift Fulfilled at a Later Date

A donor can make a commitment to the endowment campaign and support specific work or programs immediately, even though he or she cannot fulfill the commitment of the principal of the gift immediately or at a set date in the future. A formal commitment to the endowment can include a formal agreement to make an annual contribution of 6 percent of the principal amount of the commitment. The commitment is then fulfilled at a time that is beneficial to the donor or the donor's estate.

The annual payments and principal of the fund can be directed to support specific program activity. Such a commitment benefits the institution immediately and in the future, and the payment of the principal commitment to the endowment can be tailored to the donor's personal circumstances to achieve important reductions in taxes and reflect personal business and financial considerations. If it is beneficial to make partial fulfillment of the principal commitment, the annual contributions can be proportionately reduced.

Example: A donor is a principal owner in a closely held business and wishes to make a long-term commitment to an arts organization. The business may be sold or become a public company in the future. The donor makes a commitment to the endowment and makes an annual contribution of 6 percent of the total commitment. When the business is sold or goes public, the donor fulfills the commitment to the endowment before or subsequent to the transaction, to maximize tax benefits.

Life Income Gifts

The donor can irrevocably assign cash, securities, or other assets to the campaign. They are invested to pay a stated percentage or fixed amount to the donor or a person designated by the donor, as well as to a second beneficiary. Income is paid monthly, quarterly, semiannually, or annually and is generally taxable to the beneficiary. Upon the death of the last surviving beneficiary, the institution may use the assets as needed or for a specific purpose designated by the donor.

A life income gift gives a substantial charitable deduction against taxable income in the year the gift is made, even though it continues to produce income for the donor during his or her lifetime. The four main types of life income plans are

- Pooled income fund
- Charitable remainder and annuity trusts
- Charitable lead trust
- A trust under the donor's will

Each of these plans generates both tax and financial benefits to the donor and important support to the institution.

The Pooled Income Fund

Making a gift to an organization's pooled income fund is similar to investing in a mutual fund. The organization combines gifts from various donors in a single portfolio. Each gift is exchanged for "units" in the fund. Each donor's share in the fund's income is determined by multiplying the number of his or her units by the per-unit annual income. Additional contributions may be made to the fund at any time.

The principal amount contributed to the fund then supports the organization after the donor's lifetime.

Example: George, who will be 50 years old on May 1, 1997, transfers $100,000 to an organization's pooled income fund on January 1, 1998 and retains a life income interest in that property. The highest yearly rate of return earned by the fund for its three preceding taxable years is 8 percent. The current value of each share is $1,000, so $100,000 purchases 100 units in the fund. Should the fund continue to earn an 8 percent return, the beneficiary would receive $8,000 income during the first year of participation. Each year the beneficiary's earnings reflect the increase or decrease in the fund's income per unit. George would be entitled to a charitable deduction in the year of the initial contribution to the fund, calculated based on age and the return of the fund—in this case almost $20,000.

Charitable Remainder and Annuity Trusts

Donors who need investment flexibility can consider a charitable remainder trust. When establishing such a trust, the donor chooses the trustee, the length of time the donor receives income, and whether the donor receives a fixed or variable amount of income. The donor and his or her counsel create the charitable remainder trust and the donor transfers assets to the trust. The trustee invests the principal to provide the predetermined income for the term established. The organization eventually receives the remaining principal amount of the trust. A charitable remainder unitrust offers a varying return based on the gift's changing market value and performance. A charitable remainder annuity trust provides a fixed return.

Establishing either type of trust offers the donor an immediate income tax charitable deduction, as well as other tax savings based on the contributed assets. This is an interesting way to contribute property with a low cost basis, such as appreciated securities.

Example: A 59-year-old woman gives an organization stock now worth $50,000 that was originally purchased for $20,000, and the organization agrees to pay her $3,050 annually. The woman can report capital gains totaling $16,381 in equal installments over her expected lifetime, rather than the $30,000 capital gain in one sum she would have had to report if she had sold the stock and kept the proceeds. The amount of the annuity payment excluded from income is determined by multiplying the annual return by an "exclusion ratio." This exclusion ratio is computed by dividing the amount of the investment in the annuity by the expected return on the annuity.

In addition, the donor receives an immediate tax deduction for making the gift. The amount of the tax deduction is determined by the U.S. Treasury and varies. In this case it would be about $10,000.

A *deferred gift annuity* may be attractive to a donor if he or she wishes to postpone income payments until retirement, when taxable income would be lower. A deferred gift annuity is a charitable donation deduction from the donor's income in the year he or she makes the deferred gift annuity contract.

Charitable Lead Trust

If a donor wants to preserve assets for himself, herself, or heirs and still give an annual gift, the donor can create a charitable lead trust. The assets are returned to the donor or the donor's heirs after a specified period of time; during the time the assets are held by the trust, their earnings are paid to the organization annually.

This is an excellent way for a donor to fund an annual gift to an organization while ensuring that the asset will be returned at the end of the trust period.

A Trust under the Donor's Will

A donor can create a trust to take effect at a future date under the terms of his or her will. The beneficiary of such a trust would receive payments during his or her lifetime; the principal would benefit the organization after the beneficiary's death.

Outright Gifts

Cash gifts: Contributions of money without restrictions or terms of trust.

Gifts of appreciated securities or property: Transfers of securities or property for which a long-term capital gain would be realized if sold.

Gifts of real estate: Transfers of property, the value of which is determined by fair market value of the property.

Gifts of tangible personal property: Transfers of property such as artwork, books, antiques, stamps, or coins. The amount of the tax deduction is determined by the value of the gift and its relationship to the organization's tax-exempt purposes.

Deferred Gifts

Bequests: Fully deductible gifts by will, from the decedent's estate.

Life insurance: Gifts of life insurance policies, providing charitable deductions for the gifts and future premium payments, if any.

Pooled income fund: A number of life income trusts pooled for investment and management purposes, similar to a mutual fund. The donor owns a pro rata share of the pool and receives income that represents that share.

Gift annuities: Annuities, created by charitable gifts, that can pay the donor or beneficiary a rate of income for life. Part of the income is tax free, part taxable. A charitable gift is considered to have occurred when an annuity is created.

GLOSSARY OF GIVING OPPORTUNITIES

CHART 9.3

SUMMARY

It takes a tremendous commitment on the part of an institution's leaders, volunteers, and staff to successfully plan and implement a capital or endowment campaign over a number of years. Launching a large-scale campaign is not a decision that should be taken lightly. When a campaign of this magnitude is successful, however, it can have an enormous positive affect on the institution for years afterward. The organization's standing and visibility in the community has been enhanced through the excitement generated about its plans. From a financial standpoint, the institution has expanded its donor base through the campaign effort; it now has a larger pool of donors from whom to seek annual gifts, which will result in increased operating support for the institution.

CONCLUSION

· · · · · · · · ·

As two development professionals, we are acutely aware of the intense competition for funds and the financial struggle in which organizations must engage to sponsor artistic work and cultural programming. This is a particularly difficult time for fundraising, and tenacity is required from anyone working in the arts and culture field.

We can only suggest, first and foremost, not to take rejection from funders personally. Try to maintain a sense of humor and calm amidst the frequent disappointments. Good fundraisers do not necessarily succeed with every grant request, but they do have the determination to continue. Endurance and a strong sense of self-worth are necessary qualities.

- Because the fundraising profession is stressful, learning to cope with uncertainties is essential.
- Networking with other fundraisers can be helpful as well as fun, especially when sharing "war stories."
- Try very hard to negotiate attainable fundraising goals. Unrealistic projections are demoralizing and give the institution a false sense of security.
- Some donors and prospects can be intimidating, but it is always helpful to remember that funders are people, too.

Receiving a grant is a personal and institutional success that can help create something of lasting value for society. We have found that the best fundraisers believe deeply in the institutions and causes for which they seek funds. Additional joy in doing this kind of work comes from forming relationships and friendships that enrich your life.

Good luck.

APPENDIX A

Basic Fundraising Books

The ABC's of Planned Giving: A Primer for Beginners. Available from L. G. Clough, 18 Randeckers Lane, Kensington, CT 06037.

Achieving Excellence in Fund Raising: A Comprehensive Guide to Principles, Strategies and Methods. Available from Jossey-Bass Publishers, Inc., 350 Sansome Street, San Francisco, CA 94104.

Administering Grants, Contracts and Funds: Evaluating and Improving Your Grants System. Available from Oryx Press, 4041 North Central Avenue, Suite 700, Phoenix, AZ 85012.

The American Prospector: Contemporary Issues in Prospect Research. Available from The Taft Group, 835 Penobscot Building, Detroit, MI 48226.

Arts Management: A Guide to Finding Funds and Winning Audiences. Available from The Taft Group, 835 Penobscot Building, Detroit, MI 48226.

Basic Grantsmanship Library. Available from The Grantsmanship Center, P.O. Box 17220, Los Angeles, CA 90017.

Big Gifts: How to Maximize Gifts from Individuals, with or without a Capital Campaign. Available from The Taft Group, 835 Penobscot Building, Detroit, MI 48226.

Black Tie Optional: The Ultimate Guide to Planning and Producing Successful Special Events. Available from The Taft Group, 835 Penobscot Building, Detroit, MI 48226.

Business Researchers' Handbook: The Comprehensive Guide for Research Professionals. Available from Washington Researchers, Ltd., P.O. Box 19005, Washington, DC 20036.

Changing Demographics: Fund Raising in the 1990s. Available from Bonus Books, Inc., 160 East Illinois Street, Chicago, IL 60611.

Compensation in Nonprofit Organizations. Available from Abbott, Langer & Associates, 548 1st Street, Crete, IL 60417.

The Complete Guide to Corporate Fund Raising. Available from Gale Research, Inc., P.O. Box 33477, Detroit, MI 48232.

Cone/Roper Study on Consumer Attitudes Toward Cause-Related Marketing, 1994. Available from Cone Communications, Inc., 90 Canal Street, Boston, MA 02114.

Cone/Roper II: A Study of Executive Attitudes Toward Cause-Related Marketing, 1996. Available from Cone Communications, Inc., 90 Canal Street, Boston, MA 02114.

Designs for Fund-Raising: Principles, Patterns and Techniques. Available from Gale Research, Inc., P.O. Box 33477, Detroit, MI 48232.

Directory of Grants in the Humanities, new edition yearly. Available from The Oryx Press, 4041 N. Central, Suite 700, Phoenix, AZ 85012.

Double Your Dollars Matching Gifts Leaflets. Available from Council for Advancement and Support of Education, Order Department, 11 Dupont Circle, Suite 400, Washington, DC 20036.

Educational Fund Raising: Principles and Practice. 1993. Available from The Oryx Press, 4041 N. Central, Suite 700, Phoenix, AZ 85012.

The Foundation Center's Guide to Proposal Writing. Available from The Foundation Center, 79 Fifth Avenue, New York, NY 10003.

The Foundation Center's User-Friendly Guide: A Grantseeker's Guide to Resources. Available from The Foundation Center, 79 Fifth Avenue, New York, NY 10003.

Foundation Fundamentals: A Guide for Grantseekers. Available from The Foundation Center, 79 Fifth Avenue, New York, NY 10003.

FRI Prospect Research Resource Directory. Available from Fund Raising Institute, The Taft Group, 835 Penobscot Building, Detroit, MI 48226.

From Idea to Funded Project: Grant Proposals That Work, 4th ed. 1992. Available from The Oryx Press, 4041 N. Central, Suite 700, Phoenix, AZ 85012.

Gifts-In-Kind. Available from The Taft Group, 835 Penobscot Building, Detroit, MI 48226.

Giving USA Annual Report. Available from AAFRC Trust for Philanthropy, 25 West 43rd Street, Suite 820, New York, NY 10036.

Glossary of Fund Raising Terms. Available from National Society of Fund Raising Executives, 1101 King Street, Suite 700, Alexandria, VA 22314.

Handbook of Institutional Advancement. Available from Jossey-Bass Publishers, Inc., 350 Sansome Street, San Francisco, CA 94104.

Hispanics and the Nonprofit Sector. Available from The Foundation Center, 79 Fifth Avenue, New York, NY 10003.

How to Find Philanthropic Prospects. Available from The Taft Group, 835 Penobscot Building, Detroit, MI 48226.

How to Get Corporate Grants. Available from Public Management Institute, 358 Brannan Street, San Francisco, CA 94107.

The "How-to" Grants Manual: Successful Grantseeking Techniques for Obtaining Public and Private Grants, 3rd ed. 1995. Available from The Oryx Press, 4041 N. Central, Suite 700, Phoenix, AZ 85012.

How to Solicit Big Gifts. Available from Public Management Institute, 358 Brannan Street, San Francisco, CA 94107.

How to Write Powerful Fundraising Letters. Available from Precept Press, 160 East Illinois Street, Chicago, IL 60611.

How to Write Proposals That Produce. 1992. Available from The Oryx Press, 4041 N. Central, Suite 700, Phoenix, AZ 85012.

Legal Aspects of Corporate Giving to Higher Education. Available from Council for Aid to Education, 342 Madison Avenue, Suite 1532, New York, NY 10173.

The Literature of the Nonprofit Sector: A Bibliography with Abstracts. Available from The Foundation Center, 79 Fifth Avenue, New York, NY 10003.

Looking Ahead: Private Sector Giving to the Arts and the Humanities, 1996. Available from President's Committee on the Arts and the Humanities, 1100 Pennsylvania Avenue, N.W., Suite 526, Washington, DC 20506.

Managing for Profit in the Nonprofit World. Available from The Foundation Center, 79 Fifth Avenue, New York, NY 10003.

Marketing Designs for Nonprofit Organizations. Available from The Taft Group, 835 Penobscot Building, Detroit, MI 48226.

Matching Gift Details. Available from Council for Aid to Education, 342 Madison Avenue, Suite 1532, New York, NY 10173.

Maximum Gifts by Return Mail: An Expert Tells How to Write Highly Profitable Fund Raising Letters. Available from The Taft Group, 835 Penobscot Building, Detroit, MI 48226.

The Membership Mystique: How to Create Income and Influence with Membership Programs. Available from Fund Raising Institute, The Taft Group, 835 Penobscot Building, Detroit, MI 48226.

New Directions for Philanthropic Fundraising. Available from Jossey-Bass Publishers, Inc., 350 Sansome Street, San Francisco, CA 94104.

The Nonprofit Entrepreneur. Available from The Foundation Center, 79 Fifth Avenue, New York, NY 10003.

A Nonprofit Organization Operating Manual: Planning for Survival and Growth. Available from The Foundation Center, 79 Fifth Avenue, New York, NY 10003.

Philanthropic Studies Index. Available from Indiana University Press, Order Department, 601 North Morton Street, Bloomington, IN 47404.

Pinpointing Affluence: Increasing Your Share of Major Donor Dollars. Available from Precept Press, 160 East Illinois Street, Chicago, IL 60611.

Program-Related Investments Primer. Available from Council on Foundations, 1828 L Street, NW, Washington, DC 20036.

Proposal Planning and Writing. 1993. Available from The Oryx Press, 4041 N. Central, Suite 700, Phoenix, AZ 85012.

Prospect Research: A How-To Guide. Available from Council for Advancement and Support of Education, Order Department, 11 Dupont Circle, Suite 400, Washington, DC 20036.

The Raising of Money: Thirty-Five Essentials Every Trustee Should Know. Available from Third Sector Press, P.O. Box 18044, Cleveland, OH 44118.

Reinventing Fundraising: Realizing the Potential of Women's Philanthropy. Available from Jossey-Bass Publishers, Inc., 350 Sansome Street, San Francisco, CA 94104.

The Seven Faces of Philanthropy: How to Attract and Cultivate Wealthy Donors Through Interactive Marketing. Available from Jossey-Bass Publishers, Inc., 350 Sansome Street, San Francisco, CA 94104.

Solid Gold Fund Raising Letters. Available from The Taft Group, 835 Penobscot Building, Detroit, MI 48226.

Special Events: Planning for Success. Available from Council for Advancement and Support of Education, Order Department, 11 Dupont Circle, Suite 400, Washington, DC 20036.

Strategic Planning for Public and Nonprofit Organizations: A Guide to Strengthening and Sustaining Organizational Achievement. Available from Jossey-Bass Publishers, Inc., 350 Sansome Street, San Francisco, CA 94104.

Successful Capital Campaign: From Planning to Victory Celebration. Available from Council for Advancement and Support of Education, Order Department, 11 Dupont Circle, Suite 400, Washington, DC 20036.

The Third America: The Emergence of the Nonprofit Sector in the United States. Available from Jossey-Bass Publishers, Inc., 350 Sansome Street, San Francisco, CA 94104.

To Be or Not to Be: An Artist's Guide to Not-for-Profit Incorporation. Booklet. Available from Volunteer Lawyers for the Arts, 1 East 53rd Street, 6th Floor, New York, NY 10022.

A *Treasury of Successful Appeal Letters*. Available from The Taft Group, 835 Penobscot Building, Detroit, MI 48226.

Virtuous Giving: Philanthropy, Voluntary Service and Caring. Available from Indiana University Press, Order Department, 601 North Morton Street, Bloomington, IN 47404.

Where the Money Is: A Fund Raiser's Guide to the Rich. Available from BioGuide Press, P.O. Box 16072, Alexandria, VA 22302.

Women and Philanthropy: A National Agenda. Center for Women and Philanthropy, 1300 Linden Drive, Madison, WI 53706.

Writing Winning Proposals. Available from Council for Advancement and Support of Education, Order Department, 11 Dupont Circle, Suite 400, Washington, DC 20036.

APPEDIX

• • • • • • • • •

Keeping Up: Magazines, Newsletters, and Newspapers

Advancing Philanthropy: The Journal of NSFRE, quarterly. Available from National Society of Fund Raising Executives, 1101 King Street, Suite 700, Alexandria, VA 22314.

American Demographics Magazine, monthly. Available from American Demographics, Inc., P.O. Box 68, Ithaca, NY 14851.

American Philanthropy Review. Available from American Philanthropy Review, Business Office, 30021 Tomas Street, Suite 300, Rancho Santa Margarita, CA 92688.

APRA Connections, quarterly. Available from Association of Professional Researchers for Advancement, 414 Plaza Drive, Suite 209, Westmont, IL 60559.

ARTnewsletter, biweekly. Available from ARTnewsletter, 48 West 38th Street, 9th Floor, New York, NY 10018.

Arts and Culture Funding Report, monthly. Available from Education Funding Research Council, 4301 North Fairfax Drive, Suite 875, Arlington, VA 22203.

BCA News, quarterly. Available from Business Committee for the Arts, Inc., 1775 Broadway, Suite 510, New York, NY 10019.

Black Enterprise, monthly. Available from Earl G. Graves Publishing Co., Inc., 130 Fifth Avenue, 10th Floor, New York, NY 10011.

Business Week, weekly. Available from McGraw-Hill, Inc., P.O. Box 421, Hightstown, NJ 08520.

CASE Currents, monthly. Available from Council for Advancement and Support of Education, Order Department, 11 Dupont Circle, Suite 400, Washington, DC 20036.

The Chronicle of Higher Education, weekly. Available from Chronicle of Higher Education, 1255 23rd Street NW, Suite 700, Washington, DC 20037.

The Chronicle of Philanthropy, biweekly. Available from Chronicle of Philanthropy, 1255 23rd Street NW, Suite 775, Washington, DC 20037.

Corporate Giving Watch, monthly. Available from The Taft Group, 835 Penobscot Building, Detroit, MI 48226.

Corporate Philanthropy Report, monthly. Available from Capitol Publications, Inc., 1101 King Street, Suite 444, Alexandria, VA 22314.

Forbes, biweekly. Available from Forbes, P.O. Box 10048, Des Moines, IA 50309.

Fortune, biweekly. Available from TIME Customer Service, P.O. Box 60001, Tampa, FL 33660.

Foundation Giving Watch, monthly. Available from The Taft Group, 835 Penobscot Building, Detroit, MI 48226.

Foundation News and Commentary, bimonthly. Available from Council on Foundations, 1828 L Street NW, Washington, DC 20036.

The Funding Connection, quarterly. Available from Grants Link, Inc., 5650A South Sinclair Road, Columbia, MO 65203.

Fundraising Management, monthly. Available from Hoke Communications, Inc., 224 7th Street, Garden City, NY 11530.

Hispanic Business, monthly. Available from Hispanic Business, P.O. Box 469038, Escondido, CA 92046.

IEG Sponsorship Report, biweekly. Available from International Events Group, Inc., 213 West Institute Place, Suite 303, Chicago, IL 60610.

International Philanthropy, bimonthly. Available from Philanthropic Resources International Management Associates, 370 Whitney Avenue, New Haven, CT 06511.

Local/State Funding Report, weekly. Available from Government Information Services, 4301 North Fairfax Drive, Suite 875, Arlington, VA 22203.

NonProfit Insights, biweekly. Available from Whitaker Newsletters, Inc., 313 South Avenue, Fanwood, NJ 07023.

Nonprofit Management Strategies, monthly. Available from The Taft Group, 835 Penobscot Building, Detroit, MI 48226.

The NonProfit Times, monthly. Available from The NonProfit Times, 190 Tamarack Circle, Skillman, NJ 08558.

NSFRE News, bimonthly. Available from National Society of Fund Raising Executives, 1101 King Street, Suite 700, Alexandria, VA 22314.

Philanthropic Digest: The Authoritative Monthly Listing of Gifts and Grants, monthly. Available from Association of Professional Researchers for Advancement, 414 Plaza Drive, Suite 209, Westmont, IL 60559.

Town and Country Magazine, monthly. Available from Hearst Magazines, P.O. Box 7182, Red Oak, IA 51591.

Wall Street Journal, daily. Available from Wall Street Journal, 200 Burnett Road, Chicopee, MA 01020.

APPENDIX C

Research Resources

Researching Individuals

Bibliography: Resources for Prospect Development. Available from Bentz Whaley Flessner & Associates, Inc., 2150 Norwest Financial Center, 7900 Xerxes Avenue South, Minneapolis, MN 55431.

Extensive bibliography of prospect research information sources arranged alphabetically by title. Includes books, magazines, newspapers, newsletters, CD-ROM products, on-line services, and Internet resources.

CDA/Spectrum Five Percent Stock Holdings. Available from CDA Investment Technologies, Inc., A Thomson Financial Services Company, 1355 Piccard Drive, Rockville, MD 20850.

Lists the beneficial owners of 5 percent or more of the outstanding stock of any corporation publicly traded in the United States. The information is arranged by name of corporation with an index by beneficial owner.

CDA/Spectrum Insider Holdings. Available from CDA Investment Technologies, Inc., A Thomson Financial Services Company, 1355 Piccard Drive, Rockville, MD 20850.

Lists the stock held by the officers, directors, and 10 percent principal stockholders of any corporation publicly traded in the United States. The information is arranged by name of corporation.

Directory of Directors in the City of New York and Tri-State Area. Available from Directory of Directors Co., Inc., P.O. Box 462, Southport, CT 06490.

Provides names, contact addresses, and corporate and charitable affiliations of important executives in New York, New Jersey, and Connecticut. Also includes individuals outside this area who sit on two or more boards of companies of sufficient importance within the tri-state area.

Guide to Private Fortunes. Available from The Taft Group, an International Thomson Publishing Co., 835 Penobscot Building, Detroit, MI 48226.

A three-volume reference that provides brief profiles of more than 3,000 wealthy individuals.

Major Donors. Available from The Taft Group, an International Thomson Publishing Co., 835 Penobscot Building, Detroit, MI 48226.

Lists more than 20,000 donors to nonprofit organizations in the United States.

Martindale-Hubbell Law Directory, Available from Martindale-Hubbell, Inc., P.O. Box 1001, Summit, NJ 07901.

A 27-volume set that provides information on law firms and brief biographies of lawyers.

Reference Book of Corporate Managements. Available from Dun & Bradstreet Information Services, 3 Sylvan Way, Parsippany, NJ 07054.

Provides brief biographical information on the principal officers of more than 12,000 leading U.S. companies.

Social Register. Available from Social Register Association, 381 Park Avenue South, New York, NY 10016.

Provides the names, addresses, summer addresses, phone numbers, education, and club affiliations for a select group of socially prominent American families. Also provides information on births, marriages, and deaths.

Standard & Poor's Register of Corporations, Directors and Executives—Directors & Executives Section. Available from Standard & Poor's, a division of McGraw-Hill, Inc., 25 Broadway, New York, NY 10004.

Provides the names, principal business affiliations, business addresses, residence addresses, and education of over 70,000 individuals serving as officers, directors, trustees, or partners of companies listed in the corporations section of the directory.

TRW REDI Property Data. Available from TRW REDI Property Data, 1200 Harbor Blvd., 10th Floor, Weehawken, NJ 07087.

Company provides real estate ownership information in a variety of formats in 34 states and over 300 counties.

Who's Wealthy in America. Available from The Taft Group, an International Thomson Publishing Co., 835 Penobscot Building, Detroit, MI 48226.

Provides the names, addresses, education, political contributions, and stock holdings of more than 100,000 wealthy Americans with an inferred net worth of at least $1 million.

Who's Who in America. Available from Marquis Who's Who, a Reed Reference Publishing Company, 121 Chanlon Road, New Providence, NJ 07974.

Provides biographies of over 103,000 prominent individuals primarily from the United States. Other Marquis publications: *Who Was Who in America, Who's Who in the World, Who's Who in Finance and Industry, Who's Who in the East, Who's Who in the Midwest, Who's Who in the South and Southwest, Who's Who in the West, Who's Who of American Women, Who's Who in American Education, Who's Who in American Law, Who's Who in American Nursing, Who's Who in Medicine and Healthcare, Who's Who in Science and Engineering.*

Who's Who in American Art. Available from R. R. Bowker, a Reed Reference Publishing Company, 121 Chanlon Road, New Providence, NJ 07974.

Provides biographies of over 11,000 contributors to the visual arts in the United States, Canada, and Mexico.

Researching Businesses

America's Corporate Families and *America's Corporate Families & International Affiliates.* Available from Dun & Bradstreet Information Services, 3 Sylvan Way, Parsippany, NJ 07054.

America's Corporate Families provides descriptions of almost 11,000 U.S. parent companies and over 75,000 subsidiaries, divisions, and branches. *America's Corporate Families & International Affiliates* links almost 2,800 U.S. parent companies with their 19,000 foreign subsidiaries, and 3,300 foreign parents with their 12,000 U.S. subsidiaries.

America's Corporate Finance Directory. Available from National Register Publishing, a Reed Reference Publishing Company, 121 Chanlon Road, New Providence, NJ 07974.

Provides information on 5,000 American companies, including their 18,000 subsidiaries and 31,000 outside service firms. Listings include information about a company's financial service firms, including insurance brokers, insurers, pension managers, investment bankers, auditors, legal counsel, and registrars.

Corporate Foundation Profiles. Available from The Foundation Center, 79 Fifth Avenue, New York, NY 10003.

Directory provides multipage profiles of more than 200 of the largest corporate foundations in the United States.

Corporate Foundations and Giving. Available from Orca Knowledge Systems, P.O. Box 280, San Anselmo, CA 94979.

Computer-based product providing detailed information on over 4,000 U.S. giving programs.

Corporate Giving Directory. Available from The Taft Group, an International Thomson Publishing Co., 835 Penobscot Building, Detroit, MI 48226.

Provides descriptive profiles of 1,000 of the largest corporate giving programs in the United States.

Corporate Yellow Book. Available from Leadership Directories, Inc., 104 Fifth Avenue, 2nd Floor, New York, NY 10011.

Lists officers, directors, business descriptions, and financial data for over 1,000 U.S. companies. Other Leadership Directories publications: *Associations Yellow Book, Financial Yellow Book, Law Firms Yellow Book,* and *News Media Yellow Book.*

Directory of Corporate Affiliations. Available from National Register Publishing, a Reed Reference Publishing Company, 121 Chanlon Road, New Providence, NJ 07974.

Provides information on 15,000 U.S. public/private companies and international public/private companies and their 100,000 subsidiary companies. Listings include business names and addresses for parent company and subsidiaries, officers and directors of parent company, top officers of subsidiaries, and brief financial data for parent company. The master index volume includes a brand name index for companies listed in the directory.

Directory of International Corporate Giving in America and Abroad. Available from The Taft Group, an International Thomson Publishing Co., 835 Penobscot Building, Detroit, MI 48226.

Provides descriptive profiles of corporate giving programs for more that 400 foreign-owned companies doing business in the United States. Also provides information on the international philanthropy of almost 200 U.S. multinational companies.

Dun's Regional Business Directories. Available from Dun & Bradstreet Information Services, 3 Sylvan Way, Parsippany, NJ 07054.

Each directory lists the leading 20,000 businesses in a given major metropolitan area. Over 50 metro areas are covered.

Giving by Industry: A Reference Guide to the New Corporate Philanthropy. Available from Capital Publications, Inc., 1101 King Street, Suite 444, Alexandria, VA 22314.

This directory provides a detailed analysis of industry trends and how corporate giving falls into the strategies of 20 major U.S. industries. It also includes more than 200 profiles of major corporate givers.

Hoover's Handbook of American Business. Available from The Reference Press, Inc., 6448 Highway 290 East, Suite E-104, Austin, TX 78723.

Directory profiles more than 450 major U.S. public companies and more than 40 private companies. Other Reference Press publications: *Hoover's Handbook of Emerging Companies, Hoover's Handbook of World Business, Hoover's Guide to Private Companies, Hoover's Regional Business Guides,* and *Hoover's Masterlist of Major U.S. Companies.*

Million Dollar Directory. Available from Dun & Bradstreet Information Services, 3 Sylvan Way, Parsippany, NJ 07054.

Lists key officers, company size, and lines of business for more than 160,000 U.S. companies, both public and private. International version of this directory is called *Principal International Businesses* and provides information on more than 50,000 companies worldwide.

Moody's Industrial Manual. Available from Moody's Investors Service, 99 Church Street, New York, NY 10007.

Provides extensive historical and financial information on publicly traded industrial companies in the United States. Other Moody's Investors Service publications: *Moody's Bank & Finance Manual, Moody's International Manual, Moody's OTC Industrial Manual, Moody's OTC Unlisted Manual, Moody's Public Utility Manual,* and *Moody's Transportation Manual.*

National Directory of Corporate Giving. Available from The Foundation Center, 79 Fifth Avenue, New York, NY 10003.

Provides detailed portraits of over 1,900 corporate foundations and more than 650 direct-giving programs.

Standard & Poor's Register of Corporations, Directors and Executives—Corporations Section. Available from Standard & Poor's, a division of McGraw-Hill, Inc., 25 Broadway, New York, NY 10004.

Provides information on more than 55,000 corporations, both U.S. and foreign. Listings include business address, officers, directors, brief financial data, and outside services firms.

Standard & Poor's Security Dealers of North America. Available from Standard & Poor's, a division of McGraw-Hill, Inc., 25 Broadway, New York, NY 10004.

Lists addresses, phones numbers, and key individuals for 5,400 brokerage and investment banking firms and 8,000 of their branches.

Standard Directory of Advertisers. Available from National Register Publishing, a Reed Reference Publishing Company, 121 Chanlon Road, New Providence, NJ 07974.

Provides information on 25,000 companies in the United States that spend at least $200,000 on national or regional advertising. Listings include company name, address, brief business description, top officers and marketing personnel, and advertising data.

Value Line Investment Survey. Available from Value Line, Inc., 220 East 42nd Street, 6th Floor, New York, NY 10017.

This three-part weekly publication provides in-depth information and analysis of individual stocks and major industries. Part One is the summary and index. Part Two is selection and opinion. Part Three is rating and reports. A Canadian edition is also available.

Researching Foundations

America's New Foundations. Available from The Taft Group, an International Thomson Publishing Co., 835 Penobscot Building, Detroit, MI 48226.

Provides detailed profiles of nearly 2,800 recently created foundations.

Annual Register of Grant Support. Available from R. R. Bowker, a National Register Publishing Company, 121 Chanlon Road, New Providence, NJ 07974.

Describes grant programs in 11 major subject areas with 61 subcategories covering corporate, private, and government funding sources. Nontraditional sources, such as educational associations and unions, are included.

Corporate and Foundation Grants. Available from The Taft Group, an International Thomson Publishing Co., 835 Penobscot Building, Detroit, MI 48226.

Comprehensive listing of more than 95,000 recent grants to nonprofit organizations in the United States.

The Directory of Corporate and Foundation Givers. Available from The Taft Group, an International Thomson Publishing Co., 835 Penobscot Building, Detroit, MI 48226.

Provides detailed descriptions of 4,000 private foundations with assets of at least $1.8 million or grants distributions of $250,000 per year, and almost 3,900 corporate giving programs.

The Foundation Directory and *The Foundation Directory Part 2.* Available from The Foundation Center, 79 Fifth Avenue, New York, NY 10003.

The Foundation Directory provides detailed descriptions of more than 7,000 major U.S. foundations with assets of at least $2 million or grants distributions of at least $200,000 per year. *The Foundation Directory Part 2* provides detailed descriptions of more than 4,000 mid-sized foundations with assets of less than $2 million and grant distributions of $50,000 to $200,000 per year. Other Foundation Center directories: *National Guide to Funding in Arts and Culture, National Directory of Grantmaking Public Charities,* and *Directory of New and Emerging Foundations.*

The Foundation 1000. Available from The Foundation Center, 79 Fifth Avenue, New York, NY 10003.

Comprehensive profiles of the 1,000 largest foundations in the United States.

Foundation Reporter. Available from The Taft Group, an International Thomson Publishing Co., 835 Penobscot Building, Detroit, MI 48226.

Comprehensive profiles of the 1,000 largest foundations in the United States.

Grants for Arts, Culture & Humanities. Available from The Foundation Center, 79 Fifth Avenue, New York, NY 10003.

Lists hundreds of foundation grants of $10,000 or more to arts and cultural organizations, historical societies, historic preservation, media, visual arts, performing arts, music, and museums. Other Foundation Center grants listings: *The Foundation Grants Index* and *Who Gets Grants/Who Gives Grants: Nonprofit Organizations and the Foundation Grants They Received.*

Guide to U.S. Foundations, Their Trustees, Officers and Donors. Available from The Foundation Center, 79 Fifth Avenue, New York, NY 10003.

Provides brief descriptions of all 37,000+ grantmaking foundations in the United States. Includes a comprehensive trustee, officer, and donor index.

Sources of Foundations. Available from Orca Knowledge Systems, P.O. Box 280, San Anselmo, CA 94979.

Computer-based product providing detailed descriptions of U.S. foundations. Database is available in state, regional, or national versions.

Researching Government Sources

The Catalog of Federal Domestic Assistance. Available from Superintendent of Documents, P.O. Box 371954, Pittsburgh, PA 15250.

Provides detailed information on federal grants and technical assistance programs.

Congressional Yellow Book. Available from Leadership Directories, Inc., 104 Fifth Avenue, 2nd Floor, New York, NY 10011.

Provides biographical information on all U.S. senators and representatives, legislative responsibilities for key staff aides, committee and subcommittee assignments, leadership positions, and memberships in leadership and party groups. Other Leadership Directories publications: *Federal Yellow Book, State Yellow Book, Municipal Yellow Book,* and *Government Affairs Yellow Book.*

Federal Assistance Directory. Available from Carroll Publishing Company, 1058 Thomas Jefferson Street, NW, Washington, DC 20077.

Provides descriptions of federal domestic assistance programs. Other Carroll publications: *Federal Regional Executive Directory, Federal Executive Directory,* and *Federal Advisory Directory.*

Federal Grants and Funding Locator. Available from Staff Directories, Ltd., 815 Slaters Lane, Alexandria, VA 22314.

Computer-based product providing detailed information on 1,500 federally administered grants.

Federal Support for Nonprofits. Available from The Taft Group, an International Thomson Publishing Co., 835 Penobscot Building, Detroit, MI 48226.

Provides detailed profiles of more than 700 federal programs that give grants to nonprofit organizations.

Guide to Federal Assistance. Available from Wellborn Associates, Inc., P.O. Box 11369, Rock Hill, SC 29731.

Provides detailed information on funding programs administered by federal agencies.

Guide to Federal Funding for Governments and Nonprofits. Available from Government Information Services, 4301 North Fairfax Drive, Suite 875, Arlington, VA 22203.

Provides detailed descriptions of government funding programs.

On-line Information Sources

Below is a brief listing of several well known on-line information services. Information sources available on-line include: periodicals, newswires, corporate and biographical directories, television and radio transcripts, investment reports, legal and medical data, and government documents such as property records, SEC filings, and patents. The information sources available will vary depending on the vendor. Some information vendors offer access to only one database while others offer access to several databases. It should be noted that many public and/or university libraries have access to various on-line information services and can be of help in determining which database to use.

ABI/INFORM. Available from UMI, 300 Zeeb Road, P.O. Box 1346, Ann Arbor, MI 48106. E-mail: oramail@umi.com.

CDA/Investnet Insider Trading Monitor. Available from CDA Investment Technologies, Inc., 3265 Meridian Parkway, Suite 130, Fort Lauderdale, FL 33331. E-mail: wealth_id@cda.com.

CompuServe Information Service. Available from CompuServe Information Service, 5000 Arlington Center Blvd., P.O. Box 20212, Columbus, OH 43220. E-mail: 70006.101@compuserve.com.

DataTimes. Available from DataTimes, Inc., 14000 Quail Springs Parkway, Oklahoma City, OK 73134. E-mail:webmaster@datatimes.com.

DIALOG Information Services. Available from DIALOG Information Services, Knight-Ridder, Inc., 2440 El Camino Real, Mountain View, CA 94040. E-mail: customer@krinfo.com.

Disclosure Database. Available from Disclosure, Inc., 5161 River Road, Bethesda, MD 20816. E-mail: support@disclosure.com.

Dow Jones News/Retrieval Service. Available from Dow Jones Business Information Services, Dow Jones & Company, Inc., P.O. Box 300, Princeton, NJ 08543. E-mail: djnr.support@cor.dowjones.com.

Lexis-Nexis. Available from Lexis-Nexis, Reed Reference Publishing, P.O. Box 933, Dayton, OH 45401. E-mail: newsales@prod.lexis-nexis.com.

TRW REDI Property Data On-line. Available from TRW REDI Property Data, 5601 East La Palma Avenue, Anaheim, CA 92807.

Internet Sites

Association of Professional Researchers for Advancement, Internet address: http://weber.u.washington.edu/~dlamb/apra/APRA.html
Provides information about the organization and links to research and philanthropy related Web sites.

Council on Foundations, Internet address: http://www.cof.org/
Provides links to foundation and philanthropy related Web sites.

Database America Companies, Inc., Internet address: http://www.switchboard.com/
Provides database of U.S. residential and business addresses and phone numbers.

Foundation Center, Internet address: http://fdncenter.org/
Describes the organization and provides links to foundation, research, and philanthropy related Web sites.

Internal Revenue Service, Internet address: http://www.irs.ustreas.gov/
As of this writing, the IRS had plans to provide a directory of U.S. charities on its Web site.

National Assembly of State Arts Agencies, Internet address: http://www.artswire.org/Artswire/www/nasaa/nasaa.html
Provides links to state and regional arts agencies.

National Endowment for the Arts, Internet address: http://www.endow.gov/
Provides on-line version of NEA guidelines, overview, frequently asked questions, and staff contact list.

Prospect Research Page at the University of Washington, Internet address: http://weber.u.washington.edu/~dlamb/research.html
Provides links to information on companies, executives, foundations, and news sources.

Reference Press, Inc., Internet address: http://www.hoovers.com/
Provides corporate profiles for a fee. Also provides free sample of profiles and links to corporate Web sites.

Securities and Exchange Commission, Intenet address: http://www.sec.gov/
Provides database of corporate forms such as 10Ks, 10Qs and proxies. Also includes links to other related government Web sites.

United States Postal Service, Internet address: http://www.usps.gov/
Provides database of Zip+4 Codes.

APPENDIX D

Web Resources for Non-profit Fund-Raising

The following article, first published in August 1996, was written by Bob Curley for Join Together Online, a resource center and meeting place for those working to reduce the harm of substance abuse. It is reprinted here, with slight modifications, courtesy of Join Together Online and the author.* Curley based his report on tips received from participants in talk-amphilrev, an Internet mailing list sponsored by American Philanthropy Review.

I f you want to know where the best fund-raising information is on the Internet, who better to ask than the fund-raising professionals who use the 'Net as part of their day-to-day business?

Join Together Online recently asked the experts on Amphilrev, the fund-raising listserv sponsored by the magazine *American Philanthropy Review,* to tell us their favorite places to find fund-raising information on the World Wide Web, e-mail discussion lists, and other electronic resources. The response was overwhelming, with more than two dozen experts e-mailing their suggestions and comments to us.

For comprehension's sake, we've separated the best resources into some general categories. This also will give you a better idea of the breadth of fund-raising information that is available. For a more comprehensive overview, visit the links database on Join Together Online (http://www.jointogether.org/jto/forum/jtolink/links.html) or one of the other link lists noted in this article.

The site listings below are based on feedback from members of the Amphilrev discussion group. If you are a fund-raiser and interested in joining Amphilrev

*Bob Curley, Forum Editor, Join Together Online; email: hn3078@handsnet.org.
Join Together: 441 Stuart Street, 6th Floor; Boston, MA 02116; telephone: (617) 437-1500; fax: (617) 437-9394; URL: http://www.jointogether.org.

(it's free), simply send e-mail to: Majordomo@tab.com, with the following command in the body of your e-mail message: *subscribe talk-amphilrev (your e-mail address)*.

For more information on fund-raising via the Internet, you might want to check out Helen Bergan's new book, *Where the Information Is: A Guide to Electronic Research for Nonprofit Organizations*. The book is $31.95 with shipping; call 703-820-9045 for more information. Online, the *Grant Seeker's Guide to the Internet* (http://homepage.interramp.com/us002618/guide.htm), written by consultants Andrew J. Grant and Suzy D. Sonenberg, goes over the basics of using electronic information for raising money.

Links Databases

A good first step in exploring what the Internet has to offer for non-profit fund-raisers is to visit one of the excellent links databases that have been assembled around the topic. These sites contain comprehensive listings of foundation sites, private consultants, research sites, and other valuable assets that you can use to raise money using your computer.

The Web site of *Philanthropy Journal Online* (http://philanthropy-journal.org), a publication that includes news and resources on volunteers, fundraising, foundations, jobs, corporate giving, non-profits, careers, and job opportunities, also includes two of the Web's best resources for nonprofits. Peter Tavernise's Philanthropy Links (http://www.philanthropy-journal.org/plhome/plhome.htm) and Ellen Spertus's Meta-Index of Nonprofit Organizations (http://www.philanthropy-journal.org/plhome/plmeta.htm) will point you in the right direction no matter what fund-raising topic you are seeking information on.

Foundation Home Pages

If foundation officers have one piece of advice for non-profits applying for grants, it is, "Read the application and program guidelines." Dozens of foundations—national, regional, local, and corporate—now have their own sites on the World Wide Web, with more coming online every day. The best sites include the text of the foundation's annual report, recent grant-making history, news, and even online application forms.

For links to foundations and corporate giving programs, one of the best places to visit is the Foundation Center (http://fdncenter.org/). The Center's Web site includes a comprehensive list of links to online private foundations and corporate giving programs, as well as news, conference announcements, a list of Foundation Center libraries, articles, and how-to's on proposal writing.

Research Sites

Basic research is the secret ingredient to fund-raising success. And while non-profit groups are wise to explore the popular Web sites set up by grant-making foundations, the bread-and-butter for professional Internet fund-raisers are those sites containing data on companies and individuals. If you are interested in planned giving or soliciting large donations from wealthy individuals or companies, these are some of the best places to go for information.

The Prospect Research Page (http://weber.u.washington.edu/~dlamb/research.html) includes links to information on companies and executives, foundations, news sources, and more. The Securities and Exchange Commission (http://www.sec.gov/) maintains an online database of corporate form 10Ks, 10Qs, proxies, and other information that can be used by fund-raisers to gather business and biographical data on companies, salaries, stock holdings, options, board membership, and company officers.

To locate businesses and people, you don't need to go out and pay $100 for a CD-ROM with eight million addresses on it. Instead, check out the Switchboard (http://www.switchboard.com). It's a lot like the software you can buy, only free.

Resource Centers

We would be remiss if we did not mention the Funding News section of Join Together Online (http://www.jointogether.org/jto/funding/funding.html) as a resource center for fund-raising information. But there are many other such resources elsewhere on the Internet worth your research time.

Phillip A. Walker's home page (http://www.clark.net/pub/pwalker/) includes a library of articles and information on fund-raising and giving, on such topics as books and literature, coalitions, consultants, corporate contributions, and foundations. And fund-raiser Putnam Barber of the Evergreen State Society (http://www.eskimo.com/~pbarber) has compiled an extensive and excellent series of articles on topics relevant to non-profit organizations, from board and management questions to fund-raising via program fees, telemarketing, direct mail, special events, and more.

Charity Village (http://www.charityvillage.com/cvhome.html) is one of the best-regarded sites for non-profits on the Web. Highlights include the library and research sections. And the Internet NonProfit Center (http://www.nonprofits.org) is another resource center for non-profit organizations that includes an excellent collection of links and information useful for fund-raising. The Center also houses home pages for charities, addresses for non-profit groups nationally, IRS information, and many resources related to volunteerism.

International

They don't call it the "World-Wide" Web for nothing. Besides the array of domestic fund-raising sites that are online, a number of overseas organizations have established an Internet presence to help charities raise money and provide services. The German Charities Institute (http://www.dsk.de/engl/)—Deutsches Spendeninstitut Krefeld, DSK—offers nearly 16,800 pages of information on philanthropy and charitable organizations. The group's Registry of German Charities contains information on around 5,200 German charitable organizations. The UK Fundraising site at http://www.fundraising.co.uk focuses on charities in Great Britain, but it contains substantial information that can be used by fund-raisers internationally. The European Foundation Centre (http://www.poptel.org.uk/aries/efc/) is similar to the New York-based Foundation Center, but on a smaller scale.

Private Consultants

Are Web sites set up by private consultants trying to sell you something? Sure. Does that mean you should avoid them unless you are interested in buying? No way. Sites set up by private fund-raising consultants can be a great source of free advice and information on fund-raising. The best sites give you enough information to help you decide whether or not you need the services of the company sponsoring the site. Kruger Communications' CyberAdvantage Web site (http://CyberAdvantage.com/krueger/) is a good example of a private consultant providing funding information in the hopes of attracting customers. Samples from previous clients, including gif solicitation guides, case statements, video scripts, and information on conducting a feasibility study, are used to help visitors decide if they need a consultant's help.

Craig & Vartorella, Inc. (http://www.scbell.com/Marketing_&_Fundraising) raises money and secures free equipment for unusual projects, and has articles and other how-to information on its Web site. Bill Tamulonis's Web page (http://home.navisoft.com/wtamulonis/inpm.htm) includes some useful anecdotes and a good walk-though of the fund-raising process.

For specialized consulting services and information, you can check out http://www.special-event.com, Special-event.com, or the Web site of Stephen Poe (http://home.earthlink.net/~stephenpoe/), a fund-raising consultant who also happens to be a general building contractor and offers both services to clients.

Service Providers

Another piece of the private enterprise scene on the Web is sites set up by companies that provide fund-raising services to non-profits. For example,

Larry Hollingsworth's LarMar's Fundraising Bazaar (http://www.larmar.com/ bazaar/bazaar.htm) includes information on different types of fund-raising products and vendors, from candy to decorative bricks, to onions (yes, onions).

Fund-Raising.Com's site—http://www.fund-raising.com/frindex.html—includes an Idea Bank that is specifically geared toward fund-raising ideas for novices. It also is home to Web pages for fund-raising products like Scratch-n-Give (charity scratch-off cards), the Partnerships Visa Card, and Wherehouse (which lets charities earn money in the used-CD business).

Not surprisingly, many of the service providers on the Web sell products related to computers and computing. Resource Management Companies (http://www.itf.com/rmc.htm), for example, sells fund-raising tracking software, while at http://fallingrock.com you can buy Grant Writer's Assistant software and look over a listing of fund-raising consultants.

If you are daunted by the thought of poring over SEC records yourself, Target America On-Line (http://www.tgtam.com) will help you research wealthy individuals to attract donors, investors, and major gifts. Prospect Research Online (http://www.rpbooks.com) offers a similar service, and PRO's Web site has an added, excellent bonus: a news room that is regularly updated with stories and press releases on breaking fund-raising news. There also is a variety of free information available to the novice researcher.

Listservs

Would you like hot information and tips on fund-raising delivered to your mail box each day? Join a listserv. Listservs are e-mail discussion lists where members can post their questions and advice, with each posting delivered to all members of the list. Amphilrev is one example of a valuable fund-raising listserv.

Another is the Gift-PL list, supported by the National Council on Planned Giving. Postings to the list include information from universities, hospitals, and service providers regarding the field of endowment development and planned giving. To subscribe send an e-mail message to: listserv@indycms.iupui.edu, with the following command in the message area: *subscribe gift-pl (your name)*.

Finally, there is the Fund-L list, another excellent resource cited by professional fund-raisers. To subscribe, send an e-mail message to: listproc@listproc.hcf.jhu.edu, with the following command in the message area: *sub fundlist (firstname lastname)*.

APPENDIX E

State Foundation Directories

Alabama

A Grantseeker's Guide to Funders in Central Appalachia and the Tennessee Valley. Available from Appalachian Community Fund, Inc., 517 Union Avenue, Suite 206, Knoxville, TN 37902. Covers the states of Tennessee, West Virginia, Mississippi and parts of Virginia, Kentucky, Ohio, Alabama, Georgia, and North Carolina.

Alaska

Pacific Northwest Grantmakers Forum Member Directory. Available from Pacific Northwest Grantmakers Forum, 1305 4th Avenue, Suite 214, Seattle, WA 98101. Covers PNG Forum members that fund in the states of Alaska, Idaho, Oregon, Montana, and Washington.

Arizona

Arizona Foundation Directory. Available from Junior League of Phoenix, P.O. Box 10377, Phoenix, AZ 85064.

Arkansas

Guide to Arkansas Funding Sources. Available from Independent Community Consultants, Inc., P.O. Box 141, Hampton, AR 71744.

California

Guide to California Foundations. Available from Northern California Grantmakers, 116 New Montgomery Street, Suite 742, San Francisco, CA 94105.

Guide to Corporate Giving in San Mateo County. Available from Peninsula Community Foundation, 1700 South El Camino Real, Suite 300, San Mateo, CA 94402.

Guide to Los Angeles Area Foundations. Available from Volunteer Center Nonprofit Resource Library, 1000 East Santa Ana Blvd., Suite 200, Santa Ana, CA 02701.

Guide to Orange County and Inland Empire Foundations. Available from Volunteer Center Nonprofit Resource Library, 1000 East Santa Ana Blvd., Suite 200, Santa Ana, CA 02701.

Colorado

Colorado Foundation Directory. Available from Junior League of Denver, Inc., 6300 East Yale Avenue, Denver, CO 80222.

Colorado Grants Guide. Available from Community Resource Center, 1245 East Colfax Avenue, Suite 205, Denver, CO 80218.

Connecticut

Connecticut Foundation Directory. Available from D.A.T.A., 70 Audubon Street, New Haven, CT 06510.

Guide to Corporate Giving in Connecticut. Available from D.A.T.A., 70 Audubon Street, New Haven, CT 06510.

Delaware

Directory of Delaware Grant Makers. Available from Delaware Community Foundation, P.O. Box 1636, Wilmington, DE 19899.

District of Columbia

The Directory of Foundations of the Greater Washington Area. Available from The Foundation for the National Capital Region, Inc., 1002 Wisconsin Avenue NW, Washington, DC 20007.

Florida

The Complete Guide to Florida Foundations. Available from Florida Funding Publications, 9350 South Dixie Highway, Suite 1560, Miami, FL 33156.

A Guide to Florida State Programs. Available from Florida Funding Publications, 9350 South Dixie Highway, Suite 1560, Miami, FL 33156.

Georgia

A Grantseeker's Guide to Funders in Central Appalachia and the Tennessee Valley. Available from Appalachian Community Fund, Inc., 517 Union Avenue, Suite 206, Knoxville, TN 37902. Covers the states of Tennessee, West Virginia, Mississippi and parts of Virginia, Kentucky, Ohio, Alabama, Georgia, and North Carolina.

Hawaii

Directory of Charitable Trusts and Foundations for Hawaii's Non-Profit Organizations. Available from Volunteer Information and Referral Service, 680 Iwilei Road, Suite 430, Honolulu, HI 96817.

Idaho

Directory of Idaho Foundations. Available from Caldwell Public Library, 1010 Dearborn, Caldwell, ID 83605.

Pacific Northwest Grantmakers Forum Member Directory. Available from Pacific Northwest Grantmakers Forum, 1305 4th Avenue, Suite 214, Seattle, WA 98101. Covers PNG Forum members that fund in the states of Alaska, Idaho, Oregon, Montana, and Washington.

Illinois

Corporate Foundations in Illinois. Available from Illinois Association of Non-Profit Organizations, 838 Fair Oaks, Oak Park, IL 60302.

Directory of Illinois Foundations. Available from Donors Forum of Chicago Library, 53 West Jackson Blvd., Suite 430, Chicago, IL 60604.

Illinois Foundation Directory. Available from Foundation Data Center, 401 Kenmar Circle, Minnetonka, MN 55343.

Indiana

Directory of Indiana Donors. Available from Indiana Donors Alliance, Victoria Center, 7th Floor, 22 East Washington Street, Indianapolis, IN 46204.

Kansas

The Directory of Kansas Foundations. Available from Topeka and Shawnee County Public Library, 1515 SW 10th Street, Topeka, KS 66604.

Kentucky

A Grantseeker's Guide to Funders in Central Appalachia and the Tennessee Valley. Available from Appalachian Community Fund, Inc., 517 Union Avenue, Suite 206, Knoxville, TN 37902. Covers the states of Tennessee, West Virginia, Mississippi and parts of Virginia, Kentucky, Ohio, Alabama, Georgia, and North Carolina.

Louisiana

Foundation Hand Book of the Greater New Orleans Community. Available from The Greater New Orleans Foundation, 2515 Canal Street, Suite 401, New Orleans, LA 70119.

Maine

Directory of Maine Foundations. Available from University of Southern Maine, Office of Sponsored Programs, 96 Falmouth Street, 601 Law Building, Portland, ME 04103.

Guides to Corporate Giving in New England: Maine, New Hampshire and Vermont. Available from D.A.T.A., Inc., 70 Audubon Street, New Haven, CT 06510.

Maryland

Index of Private Foundation Reports. Available from Office of the Attorney General of Maryland, 200 Saint Paul Place, Baltimore, MD 21202.

Massachusetts

Massachusetts Grantmakers. Available from Associated Grantmakers of Massachusetts, Inc., 294 Washington Street, Suite 860, Boston, MA 02108.

Michigan

The Michigan Foundation Directory. Available from Michigan League for Human Services, 300 North Washington Square, Suite 401, Lansing, MI 48933.

Minnesota

The Guide to Minnesota Foundations and Corporate Giving Programs. Available from Minnesota Council on Foundations, 800 Baker Building, 706 2nd Avenue South, Minneapolis, MN 55402.

Minnesota Foundation Directory. Available from Foundation Data Center, 401 Kenmar Circle, Minnetonka, MN 55343.

Mississippi

A Grantseeker's Guide to Funders in Central Appalachia and the Tennessee Valley. Available from Appalachian Community Fund, Inc., 517 Union Avenue, Suite 206, Knoxville, TN 37902. Covers the states of Tennessee, West Virginia, Mississippi and parts of Virginia, Kentucky, Ohio, Alabama, Georgia, and North Carolina.

Missouri

Corporate Funders Operating in Missouri. Available from Grants Link, Inc., 5650A South Sinclair Road, Columbia, MO 65203.

Directory of Missouri Foundations. Available from Metropolitan Association for Philanthropy, 5615 Pershing Avenue, Suite 20, St. Louis, MO 63112.

Montana

The Montana and Wyoming Foundation Directory. Available from Eastern Montana College Library, 1500 North 30th, Billings, MT 59101.

Pacific Northwest Grantmakers Forum Member Directory. Available from Pacific Northwest Grantmakers Forum, 1305 4th Avenue, Suite 214, Seattle, WA 98101. Covers PNG Forum members that fund in the states of Alaska, Idaho, Oregon, Montana, and Washington.

Nebraska

Nebraska Foundation Directory. Available from Junior League of Omaha, 608 North 108th Court, Omaha, NE 68154.

Nevada

Nevada Foundation Directory. Available from Las Vegas-Clark County Library District, 1401 East Flamingo Road, Las Vegas, NV 89119.

New Hampshire

Directory of Charitable Funds in New Hampshire. Available from Office of the Attorney General, Division of Charitable Trusts, State House Annex, 400 Capitol Steet, Concord, NH 03301.

Guides to Corporate Giving in New England: Maine, New Hampshire and Vermont. Available from D.A.T.A., Inc., 70 Audubon Street, New Haven, CT 06510.

New Jersey

New Jersey Foundations and Other Funding Sources. Available from New Jersey State Library, CN 520, Trenton, NJ 08625.

The New Jersey Mitchell Guide: Foundations, Corporations and Their Managers. Available from The Mitchell Guide, 430 Federal City Road, Pennington, NJ 08534.

New Mexico

New Mexico Funding Directory. Available from Office of Research Administration, University of New Mexico, Scholes Hall, Room 102, Albequerque, NM 87131

New York

Guide to Grantmakers in the Rochester Area. Available from Rochester Grantmakers Forum, 55 St. Paul Street, Rochester, NY 14604

New York State Foundations. Available from The Foundation Center, 79 Fifth Avenue, New York, NY 10003.

North Carolina

A Grantseeker's Guide to Funders in Central Appalachia and the Tennessee Valley. Available from Appalachian Community Fund, Inc., 517 Union Avenue, Suite 206, Knoxville, TN 37902. Covers the states of Tennessee, West Virginia, Mississippi and parts of Virginia, Kentucky, Ohio, Alabama, Georgia, and North Carolina.

North Carolina Giving: The Directory of the State's Foundations. Available from Capital Consortium, 2700 Wycliff Road, Suite 312, Raleigh, NC 27607.

Ohio

Charitable Foundations Directory of Ohio. Available from Office of the Attorney General, Charitable Foundations Section, 101 East Town Street, Columbus, OH 43266.

Oklahoma

The Directory of Oklahoma Foundations. Available from Foundation Research Project, P.O. Box 1146, Oklahoma City, OK 73101.

Oregon

The Guide to Oregon Foundations. Available from United Way of Columbia-Willamette, 619 SW 11th Avenue, Room 300, Portland, OR 97205.

Pacific Northwest Grantmakers Forum Member Directory. Available from Pacific Northwest Grantmakers Forum, 1305 4th Avenue, Suite 214, Seattle, WA 98101. Covers PNG

Forum members that fund in the states of Alaska, Idaho, Oregon, Montana, and Washington.

Pennsylvania

Directory of Pennsylvania Foundations. Available from Triadvocates Press, P.O. Box 336, Springfield, PA 19064.

Rhode Island

Corporate Philanthropy in New England: Rhode Island. Available from D.A.T.A., Inc., 70 Audubon Street, New Haven, CT 06510.

South Carolina

South Carolina Foundation Directory. Available from South Carolina State Library, 1500 Senate Street, Columbia, SC 29211.

South Dakota

The South Dakota Grant Directory. Available from South Dakota State Library, 800 Governors Drive, Pierre, SD 57501.

Tennessee

A Grantseeker's Guide to Funders in Central Appalachia and the Tennessee Valley. Available from Appalachian Community Fund, Inc., 517 Union Avenue, Suite 206, Knoxville, TN 37902. Covers the states of Tennessee, West Virginia, Mississippi and parts of Virginia, Kentucky, Ohio, Alabama, Georgia, and North Carolina.

Texas

Analysis of Texas Foundations. Available from Funding Information Center of Texas, Inc., P.O. Box 15070, San Antonio, TX 78212.

Directory of Texas Foundations. Available from Funding Information Center of Texas, Inc., P.O. Box 15070, San Antonio, TX 78212.

Utah

Philanthropic Foundations of Utah. Published by Henry Dean, 1254 N. 1220 W., Provo, UT 84604.

Vermont

Guides to Corporate Giving in New England: Maine, New Hampshire and Vermont. Available from D.A.T.A., Inc., 70 Audubon Street, New Haven, CT 06510.

Vermont Directory of Foundations. Available from CPG Enterprises, P.O. Box 199, Shaftsbury, VT 05262.

Virginia

A Grantseeker's Guide to Funders in Central Appalachia and the Tennessee Valley. Available from Appalachian Community Fund, Inc., 517 Union Avenue, Suite 206, Knoxville, TN 37902. Covers the states of Tennessee, West Virginia, Mississippi and parts of Virginia, Kentucky, Ohio, Alabama, Georgia, and North Carolina.

Virginia Giving: The Directory of the Commonwealth's Foundations. Available from Capital Consortium, 2700 Wycliff Road, Suite 312, Raleigh, NC 27607.

Washington

Charitable Trust Directory. Available from Secretary of State's Office, Charitable Trust Division, 505 E. Union, P.O. Box 40234, Olympia, WA 98504.

Pacific Northwest Grantmakers Forum Member Directory. Available from Pacific Northwest Grantmakers Forum, 1305 4th Avenue, Suite 214, Seattle, WA 98101. Covers PNG Forum members that fund in the states of Alaska, Idaho, Oregon, Montana, and Washington.

West Virginia

A Grantseeker's Guide to Funders in Central Appalachia and the Tennessee Valley. Available from Appalachian Community Fund, Inc., 517 Union Avenue, Suite 206, Knoxville, TN 37902. Covers the states of Tennessee, West Virginia, Mississippi and parts of Virginia, Kentucky, Ohio, Alabama, Georgia, and North Carolina.

Wisconsin

Foundations in Wisconsin. Available from Marquette University Memorial Library, 1415 West Wisconsin Avenue, Milwaukee, WI 53233.

Wyoming

The Montana and Wyoming Foundation Directory. Available from Eastern Montana College Library, 1500 North 30th, Billings, MT 59101.

APPENDIX F

·········

State Arts Councils and Regional Arts Organizations

State Arts Councils

Alabama State Council on the Arts and Humanities
1 Dexter Avenue
Montgomery, AL 36130-5401

Alaska State Council on the Arts
411 West 4th Avenue, Suite 1E
Anchorage, AK 99501

American Samoa Council on Art, Culture and Humanities
P.O. Box 1540
Pago Pago, AS 96799

Arizona Commission on the Arts
417 West Roosevelt Street
Phoenix, AZ 85003

Arkansas Arts Council
1500 Tower Building
323 Center Street
Little Rock, AR 72201

California Arts Council
1300 I Street, #930
Sacramento, CA 95814

Colorado Council on the Arts
750 Pennsylvania Street
Denver, CO 80203

Connecticut Commission on the Arts
227 Main Street
Hartford, CT 06103

Delaware State Arts Council
820 North French Street
Wilmington, DE 19801

District of Columbia Commission on the Arts
410 8th Street, NW, Suite 500
Washington, DC 20004

Florida Arts Council
Department of State
Division of Cultural Affairs
The Capitol
Tallahassee, FL 32399

Georgia Council for the Arts
530 Means Street, NW, Suite 115
Atlanta, GA 30318

Guam Council on the Arts and Humanities Agency
P.O. Box 2950
Agana, GU 96910

Hawaii State Foundation on Culture and the Arts
44 Merchant Street
Honolulu, HI 96813

Idaho Commission on the Arts
P.O. Box 83720
Boise, ID 83720

Illinois Arts Council
100 West Randolph Street, Suite 10-500
Chicago, IL 60601

Indiana Arts Commission
402 West Washington Street, Room W072
Indianapolis, IN 46204

Iowa Arts Council
Department of Cultural Affairs
600 East Locust
Capital Complex
Des Moines, IA 50319

Kansas Arts Commission
700 Jackson, Suite 1004
Topeka, KS 66603

Kentucky Arts Council
31 Fountain Place
Frankfort, KY 40601

Louisiana State Arts Council
P.O. Box 44247
Baton Rouge, LA 70804

Maine Arts Commission
55 Capitol Street, Station 25
Augusta, ME 04330

Maryland State Arts Council
601 North Howard Street, 1st Floor
Baltimore, MD 21201

Massachusetts Cultural Council
120 Boylston Street, 2nd Floor
Boston, MA 02116

Michigan Council for the Arts and
Cultural Affairs
1200 6th Street, Suite 1180
Detroit, MI 48226

Minnesota State Arts Board
400 Sibley Street, Suite 200
St. Paul, MN 55101

Mississippi Arts Commission
239 North Lamar Street, Suite 207
Jackson, MS 39201

Missouri Arts Council
111 North 7th Street, Suite 105
St. Louis, MO 63101

Montana Arts Council
316 North Park Avenue, Room 252
Helena, MT 59620

Nebraska Arts Council
3838 Davenport Street
Omaha, NE 68131

Nevada State Council on the Arts
602 North Curry Street
Capitol Complex
Carson City, NV 89710

New Hampshire State Council on the Arts
Phoenix Hall
40 North Main Street
Concord, NH 03301

New Jersey State Council on the Arts
20 West State Street, 3rd Floor
CN 306
Trenton, NJ 08625

New Mexico Arts Division
228 East Palace Avenue
Santa Fe, NM 87501

New York State Council on the Arts
915 Broadway
New York, NY 10010

North Carolina Arts Council
Department of Cultural Resources
221 East Lane Street
Raleigh, NC 27601

North Dakota Council on the Arts
418 East Broadway, Suite 70
Bismarck, ND 58501

Commonwealth Council for Arts and
Culture (Northern Mariana Islands)
Department of Community and Cultural
Affairs
P.O. Box 553, CHRB
Saipan, MP 96950

Ohio Arts Council
727 East Main Street
Columbus, OH 43205

Oklahoma Arts Council
P.O. Box 52001
Oklahoma City, OK 73152

Oregon Arts Commission
775 Summer Street, NE
Salem, OR 97310

Pennsylvania Council on the Arts
Finance Building, Room 216
Harrisburg, PA 17120

Institute of Puerto Rican Culture
P.O. Box 4184
San Juan, PR 00902

Rhode Island State Council on the Arts
95 Cedar Street, Suite 103
Providence, RI 02903

South Carolina Arts Commission
1800 Gervais Street
Columbia, SC 29201

South Dakota Arts Council
Office of Arts
800 Governor's Drive
Pierre, SD 57501

Tennessee Arts Commission
Parkaway Towers, Suite 160
404 James Robertson Parkway
Nashville, TN 37243

Texas Commission on the Arts
P.O. Box 13406
Capital Station
Austin, TX 78711-3406

Utah Arts Council
617 E. South Temple Street
Salt Lake City, UT 84102

Vermont Council on the Arts
136 State Street, Drawer 33
Montpelier, VT 05633

Virgin Islands Council on the Arts
41-42 Norre Gade
St. Thomas, VI 00802

Virginia Commission for the Arts
Lewis House, 2nd Floor

223 Governor Street
Richmond, VA 23219

Washington State Arts Commission
234 East 8th Avenue
Olympia, WA 98504

West Virginia Arts and Humanities
   Division
Arts and Humanities Section
1900 Kanawha Boulevard East
Charleston, WV 25305

Wisconsin Arts Board
101 East Wilson Street, 1st Floor
Madison, WI 53702

Wyoming Council on the Arts
2320 Capitol Avenue
Cheyenne, WY 82002

Regional Arts Organizations

Arts Midwest
Hennepin Center for the Arts
528 Hennepin Avenue, Suite 310
Minneapolis, MN 55403

Consortium for Pacific Arts and Culture
2141C Atherton Road
Honolulu, HI 96822

Mid-America Arts Alliance
912 Baltimore Avenue, Suite 700
Kansas City, MO 64105

Mid-Atlantic Arts Foundation
11 East Chase Street, Suite 2-A
Baltimore, MD 21202

New England Foundation for the Arts
330 Congress Street, 6th Floor
Boston, MA 02210

Southern Arts Federation
181 14th Street, NE, Suite 400
Atlanta, GA 30309

Western States Arts Federation
236 Montezuma Avenue
Santa Fe, NM 87501

APPENDIX G

State Humanities Councils

Alabama Humanities Foundation
2217 10th Court, South
Birmingham, AL 35205

Alaska Humanities Forum
421 West 1st Avenue, Suite 210
Anchorage, AK 99501

Arizona Humanities Council
The Ellis-Shackelford House
1242 North Central Avenue
Phoenix, AZ 85004

Arkansas Humanities Council
10815 Executive Center Drive, Suite 310
Little Rock, AR 72211

California Council for the Humanities
312 Sutter Street, Suite 601
San Francisco, CA 94108

Colorado Endowment for the Humanities
1623 Blake Street, Suite 200
Denver, CO 80202

Connecticut Humanities Council
41 Lawn Avenue
Wesleyan Station
Middletown, CT 06459

Delaware Humanities Forum
1812 Newport Gap Pike
Wilmington, DE 19808

District of Columbia Community Humanities Council
1331 H Street, NW, Suite 902
Washington, DC 20005

Florida Humanities Council
1514½ East 8th Avenue
Tampa, FL 33605

Georgia Humanities Council
50 Hurt Plaza, SE, Suite 440
Atlanta, GA 30303

Guam Humanities Council
123 Archbishop Flores Street, Suite C
Agana, GU 96910

Hawaii Committee for the Humanities
First Hawaiian Bank Building
3599 Waialae Avenue, Room 23
Honolulu, HI 96816

Idaho Humanities Council
217 West State Street
Boise, ID 83702

Illinois Humanities Council
203 North Wabash Avenue, Suite 2020
Chicago, IL 60601

Indiana Humanities Council
1500 North Delaware Street
Indianapolis, IN 46202

Iowa Humanities Board
100 Oakdale Campus, North Lawn
Iowa City, IA 52242

Kansas Humanities Council
112 West Sixth Street, Suite 210
Topeka, KS 66603

Kentucky Humanities Council
206 East Maxwell Street
Lexington, KY 40508

Louisiana Endowment for the Humanities
1001 Howard Avenue, Suite 3110
New Orleans, LA 70013

Maine Humanities Council
371 Cumberland Avenue
Portland, ME 04112

Maryland Humanities Council
601 North Howard Street, First Floor
Baltimore, MD 21201

Massachusetts Foundation for the Humanities
1 Woodbridge Street
South Hadley, MA 01075

Michigan Humanities Council
119 Pere Marquette Drive, Suite 3B
Lansing, MI 48912

Minnesota Humanities Commission
987 East Ivy Avenue
St. Paul, MN 55106

Mississippi Humanities Council
3825 Ridgewood Road, Room 311
Jackson, MS 39211

Missouri Humanities Council
911 Washington Avenue, Suite 215
St. Louis, MO 63101

Montana Committee for the Humanities
P.O. Box 8036
Hellgate Station
Missoula, MT 59807

Nebraska Humanities Council
Lincoln Center Building, Suite 225
215 Centennial Mall South
Lincoln, NE 68508

Nevada Humanities Committee
P.O. Box 8029
Reno, NV 89507

New Hampshire Humanities Council
19 Pillsbury Street
P.O. Box 2228
Concord, NH 03302

New Jersey Council for the Humanities
28 West State Street, 6th Floor
Trenton, NJ 08608

New Mexico Endowment for the Humanities
Onate Hall, Room 209
University of New Mexico
Albuquerque, NM 87131

New York Council for the Humanities
198 Broadway, 10th Floor
New York, NY 10038

North Carolina Humanities Council
425 Spring Garden Street
Greensboro, NC 27401

North Dakota Humanities Council
2900 East Broadway Avenue
Bismarck, ND 58501

Commonwealth of the Northern Mariana Islands Council for the Humanities
Caller Box AAA 3394
Saipan, MP 96950

Ohio Humanities Council
695 Bryden Road
Columbus, OH 43205

Oklahoma Foundation for the Humanities
Festival Plaza
428 West California Avenue, Suite 270
Oklahoma City, OK 73102

Oregon Council for the Humanities
812 SW Washington, Suite 225
Portland, OR 97205

Pennsylvania Humanities Council
320 Walnut Street, Suite 305
Philadelphia, PA 19106

Puerto Rico Foundation for the
  Humanities
P.O. Box S-4307
Old San Juan, PR 00904

Rhode Island Committee for the
  Humanities
60 Ship Street
Providence, RI 02903

South Carolina Humanities Council
P.O. Box 5287
Columbia, SC 29250

South Dakota Humanities Council
Box 7050, University Station
Brookings, SD 57007

Tennessee Humanities Council
1003 18th Avenue South
Nashville, TN 37212

Texas Committee for the Humanities
Banister Place A
3809 South 2nd Street
Austin, TX 78704

Utah Humanities Council
350 South 400 East, Suite 110
Salt Lake City, UT 84111

Vermont Council on the Humanities
RR1, Box 7285
17 Park Stret
Morrisville, VT 05661

Virgin Islands Humanities Council
P.O. Box 1829
St. Thomas, VI 00803

Virginia Foundation for the Humanities
  and Public Policy
145 Ednam Drive
Charlottesville, VA 22903

Washington Commission for the
  Humanities
615 2nd Avenue, Suite 300
Seattle, WA 98104

West Virginia Humanities Council
723 Kanawha Blvd. East, Suite 800
Charleston, WV 25301

Wisconsin Humanities Committee
802 Regent Street, 1st Floor
Madison, WI 53715

Wyoming Council for the Humanities
Box 3643, University Station
Laramie, WY 82071-3972

APPENDIX H

Fundraising and Management Organizations

Accounts for the Public Interest
1012 14th Street, NW, Suite 906
Washington, DC 20005

The Advertising Council
261 Madison Avenue, 11th Floor
New York, NY 10016

American Association of Fund-Raising Counsel
25 West 43rd Street
New York, NY 10036

American Council on Education
One Dupont Circle, NW
Washington, DC 20036

American Management Association
135 West 50th Street
New York, NY 10020

Association of Professional Researchers for Advancement
414 Plaza Drive, Suite 209
Westmont, IL 60559

Association for Volunteer Administration
P.O. Box 4584
Boulder, CO 80306

Committee for Economic Development
477 Madison Avenue
New York, NY 10022

The Conference Board
845 Third Avenue
New York, NY 10022

Council for Advancement and Support of Education
11 Dupont Circle, Suite 400
Washington, DC 20036

Council for Aid to Education
342 Madison Avenue, Suite 1532
New York, NY 10173

Council of Better Business Bureaus
4200 Wilson Boulevard, Suite 800
Arlington, VA 22203

Council on Foundations, Inc.
1828 L Street, NW
Washington, DC 20036

Council of State Governments
3560 Iron Works Road
Lexington, KY 40578

Direct Mail Fundraisers Association
445 West 45th Street
New York, NY 10036

The Foundation Center
79 Fifth Avenue
New York, NY 10003

The Grantsmanship Center
1125 West 6th Street
Los Angeles, CA 90015

Independent Sector
1828 L Street, NW
Washington, DC 20036

National Center for Charitable Statistics
(Div. of Independent Sector)
1828 L Street, NW
Washington, DC 20036

National Charities Information Bureau
19 Union Square West, 6th Floor
New York, NY 10003

National Clearinghouse for Corporate Matching Gift Information
(Div. of the Council for Advancement and Support of Education)
11 Dupont Circle, Suite 400
Washington, DC 20036

National Committee on Planned Giving
310 Alabama Street, Suite 210
Indianapolis, IN 46204

National Committee for Responsive Philanthropy
2001 S Street, NW
Washington, DC 20009

National Society of Fund Raising Executives
1101 King Street, Suite 700
Alexandria, VA 22314

Nonprofit Coordinating Committee of New York
121 Sixth Avenue, 6th Floor
New York, NY 10013

Points of Light Foundation
1737 H Street, NW
Washington, DC 20006

Program on Non-Profit Organizations at Yale University (PONPO)
P.O. Box 208253, Yale Station
88 Trumbull Street
New Haven, CT 06520

A P P E N D I X

Arts and Cultural Service Organizations

Alliance of Resident Theaters/New York
131 Varick Street, Room 904
New York, NY 10013

American Arts Alliance
1319 F Street, NW, Suite 500
Washington, DC 20004

American Association of Community Theater
813 42nd Street
Des Moines, IA 50312

American Association of Museums
1225 Eye Street, NW, Suite 200
Washington, DC 20005

American Council for the Arts
1 East 53rd Street
New York, NY 10022

American Film Institute
The John F. Kennedy Center for the Performing Arts
Washington, DC 20566

American Symphony Orchestra League
777 14th Street, NW, Suite 500
Washington, DC 20005

Arts and Business Council
25 West 45th Street, Suite 707
New York, NY 10036

Arts International Program
Institute of International Education
809 United Nations Plaza
New York, NY 10017

Association of Hispanic Arts
173 East 116th Street, 2nd Floor
New York, NY 10029

Association of Independent Video and Filmmakers
625 Broadway
New York, NY 10012

Association of Performing Arts Presenters
1112 16th Street, NW, Suite 400
Washington, DC 20036

Business Committee for the Arts
1775 Broadway
New York, NY 10019

Center for Arts and Culture
1755 Massachusetts Ave., NW, Suite 416
Washington, DC 20036

Chamber Music America
545 Eighth Avenue
New York, NY 10018

Dance USA
777 14th Street, NW, Suite 540
Washington, DC 20005

Ethnic Cultural Preservation Council
6500 South Pulaski Road
Chicago, IL 60629

**International Society of Performing Arts
    Administrators**
2920 Fuller Avenue, NE, Suite 205
Grand Rapids, MI 49505

Meet the Composer
2112 Broadway
New York, NY 10023

National Assembly of Local Arts Agencies
927 15th Street, NW
Washington, DC 20005

National Assembly of State Arts Agencies
1010 Vermont Avenue, NW
Washington, DC 20005

National Endowment for the Arts
1100 Pennsylvania Avenue, NW
Washington, DC 20506

National Endowment for the Humanities
1100 Pennsylvania Avenue, NW
Washington, DC 20506
http://www.neh.fed.us/

Network of Cultural Centers of Color
304 Hudson Street
New York, NY 10013

Opera America
777 14th Street, NW, Suite 520
Washington, DC 20005

Poets and Writers
72 Spring Street
New York, NY 10012

Theatre Communications Group
355 Lexington Avenue
New York, NY 10017

Volunteer Lawyers for the Arts
1 East 53rd Street, 6th Floor
New York, NY 10022

Western Alliance of Arts Administrators
44 Page Street
San Francisco, CA 94102

APPENDIX

Sponsorship vs. Advertising: Comparing Return

While companies should not view sponsorship as a replacement for advertising—indeed, most sponsorships require advertising—sponsorship does offer distinct advantages that its more conventional marketing sibling does not. Below, IEG summarizes the key benefits and risks unique to sponsorship, as well as what advertising offers that sponsorship lacks.*

A dvertising is a *quantitative* medium, priced and evaluated in terms of cost per thousand. Sponsorship, on the other hand, is a *qualitative* medium; it can and should be priced and evaluated in terms of return on investment.

Sponsorship's Qualitative Value

Specific product messages such as "one-half the calories" are far more effectively communicated through a controllable medium such as advertising. But sponsorship generally outperforms advertising in its ability to establish qualitative attributes such as a consumer's image of a brand, increasing favorable ratings and generating awareness.

A major tire marketer tested this ability in a four-year study of how sponsorship compares with advertising. The company stopped advertising during the study and used sponsorship exclusively. Its two competitors used product advertising and almost no sponsorship throughout the period.

In three of the four areas measured—corporate image, propensity to purchase, and brand awareness—the sponsor fared better. The fourth area—communicating specific product attributes, such as long-wear tires—required traditional advertising.

---

*Reprinted from *IEG Sponsorship Report*, with permission of its publisher, International Events Group, Inc., Chicago.

Other areas where sponsorship's efficiency over advertising's has been demonstrated include sponsorship's ability to build

- *Credibility.* Sponsors typically receive official product designation and rights to use the sponsee's marks and logo on packaging and promotion. Because the official sponsor credential is so linked to the brand's positioning, the message works in the consumer's mind as, for example, "the sponsor's sports beverage enhances performance and is the brand to drink." Sponsorship of sports, arts and other causes generates credibility for the sponsor's brand over its competitor's, which appears not to have been sanctioned or approved.
- *Differentiation.* Unlike most measured media channels, most sponsorship properties offer companies category exclusivity. Not only is there no commercial din from competitors to undermine the message, but the sponsorship tie becomes a unique selling point not available to the sponsor's competitors.
- *Imagery.* By sponsoring, a brand can be linked immediately to a known set of image qualities, such as public service-oriented (community events), environmentally responsible (preservation causes), world-class performance (top arts and sports events), artistic excellence (performance arts institutes and museums) or durability (marathons). Advertising around the sponsorship does not have to work so hard to create image qualities for the brand, and the consumer is more likely to transfer the event's qualities to the brand.
- *Social responsibility.* The challenge facing marketers today is how to respond to consumer demand for social relevance and responsibility. Consumers view a company's sponsorship as a way to fulfill this requirement, as a form of marketing that gives something back. Through sponsorship, a company can improve a neighborhood, bring affordable entertainment to a market or provide crucial funding to the arts.
- *Lifestyle relevance.* By being where their customers are, sponsors can speak to their audiences rather than *at* them.
- *Prestige.* Only a handful of companies can afford to advertise on the most prestigious broadcasts. But with sponsorship, even a mega-event such as the Super Bowl or a city wide arts festival is accessible to smaller and local brands because they can sponsor subordinate events within the major event. Small-budget sponsors also can tie into a lesser-known event and work with the producer to develop it into something bigger.
- *Internal morale.* Unlike an ad buy, sponsorship can directly involve a company's employees. They can volunteer on site or receive special

benefits such as discounted or free event passes to share with their families.

- *Consumers' interaction.* Advertising is a monologue. Sponsorship is a dialogue, offering companies opportunities for two-way exchange with their audiences.

Sponsorship's Quantitative Value

In addition to the qualitative attributes described above, sponsorship offers quantitative benefits not available through advertising. These include

- *Live audience.* Sponsors have built-in opportunities for on-site sales and sampling, surveying, customer feedback, interaction with their sales force, and product testing.
- *Product showcase.* Sponsorship is a better showcase for brand attributes than advertising because the product or service can be used in the performance or competition. For example, photographers can shoot with a certain film and a gallery can install a sponsor's lighting system.
- *Retail extensions.* Sponsors of performances and concerts can access talent for in-store appearances, which they can tie to incremental display and case orders. Sponsors of festivals and ticketed events can drive retail sales by offering a point-of-sale or ticket discount with proof-of-purchase. Sponsors of venues have access to special tickets and backstage tours so they can leverage with trade customers. Often, sponsors can share benefits with their retail customers.
- *Guaranteed delivery.* With sponsorship, a company's message is incorporated into the action; with advertising, it is added on and can be screened out. When an ad interrupts a TV program, viewers can switch to another station. For messages at the start of a rented movie, there's fast forward. And, for unsolicited direct mail or telemarketing, there's the garbage bin and disconnect button, respectively.
- *Client entertainment.* Several hours in the company of clients and potential clients away from ringing phones can be an invaluable sales tool. Events make great settings for informal networking; they are unusual and desirable—two attributes absolutely necessary to entice a business contact to join during non-business hours.

Why It's Easier to Stick with Advertising

Despite sponsorship's many advantages, the process of buying, managing, and measuring sponsorship is far more time-consuming, complex, and risky than other forms of marketing. Among the efficiencies advertising offers that sponsorship does not are:

- *Standardization.* Unlike measured media, where what's delivered is consistent—all broadcast media deliver time, all print outlets offer space—sponsorship benefits vary dramatically from one property to another. Although two properties might deliver the same audience and numbers in identical markets, they offer sponsors different benefits. Pro-am spots or title of a stage are benefits that make comparing like and like difficult.

- *Evaluation.* Flawed as it is, cost per thousand is a universally accepted measure providing advertisers with built-in evaluations of their media buys. While sponsorship can be measured, evaluation by an objective third party usually requires extra spending and work on the part of the sponsor.

- *Turnkey operation.* Ad buys usually do not require additional promotion for effectiveness. This is not the case with sponsorship. Companies looking for a payoff derived solely from the automatic rights that come with the sponsorship package will be disappointed. On a straight-ahead, cost-per-thousand basis, sponsorship rarely outperforms measured media. To garner a return from sponsorship, the company must view the property as a promotional platform for building trade, consumer and client programs.

- *Make-goods.* If ratings are lower than projected, the advertising seller can provide additional time or space compensation. With sponsorship, where the seller often controls only one property and has no access to a year-round inventory, this rarely happens.

- *Known cost.* With advertising, a company knows what its total spending will be. But in sponsorship, fees are just the beginning. Sponsors also must budget for managing the process, the agency, the travel and entertainment, the evaluation, contingencies and leveraging. The rule of thumb (as determined by the International Events Group, author of this article) is that for every dollar a sponsor spends on rights, it will need to spend two dollars to exploit the sponsorship and another dollar on TV advertising if the event is televised. Most spending is not incremental, but rather a conversion of existing media dollars.

- *Easier implementations.* A media buy can be implemented without the participation of the rest of the company. Sponsorships cannot. For example, a company must sell its sales force on the sponsorship because they are the people who will get the sponsorship implemented at retail. If they are not behind it, chances are the sponsorship will not work. Similarly, companies that rely on dealers to sell product require dealer participation in their sponsorship or they will not succeed.

- *Less risk.* Advertising generally is taken at face value with no questioning of motivation. Unless a sponsor is genuinely seen to be "enabling" a recipient organization, the strength of feeling engendered by its involvement easily can turn against the company and portray it as exploiting the situation.

APPENDIX K

Fundraising Materials

ANNUAL REPORT

The annual report of an institution chronicles its program activities and financial status during a complete fiscal year. The annual report featured here (courtesy of the Brooklyn Academy of Music) included letters from the president and the chair of the board of trustees, a list of performance events, narratives and photographs relating to each major program initiative, a donor listing, and a financial summary based on the institution's audit. The cover displayed a photograph of a performance highlight from the past year.

The annual report is an extremely useful tool in fundraising because it provides a comprehensive glance at the institution's full programmatic and financial performance in any given year. The annual report also establishes credibility and shows that the organization has a track record in its area of specialization. All organizations, large and small, should produce an annual report.

An annual report need not be expensive or include pictures and elaborate graphics to be effective. The report mainly needs to provide solid information about the organization and how it met its goals during the fiscal year just completed. The report should be mailed to donors, government officials, and selected prospects, no later than six months after the close of the year it reports.

Letters from the President and the Board Chair

The Chairman

I AM PLEASED TO REPORT that Brooklyn Academy of Music, after successfully completing an ambitious season, remains ready to face new challenges and has created a comprehensive stabilization strategy for the future of the institution.

A vital component of this strategy is The Campaign for BAM which has raised $61.2 million in combined operating, capital and endowment funds since 1992. We now look forward to launching a second phase of that campaign. Once again, I want to thank our Campaign Chair, Bettina Bancroft for her tireless efforts, and I am happy to welcome Alan Fishman, our Co-Chair of the Campaign as we prepare for our next phase of work. Many thanks also to our dedicated committee members and our generous contributors for their special commitment to BAM.

Our staunchest ally, The City of New York, again provided support for BAM's annual operations. We extend our sincerest thanks to The Mayor and to the City's Department of Cultural Affairs, to the Brooklyn Delegation of the New York City Council led by Councilman Herbert E. Berman, and Brooklyn Borough President Howard Golden for their support during the past year.

Additionally, the introduction of the Cultural Challenge Initiative, a joint funding program of the City and State designed to spur private giving, helped BAM present Peter Brook's The Man Who, The Kronos Quartet, our first International Children's Festival and the Baroque Music Festival featuring Les Arts Florissants.

Our operations would not be possible without the participation of State agencies including the New York State Council on the Arts, the Natural Heritage Trust and the Brooklyn Delegation of the New York State Assembly; Significant Federal support from the National Endowment for the Arts and generous private contributions from our foundation, corporate and individual sponsors have also been vital and are greatly appreciated. Finally, we thank the BAM Board of Trustees for their continued enthusiasm and dedication.

During that past season, we warmly welcomed new Trustees; Andrew Blesley, Vice Chairman and Chief Operating Officer of National Westminster Bancorp; Thomas Florio, President of The New Yorker; Jean-Louis Ginibre, Executive Vice President and Editorial Director of Hachette Filipacchi Magazines; and Arthur Shapiro, Executive Vice President-Marketing of The House of Seagram.

For the ninth consecutive year, Philip Morris Companies Inc. served as the major corporate sponsor of the Next Wave Festival and Gala.

In the spring, Their Majesties King Carl XVI Gustaf and Queen Silvia of Sweden, and The Speaker of the Swedish Parliament, Birgitta Dahl, joined us for the Bergman Festival's Royal Gala celebrating the opening night performance of The Winter's Tale. Our sincere thanks to the Festival's principal sponsor Absolut Vodka, Festival/Gala Chairmen Michael Fuchs and Christina Ohrstrom Moliteis, and Swedish Consul General Dag Ahlander.

With the help of corporate sponsor AT&T, BAM's Danse Africa America has become. BAM and its seven partner institutions secured a $600,000 Challenge Grant from the National Endowment for the Arts, plus major national support from Target Stores and the John S. and James L. Knight Foundation.

In closing, and on a personal note, I want to salute BAM Trustee Stanley Kriegel and his wife Claudette, who celebrated their 60th wedding anniversary with a gathering of family and friends on the Opera House stage this past June. An opening night at BAM is not complete without the Kriegels.

In short, another year of landmark achievements, new partnerships, and of course, great nights in the theater. Bravo to everyone who made it possible!

Bruce C. Ratner

The President

RADICAL GRAHAM TO INGMAR BERGMAN, the opening and the final offering of the season. I do not mean to drop names, but it was a memorable season with such artists as Peter Brook, Giorgio Strehler, Jiri Kylian, Pina Bausch, Philip Glass, William Christie, Twyla Tharp, Valerie Gergiev, The Kronos Quartet, John Adams and Robert Ashley; and such singer or known artists as Bill T. Jones, Susan Marshall, Saburo Teshigawara, Declan Donnellan, Michael Nyman, Lev Dodin and many others. And, of course, Martha Graham and Ingmar Bergman.

It was our most expansive season ever. Audiences were responsive and houses were full (mostly), and we were pleased to have so much extraordinary work at BAM. A particular favorite of mine was the Kirov Opera production of Rimsky-Korsakov's, The Legend of the Invisible City of Kitezh, which was a memorable discovery.

The work on the stage is the cornerstone of BAM. But it is a partnership: performer and audience. And how we treat artists at BAM and how we take care of our audiences are of equal importance. We now have an audience services department to be responsive to audience needs and problems.

We are examining every area where we have contact with our ticket buyers: on the phone, at the box office, in the lobby, in the theater, the parking lot, etc. We will continue to give better service, and welcome your input. We understand that we cannot take whatever success we have achieved, for granted.

So what is in our future? The answer is lots; there will be many changes to expand our repertoire and serve our patrons better. You will be hearing about them. Some will creep up on you, and some will create a stir. Keep tuned.

To my colleagues at BAM, my thanks for making this journey so incredibly exciting, and interesting and diverse. To our dear Trustees, to our City fathers, our patrons and our audiences, thank, many thanks, for giving us the opportunity to serve you. As Karen Hopkin has been known to say, BAM is not a job, it is a crusade.

Harvey Lichtenstein

Program Listing

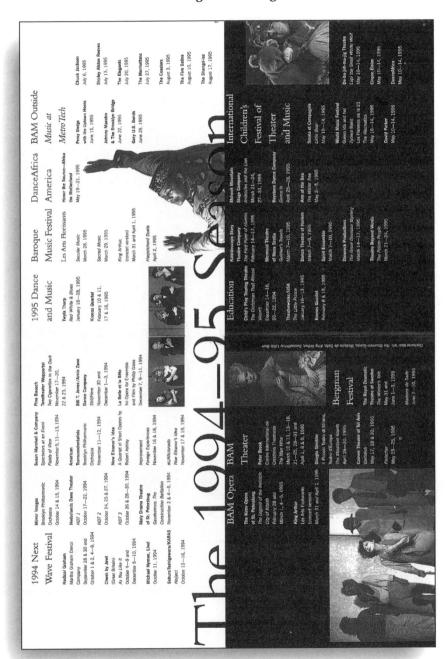

Description of Major Programs

Kronos Quartet
David Harrington, violin
John Sherba, violin
Hank Dutt, viola
Joan Jeanrenaud, cello
BAM Majestic Theater

George Crumb, *Black Angels: Thirteen Images from the Dark Land*
(New York staged premiere)
Philip Glass, *Quartet No. 5*
Henryk Gorecki, *Quartet No.2 (Quasi una Fantasia)*
February 10, 1995

LaMonte Young, *Chronos Kristalla*
(New York premiere)
February 11, 1995

Dmitri Yanov-Yanovsky, *Chang Music V*
(US premiere)
Scott Johnson, *Cold War Suite* (New York premiere)
Jihad Racy, *Zaman Suite*
(New York premiere)
Tan Dun, *Ghost Opera*
(world premiere)
February 17, 1995

John Adams, *John's Book of Alleged Dances*
(New York premiere)
Don Byron, *There Goes the Neighborhood*
(New York premiere)
Brent Michael David, *Tunpao Nenangpe*
(world premiere)
Ingram Marshall, *Fog Tropes II*
(New York premiere)

Louis Harden (Moondog), *Synchrony*
(world premiere)
Elliot Carter, *Fragment*
(New York premiere)
February 18, 1995

Matinee performances for young people
February 8 & 15, 1995

This program was supported by the Cultural Challenge Initiative, a program administered jointly by the New York State Council on the Arts, a state agency, and the New York City Department of Cultural Affairs; additional support was provided by Nonesuch Records

THE KRONOS QUARTET BEGAN an exclusive New York residency at Brooklyn Academy of Music in February 1995. This marked their first BAM engagement since the 1986 Next Wave Festival. Over the course of the residency, the quartet presented four different programs of work from the widest possible array of composers, including a number of world premieres and works commissioned expressly for the group. In addition, Kronos performed two special matinee concerts for young audiences as part of BAM's ongoing effort to integrate mainstage artists into the education programs offered to school groups. See page 22 of this report for more information on BAM's education programs.

Red White & Blues
New works choreographed by Twyla Tharp
January 16—28, 1995
BAM Opera House

CHOREOGRAPHER AND DIRECTOR Twyla Tharp returned to BAM, after an eight-year absence, renewing a relationship with the Academy that spans more than a quarter of a century. The special two-week season showcased a company of seven dancers in a program of new work that celebrated the art of making dances. The BAM performances were the final product of an experiment that began in Washington D.C. when Ms. Tharp agreed to do an informal residency with the John F. Kennedy Center for the Performing Arts in 1994.

Special support provided by
Hachette Filipacchi Magazines
and The Harkness
Foundations for Dance.

Clockwise from bottom left; *Red White & Blues*; Kronos Quartet; *King Arthur*

Donor List

Annual Supporters

Leadership ($100,000 or more)
Absolut Vodka
AT&T
Booth Ferris Foundation
Brooklyn Borough President
  Howard Golden
Brooklyn Delegation of the New
  York City Council
Richard B. Fisher
The Ford Foundation
Forest City Ratner Companies
The Howard Gilman Foundation
The Florence Gould Foundation
The Harkness Foundations
  for Dance
The Andrew W. Mellon Foundation
The MetroTech Downtown Fund
National Endowment for the Arts
New York City Department of
  Cultural Affairs
New York State Council
  on the Arts
The Pew Charitable Trusts
Philip Morris Companies Inc.
Bruce C. Ratner
Fan Fox & Leslie R. Samuels
  Foundation, Inc.
Starrett at Spring Creek, managed
  by Grenadier Realty Corp.
Trust for Mutual Understanding
Robert W. Wilson

**President's Circle
($50,000 or more)**
The Bohen Foundation
Brooklyn Union
The Chase Manhattan Bank
Con Edison
The Charles E. Culpeper
  Foundation
The Eleanor Naylor Dana
  Charitable Trust
The Gladys Krieble Delmas
  Foundation
Dow Jones Foundation
Hachette Filipacchi Magazines
Frederick B. Henry
Independence Savings Bank
Israel Expo '95
John S. & James L. Knight
  Foundation

Arthur & Marylin Levitt
The Henry Luce Foundation, Inc.
NYNEX
Pharmacia
Republic National Bank
  of New York
Republic Bank for Savings
The Rockefeller Foundation
Samuel and May Rudin
  Foundation, Inc.
The Shubert Foundation, Inc.
Skandinaviska Enskilda Banken
  Corporation
Skanska
Target Stores
Volvo North America
The Norman & Rosita Winston
  Foundation

Guarantors ($25,000 or more)
Aero Studios Limited
The Vincent Astor Foundation
The Louis Calder Foundation
Cultural and Scientific Relations
  Department, Ministry of Foreign
  Affairs, Jerusalem
The Nathan Cummings Foundation
The Department Store Division by
  the Dayton Hudson Corporation
The Educational Foundation
  of America
European American Bank
French Ministry of Foreign Affairs
  through AFAA and the Cultural
  Services of the French Embassy
  in New York
Forbes Inc.
The Georgetown Company
The Horace W. Goldsmith
  Foundation
The Francena T. Harrison
  Foundation Trust
The Hearst Foundation, Inc.
Mrs. Alex Hillman
Home Box Office, Inc.
Kaufmann, Feiner, Yamin,
  Gildin & Robbins
Lincoln Continental
Lufthansa
Estate of Arthur Miller
Morgan Guaranty Trust Company

Morgan Stanley Group Inc.
Natural Heritage Trust
NatWest Bank
Samuel I. Newhouse
  Foundation, Inc.
The New Yorker
Bernard Osher Foundation
Pfizer Inc.
Prada
Premier Party Servers
Salomon Foundation Inc
Scandinavian Airlines
Simon & Schuster
The Starr Foundation
Stockholm Information Service
Consulate General of Sweden
  in New York
Swedish Travel & Tourism Council
Time Warner Inc.
The Isak and Rose Weinman
  Foundation, Inc.
Anonymous

Pacesetters ($10,000 or more)
The Aeroflex Foundation
American Express Company
The American-Scandinavian
  Foundation
AREA Inc.
Andin International Inc.
Bettina Bancroft & Andrew Klink
Bear Stearns & Co., Inc.
BMG Music International
Bowne of New York
Bristol-Myers Squibb Company
Mary Flagler Cary Charitable Trust
Chemical Banking Corporation
Citibank
Robert Sterling Clark Foundation
Credit Lyonnais
Dance Ink
The Dime Foundation
The Equitable Foundation
Mr. & Mrs. Alan Fishman
France Telecom, Inc.
Mr. Michael Fuchs
Ministry of Foreign Affairs of the
  Federal Republic of Germany
  through the German Consulate
  General in New York
The Green Fund Inc.
The Greenwall Foundation
The House of Seagram
The Italian Cultural Institute
Heckscher Foundation for Children
ING Capital
Rita J. and Stanley H. Kaplan
  Foundation
Robin & Edgar Lampert
John Phillip Lipsky
  & Zsuzsanna S. Karasz
Mr. & Mrs. Hamish Maxwell

Financial

Treasurer's Report

Extracted
Financial
Statements
Operating Funds
Balance Sheet
Year Ended
June 30, 1995

Extracted
Financial
Statements
Operating Funds
Year Ended
June 30, 1995

	FY 1995	FY 1994
ASSETS		
Current		
Cash	128,638	698,925
Accounts Receivable	620,333	514,929
Grants Receivable	2,029,086	1,664,514
Prepaid Expenses & Other Assets	929,890	641,633
Marketable Securities & Works of Art	101,654	100,737
Total Current	$3,809,501	$3,610,738
Non-Current		
Grants Receivable	25,000	52,500
Fixed Assets (Net of Accumulated Depreciation)	2,019,652	2,086,264
Total Assets	**5,854,253**	**5,749,502**
LIABILITIES		
Current		
Accounts Payable	1,628,834	1,072,746
Grants for Future Periods	1,000,032	1,203,500
Notes Payable	1,460,389	910,000
Advance Box Office & Rentals	0	126,035
Advance Distribution from BET	0	300,000
Capital Lease Obligation	13,184	13,052
Total Current	$4,102,389	$3,625,333
Long Term		
Grants for Future Periods	50,000	177,500
Capital Lease Obligation	12,857	26,050
Total Liabilities	$4,165,256	$3,828,883
Fund Balances	1,688,997	1,920,619
Total Liabilities and Fund Balances	$5,854,253	$5,749,502

The Brooklyn Academy of Music, Inc. is tax-exempt under Section 501(c)(3) of the Internal Revenue code, and is not a private foundation. Contributions are tax deductible to the extent provided by law

	FY 1995#	FY 1994#
REVENUE		
Box Office, Rentals & Concessions	5,735,421	4,923,333
Appropriations & Contributions:		
New York City	3,100,302	2,704,708
New York State	332,500	267,815
Federal Support	304,000	636,300
Private Support*	6,074,162	5,872,405
Endowment Income	300,000	300,000
Total Revenue & Public Support	**$15,846,385**	**$14,704,561**
EXPENSES		
Program, Rentals & Concessions	6,573,484	8,349,972
Artistic Development	914,229	580,748
Program Related:		
Stage & Producer	977,995	962,534
Promotion, Advertising & Community Relations	763,309	647,679
House Management & Box Office	632,725	574,438
Building Maintenance & Operations	1,097,839	1,118,511
Majestic Theater Operations	171,951	196,673
Supporting Services:		
Administration	1,698,292	1,414,316
Development	600,850	718,064
Operating Expenses	**$15,632,860**	**$14,562,935**
Operating Surplus/(Deficit) before depreciation	$213,525	$141,626
Additional Information		
Appropriation for Capital Acquisitions**	195,230	133,911
Surplus/(Deficit) After Capital Acquisitions	$18,295	$7,715

*Includes Benefit Income net of direct expenses

**In addition to BAM's own capital purchases, during FY 95 the City of New York has made appropriations for building renovations and computer purchases in the amount of $1,960,000

#These pre-extracted statements. Copies of the Audited Financial Statements may be obtained upon request

40

GENERAL-SUPPORT RENEWAL LETTER

Date

Address

Dear:

Through the generous support of donors like, _____ the Museum of
Contemporary Art continues to contribute to Chicago's cultural life as one of the
city's leading arts institutions. Our ability to serve even larger audiences will grow
in 1996, as the Museum opens its new building on Chicago Avenue! I am writing to
request that _____ renew its support of the Museum with a contribution of
$5000. Your operating support is especially needed at this time as we move into our
new, larger facility and expand our operating budget from $4.4 million to $7.1
million.

The generous charitable support of corporations and foundations who understand the
importance of cultural organizations to our city's vitality continues to enable the
Museum to maintain and expand its exhibition programming and outreach to the
community. During the past fiscal year your support has made the following
achievements possible. Your renewed gift will help us realize our plans for this
momentous year.

♦ The Museum of Contemporary Art celebrated structural completion of
the new building with a Topping Out Ceremony in late 1994, drawing
750 Chicago area residents to mark this construction milestone. In the
Spring, 1995, the building was enclosed and work on the interior
partitions, with the completion of the monumental grand staircase.
Work on the parking garage and the sculpture garden began in March
and peripheral landscaping is underway in the parkways and garden.

♦ A ten-day period of inaugural celebrations has been planned to mark
the building's opening. The Grand Opening and Summer Solstice
Celebration will begin Friday, June 21, 1996, with a dedication and the
ceremonial opening of doors to the public. The opening festivities will
continue for more than 24 hours, with free events and activities held
every hour on the hour.

♦ The Education Department reached broader and more diverse audiences
through both interpretive and public programs. The Museum hosted
in-gallery artist lectures in conjunction with the exhibitions **Options
47: Gabriel Orozco** and **Gary Hill**. Public lectures were presented in
conjunction with exhibitions **Options 49: Hiroshi Sugimoto** and
Franz Kline: Black and White, 1950-1961. Over the past fiscal
year, _____ was appointed Director of Education. Prior to this
appointment, _____ completed a highly successful tenure as
_____.

♦   Education and community outreach programs will reach new heights as the primary beneficiary of the MCA's new education center and theater. Education facilities in the new building will provide state-of-the-art classrooms, workshop spaces, and orientation galleries. Education will be a central, highly-visible part of Museum operations as the MCA touches the lives of ever-growing numbers of Chicago residents and school children.

♦   The Curatorial Department presented a number of noteworthy exhibitions in the past year, bringing select contemporary art to our diverse audiences. MCA-organized exhibitions presented this past fiscal year include **Kay Rosen: Home on the Range, Vincent Shine, Hollis Sigler, Jeanne Dunning, Jim Lutes** and **Dan Peterman.** All of these artists live and work in the Chicagoland area, and the MCA is proud to exhibit these talented local artists. The MCA hosted the only North American presentation of **Some Went Mad...Some Went Away,** a touring exhibition from London of work by 15 international artists. Two noteworthy traveling exhibitions, **Gary Hill** and **Franz Kline,** impressed MCA audiences.

♦   For the first time in MCA history, the Permanent Collection will be continuously displayed on the fourth floor of the new building. The Curatorial Department is developing plans for blockbuster programming that will excite and educate hundreds of thousands of Chicagoans and other visitors to the new museum. **Negotiating Rapture: The Power of Art to Transform Lives** and **Art in Chicago, 1945-1995** will be the first two major exhibitions in the new building and promise to attract national and international recognition.

The Museum of Contemporary Art continues to contribute to the cultural vitality of the Chicago area and beyond. I have enclosed an informational packet including materials on the museum's activities including our schedule of grand opening events. Please mark your calendar now for our June 21 Grand Opening. It will be a historic moment in Chicago's cultural history and we would like for you to be there. If I can provide additional information, please do not hesitate to call me at 312.280.2666.

Thank you for the support you have generously provided in the past, and for your consideration of this request.

Sincerely,

Enclosures

(Courtesy of the Museum of Contemporary Art, Chicago)

CORPORATE GENERAL-SUPPORT LETTER

Date

Name
Title
Company X
Address

Dear Name:

On behalf of everyone at the Brooklyn Academy of Music, I want to let you know how much we appreciate Company X's loyal and generous support since 1985. At this time, I am sending you our proposal for the 1997/98 season.

Established in 1861, the Brooklyn Academy of Music (BAM) has since become the nation's largest and arguably most influential presenter of alternative performing arts, presenting work that cannot be seen elsewhere. The Academy's primary mission is to develop and present new work in the performing arts; to encourage innovative approaches to the traditional repertory of dance, opera, music, and theater; to promote unusual collaborations with visual artists; and to reach out to the local community through educational activities and multicultural experiences that specifically serve the interests of a culturally diverse, urban population. BAM accomplishes this mission through four basic programming areas: the Next Wave Festival of the contemporary performing arts; BAM Theater and other special international events; BAM Opera; and the Academy's educational and community programs.

Currently, we are in the final weeks of a spectacular Next Wave Festival, whose highlights have included productions by director Robert Wilson, choreographer David Rousseve, and Taiwan's acclaimed Cloud Gate Dance Theatre. This week, London's Cheek by Jowl theater troupe returns to BAM with John Webster's *The Duchess of Malfi,* and the Mark Morris Dance Group will present eight New York premieres. The reviews for this year's Festival have been terrific and ticket sales are stronger than in any season in recent memory.

The spring season promises to be among our most innovative and ambitious yet. BAM Opera will present three fully staged works including the Glimmerglass Opera Company's acclaimed production of Monteverdi's *L'Incoronazione di Poppea,* while BAM Theater will focus on French playwrights and companies, featuring two productions by the Comédie Francaise, Patrice Chéreau's staging of Bernard-Marie Koltès' *Dans la Solitude des Champs de Coton,* and an encore presentation of the Royal Dramatic Theatre of Sweden in a Bergman-directed production of Molière's *The Misanthrope*.

BAM also continues to offer a wide range of community and educational programs in the 1997/98 season. The 35-year-old Performing Arts Program for Young People (PAPYP) will present a total of 78 school-time performances of 15 productions, and the Academy's Arts Bridge program, which establishes artist residencies in local public schools, will offer in-depth study units linked to BAM performances as well as teacher workshops designed to encourage the arts in the classroom. In May, BAM will host both its nineteenth annual Dance Africa Festival and its second annual International Children's Festival.

As government funding for the arts continues to be cut at the state and federal levels, support from the corporate world has become increasingly important. In light of the quality and scope of BAM's programming in the 1997/98 season, as well as the difficult funding climate in which we are operating, we are asking that Company X consider increasing its general support of the Academy to the level of $7,500.

Thankfully, city funding remains solid. We are pleased to announce that the Academy was recently awarded a 1995–96 Cultural Challenge Grant from the New York City Department of Cultural Affairs. A stipulation of this $242,000 grant is that it be matched by gifts from private sources. An increased contribution to BAM's general operating fund would be especially valuable at this time, as it would help BAM meet this important challenge from our city government.

Thank you in advance for your consideration of this request. I hope to see you at BAM soon!

Sincerely,

Karen Brooks Hopkins
Executive Vice-President

(Courtesy of the Brooklyn Academy of Music)

CORPORATE GENERAL-SUPPORT PROPOSAL

Brooklyn Academy of Music

1995/96 Season

A General Support Proposal

BROOKLYN ACADEMY OF MUSIC
30 Lafayette Avenue
Brooklyn, New York 11217

Harvey Lichtenstein, President & Executive Producer
Karen Brooks Hopkins, Executive Vice President
Joseph V. Melillo, Producing Director

INTRODUCTION

The Brooklyn Academy of Music (BAM), established in 1861, has become one of the nation's most significant forums for innovation in the arts. BAM is a national model of an urban arts center in the nineties, addressing both global issues in the arts and local community needs. The Academy's primary mission is to develop and present new work in the performing arts; to encourage innovative approaches to the traditional repertory of dance, opera, music, and theater; to promote unusual collaborations with visual artists; and to reach out to the local community through educational activities and multicultural experiences that specifically serve the interests of a culturally diverse, urban population. BAM provides Brooklyn, the City of New York, the tri-state area, and visitors from this country and abroad with a shining example of an urban arts institution of exemplary entrepreneurial energy and community commitment.

All of the Academy's programming areas - - the NEXT WAVE Festival, BAM Opera, BAM Theater and other special international events, and the Academy's Community and Education Programs - - serve as catalysts for change. Whether the result is to expose traditional audiences to non-traditional works or to expose New York City school children to the performing arts for the first time, BAM has concentrated primarily on innovation in the performing arts by finding alternative ways to explore traditional repertory and by commissioning and producing newly created works for the stage. As the only large, independent performing arts center in New York City outside Manhattan, BAM has addressed many of the new, pressing issues facing urban arts institutions. BAM has been a national leader in creating programs that serve local communities, provide arts education, address multiculturalism, present artists from different cultures around the world, and encourage contemporary work, collaborations, and new forms in the performing arts.

BAM's activities also encompass one of the largest performing arts programs for young people in this country, with programming that has particular relevance to Brooklyn audiences, supplemented by specially developed humanities materials that assist in promoting an appreciation and understanding of the work presented. In addition to performance-related activities, the Academy hosts numerous community events and has organized extensive local development initiatives.

BAM'S 1995-96 SEASON

NEXT WAVE FESTIVAL (Fall 1995): In 1983, BAM produced the first annual NEXT WAVE Festival to commission, develop, and present new work in the performing arts from national and international artists in all disciplines. The 1995 NEXT WAVE Festival opens with the American premiere of visionary director Robert Wilson's *Alice*, marking the return of Robert Wilson, composer Tom Waits and the Thalia Theater of Hamburg to the NEXT WAVE. Other NEXT WAVE theatrical events are: British actor/director Steven Berkoff's surrealistic staging of Oscar Wilde's *Salome*; Ping Chong's *Chinoiserie*, a multi-disciplinary performance work that explores relations between China and the West from the eighteenth century on; and the return to BAM of England's Cheek by Jowl company in its new production of John Webster's Elizabethan tragedy *The Duchess of Malfi*.

Dance programming in the NEXT WAVE encompasses a range of styles. Taiwanese choreographer Lin Hwai-min and his Cloud Gate Dance Theatre make their BAM debut with a full-length dance piece entitled *Nine Songs*, which Lin created to celebrate Cloud Gate's 20th anniversary and premiered in Taiwan in August 1993. Choreographer David Rousseve and his company REALITY return to BAM with a new dance/theater work entitled *The Whispers of Angels*, the second and final part in the *Dream Series* that began with the 1994 piece *Pop Dreams*. The NEXT WAVE also welcomes the Mark Morris Dance Group in two evening-length programs of new pieces, marking the company's ninth visit to the Academy.

Musical events include two weekends of alternative jazz hosted by acclaimed jazz clarinetist Don Byron and showcasing, among others, Bill Frisell, Vernon Reid and Frank Lacy. In addition, a screening of Danish filmmaker Carl Dreyer's 1927 masterpiece *The Passion of Joan of Arc* features the New York premiere of *Voices of Light*, Richard Einhorn's newly composed score for the film.

Each year BAM presents the Academy's resident Brooklyn Philharmonic Orchestra as part of the NEXT WAVE. For 1995, the BPO performs in two separate three-concert engagements: The first program, *From Gospel to Gershwin*, surveys African American and African American-influenced music after World War I, while the second three-concert performance series features the Kronos Quartet.

Artists in Action is a new initiative, under the auspices of the NEXT WAVE Festival, in which visual artists conceive and develop new works for performance in theater, museum and alternative exhibition spaces. The program grows out of BAM's successful history of commissioning and presenting collaborative projects involving visual artists. The initiative reverses the roles generally held by visual and performing artists in these projects, giving visual artists the leadership role. In the 95/96 season, the participating visual artists are Ilya Kabokov, Vito Acconci, and the collaborative team of Kristin Jones and Andrew Ginzel, presenting works at the BAM Majestic Theater, the DIA Center for the Arts, and the Queens Museum of Art, respectively.

BAM OPERA (Winter/Spring 1996): In 1989, the Brooklyn Academy of Music inaugurated a formal opera program to foster innovation in the field of opera and promote an alternative vision of opera for American audiences. BAM Opera's eighth season features three fully-staged productions. BAM Opera presents the Glimmerglass Opera Company's production of Monteverdi's *L'Incoronazione di Poppea*, a passionate tale of love and scheming, honor and death, considered among the greatest works of the first half of the seventeenth century. To continue the season, as part of the Academy's ongoing French Baroque Opera Project BAM presents William Christie and Les Arts Florissants in an innovative new conceptualization of Handel's three-act *Orlando*, directed by Canadian-born artist Robert Carsen. Finally, the Mark Morris Dance Group performs choreography specially created by Morris for Gluck's *Orfeo ed Euridice* alongside the Handel & Haydn Society chorus and period orchestra.

BAM THEATER (Spring 1996): For over twenty years, BAM has provided an American home for important international theater directors and companies whose work is not frequently seen in the United States, establishing a reputation as a leading presenter of international artists and work. The 1996 BAM Theater season focuses on French artists and work. The season opens in February with Patrice Chereau's staging of Bernard-Marie Koltès' two character play *Dans la Solitude des Champs de Coton* (In the Loneliness of the Cotton Fields). In May, with the full cooperation of the French government, BAM presents the legendary Comédie-Française in two extraordinary productions - - Moliere's *Dom Juan* and Marivaux's *La Double Inconstance* - - marking the company's first New York engagement since 1979. The season closes with the Royal Dramatic Theatre of Sweden's return to the Academy after its critically acclaimed appearances in 1988, 1991, 1993 and 1995, with Ingmar Bergman's rendition of Moliere's French classic *The Misanthrope*. In conjunction with the Alliance Française, the Board of Education's French department and others, BAM is developing a full roster of educational activities to complement the productions including an exhibition of sets, costumes, scripts and posters chronicling the 315 year history of the Comédie-Française.

EDUCATIONAL PROGRAMS: Since 1960, BAM's Performing Arts Program for Young People (PAPYP) has been committed to developing and expanding the social, cultural and aesthetic awareness of New York City's school children by offering a comprehensive arts education program including multicultural performances, preparatory student/teacher study guides, post-performance workshops, and in-school residencies. Initiatives for the 95/96 season include the ongoing schooltime performance series and in-school program *Arts Bridge*, and the second International Children's Festival of Theater and Music. In total, BAM expects to serve over 70,000 children in the 1995/96 season.

COMMUNITY PROGRAMS: BAM's community programs include: the 19th anniversary season of DanceAfrica, which, with the theme *Salute to Women of the African Diaspora*, features performances, the annual Bazaar, and educational, outreach and humanities components; music, dance and theater events as part of the eighth season of 651, an independent organization founded under BAM's auspices and named for the address of the BAM Majestic Theater at 651 Fulton Street; and special projects of BAM's Public Affairs Department including Brooklyn's annual Tribute To Dr. Martin Luther King, Jr., the Community Arts Partnership Project (CAPP), and the Ticket Assistance Program.

FINANCIAL PROFILE

BAM is currently projecting a balanced budget for FY96 that will total $XX in expenses: with $XX representing direct program expenses and $XX representing building maintenance, security, and administrative overhead to support the programming. The balancing income is projected to come from the following sources:

1) $XX in earned revenue including box office receipts, co-production income, advertising sales, and the sale of art. BAM continues to package special discounts and greater flexibility in ticket ordering to encourage increased ticket sales.

2) $XX in contributed income, representing $XX from foundations, $XX from corporations, $XX from individuals, $XX from special events, and $XX from city, state, and federal government sources.

BAM's Development Office continues to focus special initiatives on income areas with significant growth potential, namely corporate sponsorships and individual giving.

THE CAMPAIGN FOR BAM

The Campaign for BAM is the Academy's first major comprehensive fundraising effort, designed to: ensure financial security; continue program integrity; allow program expansion; improve audience amenities; preserve the institution's heritage; and maintain the institution's cutting edge.

The Campaign is presenting BAM's constituency with a comprehensive needs assessment of the institution's priorities and goals that combines private annual operating support, endowment and cash reserve funds, and capital improvements through the year 2000. In a time when government support for the arts continues to decline and the competition for private support increases, such an approach will help to focus and clarify BAM's current and future needs.

In its first phase (1992-1995) the Campaign achieved a combined total of 61.2 million dollars including: XX million endowment and completed cash reserve (XX million); XX million in private annual operating support; XX million in government operating appropriations; and XX million in capital appropriations from New York City that will improve the Academy's infrastructure, elements of its immediate geographic environment, and audience amenities including lobby renovation, in-house restaurant facilities, expanded parking, and new chairs and carpeting in the Opera House.

The goal of Phase Two (1996-2000) is to achieve a combined total of XX million dollars including: an additional 6 million in private endowment funds; XX million in annual private operating support; XX million in new government operating appropriations; and XX million in capital appropriations from New York City, of which XX million is currently secured for infrastructure/building interior needs, an upgraded communications/computer system, and a facility for BAM's new film program.

With the successful completion of Phase Two in the year 2000, BAM will have realized XX million dollars over an eight year period.

BAM has established The BAM Endowment Trust as an independent 501(c)(3) organization that will maintain, augment and supervise investment of endowment monies. (name), Chairman, Company B, is Chairman of The BAM Endowment Trust, and BAM Trustees (name), Director, Company C and (name), Managing Partner, Company D are co-chairs of *The Campaign for BAM*.

GOVERNANCE

The development and expansion of the BAM Board has been a primary goal for the Academy over the past decade. Currently, the Board has 47 active members consisting of leadership that represents BAM's broad constituency. The BAM Board meets five times per year to review current and future issues involving programming, finances and policy and is advised in specialized areas through the work of its Executive Committee and standing committees. The BAM Board is currently responsible for 20% of BAM's annual contributed income.

(name), President of Company A, is Chairman of the BAM Board. As developer of X Center in downtown Brooklyn, (name) has harnessed the forces of the private and public sectors to realize one of New York City's most successful development projects. (name) is committed to developing new alliances for the arts at BAM.

CORPORATE SPONSORSHIP BENEFITS

Each contributor has the opportunity to affiliate itself with specific artistic, educational, and community programs. The range of benefits for these affiliations is based on the scope of the individual program and the level of financial commitment.

Corporate benefits may include: prominent billing in program brochures, program print advertising, and title page credit in BAMbill House Programs; prominent credit in all related program press releases; acknowledgments in BAM's Program Donor Listing and Annual Report;
acknowledgment and executive participation at program special events; complimentary tickets for opening night performances and receptions, and subsequent performances; discounts on tickets above the complimentary allotment; and opportunities for corporate entertaining in BAM spaces during the engagements.

In addition, employees of corporate contributors at the $5,000 level and higher are eligible to participate in the BAMbucks ticket program, which provides a discount of 15% off single ticket prices for most BAM, Brooklyn Philharmonic Orchestra, and 651 events. This benefit is extended to employees, their families, and company retirees. As a special bonus, each discounted ticket purchased will include a chit for a complimentary drink in the BAM lobby.

The sponsorship packages offered by the Academy are flexible and designed to provide a corporation with maximum visibility. BAM tailors each package to the specific needs and interests of the individual sponsor.

CONCLUSION AND REQUEST FOR SUPPORT

The Brooklyn Academy of Music sincerely appreciates Company X's loyal support and is now asking that Company X consider renewing its support of the Academy at the level of $XX. Your contribution will assist the Academy in stabilizing its financial position in these uncertain times, thus safeguarding its important cultural, educational and community initiatives.

(Courtesy of the Brooklyn Academy of Music)

CORPORATE SPECIAL PROJECT PROPOSAL I

Date

Address

Dear :

We would like to thank you once again for taking the time to come to the MCA. We appreciate the opportunity to discuss with you our plans for the new MCA. It is a pleasure to present you with the enclosed proposal requesting a grant of $200,000, payable over four years, to help us provide important educational programs.

As our move into the new building in 1996 approaches, the MCA is planning exciting programming to serve children and adults. As you know, our location on Chicago Avenue will increase the numbers of first-time visitors to the MCA, including school children in need of art education. Your grant to the MCA as we expand will assist large numbers of people seeking to bring the visual arts into their lives. In addition, support for the MCA strengthens Chicago's cultural offerings and adds to the vitality of our community.

Thank you for your consideration of our request. We would be honored to see the (company) name associated with education programming in the new MCA. Please do not hesitate to contact us if we may provide you with any additional information.

Sincerely,

Director   Trustee

A Proposal to

(Name of Company)

The Museum of Contemporary Art

August, 1994

Support for Educational Programs at the
Museum of Contemporary Art

Education experts agree that the arts encourage active learning and promote critical thinking and problem-solving skills in students. Art education, especially in a museum setting, requires participation by students as they learn about artists and art through discussing and seeking to understand what art can teach about the human condition. Because the participatory nature of art education often elicits positive responses from students who do not respond to other modes of education, art education is vital to many students.

A cornerstone of the Museum of Contemporary Art's (MCA) mission is the responsibility to introduce and teach children and adults about contemporary art, enabling them to integrate the visual arts into their lives. The Museum of Contemporary Art requests that _____ consider making a grant of $200,000, payable over four years, to support MCA educational programming.

Both the School Outreach Program and educational programming for the "Art in Chicago" exhibition are two crucial programs which will help define the MCA's success in the new building. We are proud to offer you a choice of funding either of these programs. Following is a description of the new facility and these two funding options.

The New Museum of Contemporary Art

With the whole world watching, Chicago will celebrate one of its most momentous cultural achievements as the Museum of Contemporary Art builds its much-heralded showcase for contemporary art on the site of the Chicago Avenue Armory. According to the Chicago Tribune, "with a striking prime location, striking design, expanded gallery space and new opportunities for education programs, the facility should allow the MCA finally to move into the most prominent echelon of Chicago cultural institutions, and of contemporary art museums nationally."

The new museum building will be a cultural landmark. It will contribute to the architectural legacy of Chicago, providing a magnificent aesthetic link between the historic Water Tower and Lake Michigan. It will, in itself, represent one of Chicago's greatest works of art.

The new building will incorporate the latest technologies for museum design into a structure uniquely suited to the mission of the MCA. Grand stairs will rise to a soaring glass-fronted curtain-wall through which passersby may catch a glimpse of the galleries inside. A central atrium bisecting the building vertically will allow visitors to look through the building onto vistas of Lake Michigan and the surrounding Chicago environs. The 148,000-square-foot facility and sculpture garden will become an internationally-recognized landmark.

Page 2

The new building will encourage a vibrant institutional life through special event facilities, bookstore, cafe and museum shop. Together, each of these components will work to create an atmosphere which opens up the transforming world of contemporary art to the broadest possible audience.

School Outreach Programming in the new MCA

Education and community outreach programs will reach new heights as the primary beneficiary of the MCA's new education center and 300-seat theater. Education facilities in the new building will provide state-of-the-art classrooms, workshop spaces, and orientation galleries. Education will be a central, highly-visible part of Museum operations as the MCA touches the lives of ever-growing numbers of Chicago residents and school children.

One of the most exciting aspects of the new Museum will be the opportunity to provide substantial free educational programs, helping to partially fill the gap in art education in Chicago public schools. A grant from _____ in support of the School Outreach Program will help enable the MCA to serve 25,000 to 30,000 Chicago public school children in need of art education annually. The School Outreach Program has been designed in cooperation with the Chicago Board of Education with input from a panel of Chicago-area teachers to assure maximum service and value to participating schools. The School Outreach Program will have several components:

o   **Teacher Training** In the first year in the new building, the School Outreach Program will begin with an intensive training program for approximately 800 to 1,000 Chicago public school teachers. The MCA will provide them with free teacher packets, which include slides to use in their classrooms and other art materials connected to the current exhibition. Art training the MCA offers public school teachers will include workshops in which MCA education professionals guide teachers through exhibitions, deliver lectures on art history and aesthetics, and conduct multi-disciplinary hands-on activities that the teachers can duplicate back in their own classroom with their students. In the new facility, the MCA expects to hold four workshops per exhibition block, possibly held in the new 300-seat auditorium.

o   **Transportation** Students and teachers will then be brought to the Museum. The MCA will provide free bus service to the Museum for School Outreach Program tours.

o   **Guided Tours** MCA education professionals and trained volunteer docents will provide guided tours for students which will give them a friendly introduction to learning about the visual arts. The tours will introduce students to the works of art on display and invite students' responses during interactive, lively question and answer

Page 3

    sessions. These tours will begin with a video orientation and conclude with a studio art experience. Students will realize there is a place for them in the art world and learn that art can be a joyful experience.

o   **Follow-up Visits** The School Outreach Program will also provide opportunities for students to return with family members and renew the connections to art forged during their school instruction and tours. For example, students will receive free Museum passes to encourage them to continue to explore the world of contemporary art.

o   **New Education Partnerships** The MCA is currently developing partnerships with some of Chicago's neediest schools. For example, this fall the MCA will initiate a program with Farren Elementary School which serves children living in the Robert Taylor Homes, a public housing development labeled a "war zone" by many. Residents there will benefit greatly from the MCA's involvement in the education of their children, many of whom are raised in households headed by single parents who have not graduated from high school. The MCA, with support from the Chicago Housing Authority and the _____, is working with officials at the Farren School to create a program that will offer Farren upper-elementary students the unique opportunity to become trained docents, delivering their own tours of the MCA.

School Outreach Programming will answer the community's need for greater resources in the area of art education. At Farren Elementary School, for example, one teacher is responsible for teaching art to 800 students. The MCA has worked recently with schools such as Howland School of the Arts, Solomon School, Bright Elementary School, and Ray School. The MCA will continue to develop partnerships with Chicago's neediest schools.

    A grant of $200,000 from _____ to support the School Outreach Program will enable the MCA to reach a significant segment of Chicago's public school population, and help them meet the educational challenges they confront on a daily basis.

"Art in Chicago" Educational Programming

    The "Art in Chicago, 1945 - 1995" exhibition will be the major fall show for the inaugural year of the new building. The exhibition will include substantial educational programming benefiting new audiences of children and adults. A $200,000 grant from _____ would support educational programming for the entire five months of the exhibition, which focuses on Chicago's contemporary artists and their work. "Art in Chicago" will highlight Chicago's creative genius over the past 50 years and the extraordinary creative talent existing in the city today.

Page 4

The educational programming for the exhibition is a crucial part of the Museum's efforts to bring contemporary art into the lives of thousands of Chicago area residents and visitors who have perhaps never participated before in MCA programming. As one of the first year's major shows in the new building, "Art in Chicago" provides the MCA with an important opportunity to reach out to new audiences. Linking this exhibition with education will enrich the lives of children and adult students as they become a vital, active part of the Museum community.

A special emphasis of "Art in Chicago" education programming is on the diversity of Chicago art. With a large population of Latinos and other ethnic minorities, Chicago offers a wide range of art in a variety of mediums, and the "Art in Chicago" educational programming will focus on this diversity, to the benefit of all participants. The complexity of what can be named "Chicago art" will be explored in all of the following programs.

"Art in Chicago" educational offerings will include the following:

o   **Family Day Programs** On selected weekends during the exhibition, parents, grandparents, and guardians will accompany children on tours and participate in hands-on studio experiences in the MCA's new classrooms. Docent-led tours will bring participating families to art objects in the show, generate lively inter-generational discussion, and lead participants into classrooms where they will together explore different media and create their own art. Linked to the "Art in Chicago" exhibition, family programming will explore expressions of Chicago art that were previously overshadowed by the focus on more widely-known aspects of Chicago art, such as Imagist painting. Family Day activities will include storytelling, puppetry, acting, and music for younger children.

o   **Artist Studio Visits** Open to all interested children and adults, these MCA-sponsored visits will afford an intimate and instructive glimpse into the working life of practicing local artists. The artist will conduct a tour of his or her work space and answer audience questions. This program offers an opportunity for the MCA to include ethnic neighborhoods in its programming arena, while encouraging the Museum's members to partake of the vibrant cultural life of the city.

o   **Two-Day Symposium** Held on the opening weekend of the exhibition, this symposium will be open to all and conducted in the new building's theater. Approximately 300 attendees will hear artists and scholars from throughout the country and Chicago discuss the last fifty years of artistic activity in Chicago. These two intensive days of scholarly dialogue will add to our knowledge of American art, acting as a catalyst for future research with a focus on the art created in Chicago.

Page 5

o   **Chicago Artists Videos** During the run of the exhibition, a series of videos will be
     shown in the MCA's orientation spaces. These videos will illuminate the creative
     process and lives of the Chicago artists represented in the exhibition, and will provide
     compelling counterpoint to art on view. After the exhibition, the videos will become
     part of the MCA archive of videos and available for study by interested individuals
     and organizations.

o   **Artists-in-Residence** Three artists active in Chicago at some time since World War
     II will be in residence at the MCA. Not only will these artists create their own
     original works during their stay, but they will discuss the exhibition, give talks about
     their work and meet with students and young artists, thereby providing once-in-a-
     lifetime learning opportunities for these young people to interact with working artists.

o   **Other Programming** These include augmented lectures, tours of the exhibition, art
     courses for college credit, a film series, and outdoor walking tours. For example, a
     walking tour of Chicago's outdoor murals created by Latino artists in Latino
     neighborhoods could provide audiences with new insight into Chicago's contemporary
     art community.

Recognition

A gift of $200,000 represents a significant vote of confidence in the Museum of
Contemporary Art. _____ will be recognized as lead supporter of either the School
Outreach Program or "Art in Chicago" education programming on all program literature
distributed to the public during the inaugural year, when attendance is expected to reach
500,000. These materials include teacher packets, gallery guides, brochures, press releases
and publicity packets sent to members of the national press, and calendars and other
documents produced for MCA members and trustees.

These recognition opportunities will link _____ with inspiring educational
programming during the first year of operation in the new building, when MCA programs
will be in the national spotlight and reach a larger and more diverse audience than ever
before in its history.

The Request

The Museum of Contemporary Art in Chicago stands ready to take its place among
the great museums of the world. The participation of _____ in educational
programming in the new MCA building will greatly benefit the MCA and its audiences and
link the _____ name with a high-profile program. A grant of $200,000 to support
educational programming can be earmarked either for expanded School Outreach
Programming or to fund educational programs for "Art in Chicago." By supporting either of
these fine programs, _____ will affirm its commitment to bettering peoples' lives and
to enriching the educational and cultural life of the Chicago area.

(Courtesy of the Museum of Contemporary Art, Chicago)

CORPORATE SPECIAL PROJECT PROPOSAL II

Bergman Festival
New York
May–June 1995

I.   Introduction

In the spring of 1995, seven of New York City's cultural institutions will present a singular retrospective of the life and multifaceted work of Ingmar Bergman. Jointly, the Brooklyn Academy of Music, the Film Society of Lincoln Center, the Museum of Modern Art, the Museum of Television and Radio, WNET/Thirteen, the New York Public Library for the Performing Arts, the American Museum of the Moving Image, and Arcade Publishing, literary agents for Bergman in the United States, will collaborate to show the entire range of Bergman's screen, stage, and literary work. The Festival, running from the beginning of May to the end of June, will explore Bergman's role as a twentieth-century giant of film and stage, examining his influence on both genres, as well as the forces that helped to shape his work. The festival will include film screenings, live performances, exhibitions, lectures, symposia, and informal discussions with leading scholars, critics, and film and stage artists from Sweden and the United States. Taken together, these elements provide an overview of Bergman's film career and his current theatrical work, highlighting the importance of Swedish culture and history on his direction and writing. Altogether, it will be one of the largest celebrations of any international artist's life and work ever held in the United States.

THE BERGMAN FESTIVAL

II.   Screenings and Performances

1.   Bergman on Stage
   Royal Dramatic Theatre of Sweden
   Brooklyn Academy of Music
   June 1995

With its critically acclaimed appearances at BAM in 1987, 1991, and 1993, the Royal Dramatic Theatre of Sweden (Dramaten) has developed an ongoing relationship with BAM. In essence, the Academy now serves as an American home for the company. In total, Dramaten has presented six critically acclaimed productions at BAM, all directed by Ingmar Bergman, including Strindberg's *Miss Julie* with Lena Olin, O'Neill's *Long Day's Journey Into Night* with Bibi Andersson, and Ibsen's *Peer Gynt* with Borje Ahlstedt. In the spring of 1995, BAM is planning to bring three productions directed by Ingmar Bergman to the United States. These plays include: Shakespeare's *The Winter's Tale*; set in the world of *Fanny and Alexander*; Moliere's *The Misanthrope*, and the return of Yukio Mishima's *Madame de Sade,* which in its 1993 limited engagement of three performances played to capacity audiences at BAM.

In celebration of the Dramaten's return to the Academy and of the Bergman festival, BAM will have the honor of hosting the King and Queen of Sweden at a Royal Gala on May 31.

2.   **Ingmar Bergman Film Retrospective**
      The Film Society of Lincoln Center
      May 1995

The Film Society of Lincoln Center is one of the oldest and largest not-for-profit film societies in the United States. The Film Society's annual events include the acclaimed New York Film Festival, attended last year by over 64,000 people. For the 1995 Bergman celebration, the Film Society plans to mount a retrospective of Bergman's films that promises to be "as complete as possible," screening at least 30 of Bergman's 40 films. The series will include such classics as *The Seventh Seal*, *Wild Strawberries*, and *Fanny and Alexander*, as well as other, lesser-known works rarely shown in this country, such as *Summer with Monika*, *Thirst* and *Crisis*. As part of the retrospective, the Film Society hopes to use many newly restored and subtitled prints of Bergman films. The creation of such a complete film archive would open up the possibilities for a national and international tour of the retrospective. The screenings at Lincoln Center will take place in the 268 seat Walter Reade Auditorium.

In addition to its comprehensive screening series, the Film Society will host an exhibition of still photos from 7 of Bergman's 40 films. This exhibition, taken from restored films, has already toured with great success in other parts of the United States and Europe. The collection will remain at Lincoln Center throughout the run of its screening series.

3.   **Alf Sjoberg Film Retrospective**
      The Museum of Modern Art
      June 1995

The Museum of Modern Art (MOMA) will present a retrospective of the films of Alf Sjoberg, Sweden's first internationally acclaimed director and the first Swede to win the Palme d'Or at the Cannes Film Festival (*Miss Julie* in 1951). Sjoberg also directed Ingmar Bergman's first screenplay, *Torment* (1944), and is widely regarded as a major influence on Bergman as both a theater and film director. As an act of homage to his friend and colleague, Bergman made a television film of Sjoberg's final stage production. This version of Moliere's *School for Wives* will be part of the television programming described below. For this Sjoberg retrospective, MOMA hopes to show as many films as possible from newly subtitled prints that they commissioned solely for this exhibition. Following the New York showing, the films would be available for a national and international tour.

4.   **Bergman on Television**
      The Museum of Radio and Television
      May - June 1995

New York's Museum of Television and Radio is devoted to the preservation of classic works of television and radio from this country and abroad, and frequently features retrospectives of the lives and works of individuals who have shaped the medium. In the course of his career, Bergman directed numerous works for Swedish television. The Museum of Television and Radio, which currently has 10 Bergman television works in its collection, will present an ongoing screening series of these works, including the complete six-hour *Scenes from a Marriage*, as well as selected documentaries and television biographical profiles of Bergman. The Museum hopes to acquire additional material for the 8 week series.

5.   Bergman on Television
Thirteen/WNET TV
June 1995

Thirteen/WNET the New York PBS station will present *Bergman on Thirteen*, a two-day marathon of Ingmar Bergman's television and film works. On June 10, Thirteen will present Bergman's 1992 three-part television adaptation of his acclaimed novel The Best Intentions (directed by Bile August), a story based on Bergman's parents. On June 17, Thirteen will offer a thirteen-hour extravanganza of Bergman film masterpieces, including *Wild Strawberries* and *Through a Glass Darkly*. Thirteen will also air *World of Film: Sweden*, a documentary exploring Swedish cinema from Bergman to the new generation.

6.   Bergman in Print
May - June 1995

Since retiring from film in 1986, Bergman has directed much of his energies towards writing, publishing two novels (Best Intentions and Sunday's Children) and two autobiographical works (The Magic Lantern and Images). The festival will work closely with Arcade Publishing, the publisher of Bergman's work in the United States. Collaborative efforts with Arcade would make Bergman's literary works available at exhibitions, screenings, and theater events. Arcade will also publish Ingmar Bergman: An Artist's Journey, edited by Dr. Roger W. Oliver, in conjunction with the Festival. This collection of interviews and articles will encapsulate Bergman's artistic life and serve as the catalogue for the Festival. Along with photos from the artist's life and work, the book will include reprinted essays by James Baldwin and Woody Allen, interviews with Liv Ullmann and Lasse Bergstrom, and tributes by Kurosawa, Fellini, and Godard. In addition, An Artist's Journey will also include new interpretive essays by leading Swedish and American scholars.

7.   Bergman and Cinematography
Museum of the Moving Image
June, 1995

As part of their regular programming, the Museum of the Moving Image often programs weekend retrospectives devoted to one cinematographer. As part of the festival, they will devote a weekend to the work of Sven Nyqvist, who has photographed all of Bergman's film and television work since 1961. Several of Bergman's films will be shown and Nyqvist will comment on his work and analyze several sequences in detail.

III. Humanities Programs

1. Exhibition

In order to present the American public with a clear and comprehensive view of Ingmar Bergman's career as a filmmaker and theater director -- and the relationship between the work in the two media-- The New York Public Library for the Performing Arts will host an exhibition of materials documenting and interpreting his film and theater work. Most of these materials, which include production photographs, programs, posters, unpublished and annotated scripts and promptbooks, as well as scene and costume designs and set models, costumes and masks, will be drawn from the archives of the Swedish Film Institute and the Royal Dramatic Theater. Since these archives are not accessible to the public, this will provide a rare opportunity for an examination of Bergman's career in this way. The exhibition will be structured along themes that reccur in Bergman's work, such as the use of myth and ritual, Bergman's relation to Sweden, and his relation to Shakespeare.

2. Symposium

In order to develop and expand upon some of the central themes of the exhibition, a day-long symposium will be held on Saturday, June 10, 1995 at The New York Public Library for the Performing Arts. Although most of participants will be drawn from the academic community, the emphasis will be on an exchange of ideas that will be of interest to the general public. Themes for discussion will include: the influence of Sweden and Scandinavia on Bergman and his work; and the Dramaten and the emergence of a national theater. People attending the symposium from outside the New York City area will be able to attend a performance of Bergman's production of *Madame de Sade* that evening and attend film and television screenings during the weekend. The symposium will be videotaped and copies of the tape will be made part of the Library's collection. Like all aspects of the Festival, it will be listed and described in the program brochure.

IV. MARKETING AND PROMOTION

The festival will be supported by a full-scale marketing and promotion campaign beginning in the fall of 1994, one which will involve all participating institutions as well as local and national print and broadcast media. The promotional campaign will be executed in a two-tiered plan, which will involve both individual efforts on the parts of the participating institutions, as well as an overall, comprehensive campaign that will promote the festival itself. The marketing strategies of the individual institutions will include regular season mailing campaigns as well as special festival announcements sent out in target mailings to over 400,000. It is estimated that over 50,000 people from New York and other parts of the nation will attend the Festival events.

Key elements of the comprehensive marketing and promotion campaign will include:

- The creation of a festival logo and comprehensive design strategy.
- Artwork and design for brochures, posters, and support materials.

·   An all-inclusive press kit that will provide information about all of the festival's events and participants.

·   A festival brochure that will provide a complete schedule and listing of all of the festival's main and ancillary events.

·   Scheduling of a major festival press conference with local and national media to launch the festival, approximately 2 weeks prior to the opening event (this would include T.V. coverage from possibly the CBS Evening News, CNN, ABC).

·   An advertising supplement with a national magazine such as <u>The New Yorker</u> .

·   Coordination of all other media campaigns with major ads purchased in the <u>New York Times</u>, <u>Stagebill</u> and <u>Playbill</u>.

·   The development and design of a festival merchandising strategy.

V.   Benefits of Sponsorship

Benefits of sponsorship for 1995's Bergman festival will include:

- prominent billing in program brochures,
  program print advertising, and title page credit in house programs, each with logo designed for the program;

- prominent credit in all related program press releases,
  including the comprehensive festival press kit;

- acknowledgments in Program Donor Listing and
  individual institutional annual reports;

- opportunities for major sponsor product displays
  (cars, etc.) at performance sites;

- acknowledgment and executive participation at program
  special events such as the Royal Gala on May 31;

- complimentary and discounted tickets for opening night
  performances, reception, and subsequent performances;

- discounts on tickets above the complimentary allotment;

- opportunities for corporate entertaining in festival
  performance spaces during the engagements;

The sponsorship packages offered by the festival participants are flexible and designed to provide corporate sponsors with maximum visibility. Each package can be tailored to meet the specific needs and interests of the individual sponsor.

VI. FUNDRAISING AND LEADERSHIP

This celebration of Bergman and his work promises to be one of the largest collaborative cultural events that New York has ever produced, and certainly the most comprehensive celebration of the artist's work ever conceived. A project of this magnitude and scope requires vision and commitment from its leaders and its supporters. At this point, the festival has secured the leadership of (name) and (name) to serve as Festival Chairmen. Together (name) and (name) will work with the Swedish and American cultural and business communities, including the Swedish and American theater and film communities, to coordinate their involvement in the festival.

The success of this unprecedented project is also dependent on meeting its fundraising objectives. The collaborating institutions are currently working to build a consortium of funders that will hopefully include the Swedish Ministry of Culture, the National Endowment for the Humanities, and a select group of leading corporations from both Sweden and the United States. The Swedish government will also provide funds for the restoration of the films of both Bergman and Sjoberg, which would then make them available to a wider audience and would provide prints suitable for Sweden's national archives and subsequent international touring.

VII. Conclusion

The Bergman Festival will be an unprecedented citywide program, and will be a unique opportunity for the Swedish and American communities to join together in what promises to be the cultural event of the year. This celebration, hosted by the Swedish Consulate in cooperation with seven of New York's most prominent cultural institutions and Bergman's American publisher, will pay fitting tribute to Sweden's greatest artist. It promises to be an unparalleled event highlighting every aspect of this seminal artist's work.

The Festival depends on a strong partnership between the Swedish and American corporate and cultural communities. At this time, we respectfully request support for the festival at the level of $XX. Your support will ensure that this triumphant celebration of the artistry of Ingmar Bergman will succeed.

Attachments

I.	Projected Summary Budget
II.	Key Biographies
III.	Institutional Mission Statements
IV.	Institutional Press
V.	Selected Brochures, etc.

(Coutesy of the Brooklyn Academy of Music)

FOUNDATION SPECIAL PROJECT PROPOSAL

A PROPOSAL

For

ARTISTS IN ACTION

to

The EFG Foundation

From

THE BROOKLYN ACADEMY OF MUSIC
30 Lafayette Avenue
Brooklyn, New York 11217-1486

October 1995

Submitted by

Harvey Lichtenstein, President and Executive Producer
Karen Brooks Hopkins, Executive Vice President
Joe Melillo, Producing Director

Overview

The Brooklyn Academy of Music has developed a new Visual Arts Initiative: *Artists in Action*, a collaborative workshop program that places primary emphasis on the role of visual artists in conceiving and developing new work for the performing arts. *Artists in Action* offers visual artists a leadership role in creating collaborative performance projects, effectively reversing the roles generally held by visual artists and performing artists in these projects.

Artists in Action also creates a unique model for collaboration between performing and visual arts organizations (including museums and alternative venues). It has brought together performing and visual arts professionals to establish program guidelines, to nominate and select artists, and to host and support the presentation of the new works created through the program. In addition to promoting the sharing of institutional resources, *Artists in Action* facilitates the development of new audiences for both visual and performing arts institutions. Ultimately, BAM hopes to expand this program nationally, working with select partners across the United States, setting the stage for the creation of a national model for the commission, development, and production of visual artist-initiated performance projects. Using methodology developed during the first program year, BAM is developing a structure for institutional collaboration that can be successfully replicated by arts facilities in other cities across the country. During future program years, BAM will work with representatives from institutions in other cities to analyze the effectiveness of its model and to expand the program nationally.

Detail

Artists in Action has been designed as a four-year pilot program (one planning year in 1994 followed by three program years from 1995-1997) leading to the development of a new national model for artistic and institutional collaboration. Each year three visual artists are selected to develop their ideas for performance-related projects. These artists and their performing artists collaborator(s) work with BAM to develop their projects in a workshop format over a six-to nine-month period. At the end of the workshop period, the artists present their "works-in-progress" to the public as a mini-series programmed as part of BAM's NEXT WAVE Festival.

Thanks to a planning grant received from XYZ in 1992, BAM developed an ongoing structure for the operation of this program. Following preliminary planning meetings, an Advisory Committee (see attached list) was established to serve in an advisory capacity to BAM's Visual Arts Initiative on a regular basis. Advisory Committee members were asked to nominate artists, to make recommendations with regard to the artists selection process, and to recommend sites for workshop presentations. They also serve on the Selection Panel that chooses the artists who participate in this program.

As *Artists in Action* has evolved, membership on the Advisory Committee has rotated so that other individuals, as well as representatives from a variety of visual arts organizations (including a diverse range of institutions from across the country), have the opportunity to participate on this Committee. Additionally, individuals from both local and national visual arts organizations that were not originally represented on the Advisory Committee have also been included in the program as Visual Arts Advisors. The Visual Arts Advisors, selected on the basis of criteria which included their organization's location, ethnic focus, size, and prior experience with performing artists, have provided general program advice and nominated additional artists.

During each year of the program's operation, BAM will work with two separate visual arts organizations, or "art partners" selected from among the Advisory Committee members and Visual Arts Advisors. In conjunction with its art partners, the Academy will mount the works-in-progress at BAM and at the locations of each of its partners. Thus, each of the three "works-in-progress" will be presented at a separate site. Although BAM's involvement will remain constant, the two visual arts partners will rotate from year to year. This rotation will increase the opportunities available to artists, facilitate a variety of organizational collaborations, and develop new audiences for each of the participating institutions. The Project Director of *Artists in Action* acts as a liaison between BAM, the visual arts partners, and the artists, and also works with BAM to fundraise for the Initiative and to administer grants. Because most visual arts organizations are not equipped to handle ticket reservations and sales, BAM also administers this aspect of the program.

The works-in-progress resulting from the workshops are introduced as a mini-series during BAM's NEXT WAVE Festival. The "Works-in-Progress" mini-series has been launched as part of the 1995 NEXT WAVE Festival, which takes place from October through December 1995, and has been publicized as part of the NEXT WAVE Festival. BAM is also working with its partners and the program Advisory Committee to reach visual arts audiences through organizational newsletters, their membership mailings, and other promotional mailings. The works-in-progress are performed a total of three to five evenings and/or matinees at their designated sites.

Each work-in-progress will be documented by slides and videotape. Following the program's third year, BAM will produce a catalog containing text, photographs, artists' sketches, and other materials which trace the development of the project and document the artists' presentations. Based upon the success of the artist presentations created through *Artists in Action*, BAM may choose to develop one or more of the works-in-progress for full production as part of a future NEXT WAVE Festival.

The "Works-in-Progress" series offers an unprecedented opportunity for audience development at each of the participating sites. Because each performance and each site are part of a single series, and because audience members will encounter many of the same people at each location, audiences will be easily introduced to organizations in unfamiliar locations. It is hoped that people who visit a new organization as part of this series will be encouraged to return to the organization again and again, and perhaps, in time, become a member of that organization.

Project Timetable

Artists in Action will commence in 1994 with an initial planning year. In January of 1995, BAM will publicly launch *Artists in Action* with the announcement of the first set of program artists. At the end of 1995 the program will be evaluated and alterations made as needed to ensure the program's successful operation during the next two years. Using the methodology developed during the first year of implementation, BAM, in conjunction with its Advisory Committee, will work during the next year (1996) to plan and design a national expansion of *Artists in Action*. This process will involve developing selection criteria and identifying cities and institutions across the country where the program can easily be replicated. During 1997, BAM will help plan and develop *Artists in Action* in the nationally targeted city or cities.

The Artists Selection Process

Several criteria were developed to identify appropriate artists for *Artists in Action*. Advisory Committee members recommended that an artist's work should have the following characteristics: (1) a strong narrative basis or evocative content; (2) an innate sense of theater or drama; and (3) a powerful visual presence. It was also recommended that the following factors be taken into consideration: (1) the artist's interest and/or previous experience with performance, and (2) the artist's ability, based on a nominator's previous experience with that artist, to work well in collaboration with other artists.

The Advisory Committee also recommended that three distinct groups of artists be considered for participation in *Artists in Action*: (1) artists who may have previously utilized performance in their work but who have not yet had the opportunity to design work on a larger scale in a performing arts context; (2) artists who presently create installation-oriented work, for whom the addition of a performance component would be the next logical step; and (3) artists who have worked exclusively in painting or sculpture, but who have expressed an interest in expanding the boundaries of their work.

Visual Arts Advisors and Advisory Committee members were asked to recommend up to three visual artists to be considered for participation in the Visual Artists Initiative. Through this nomination process, over forty artists have been recommended to participate in the Visual Artists Initiative (see attached list of artists' names). Selection criteria for both the nominators and nominated artists were designed to encompass the broadest possible spectrum of contemporary visual artists, including artists of color and other artists who do not have access to mainstream cultural facilities and audiences.

Artists Payment Plan

Participating visual artists will be each paid a fee of $X to cover time and effort expended in the creation of their artworks. Their performing artists collaborator(s) will also receive fees of $X each. An additional $X-$X will be allocated for each of the three projects to pay dancers, musicians, and other performers required for the workshop presentations (the "Works-in-Progress"). The artists will receive half-payment of their fees upon the selection and signing of their contract and will receive the balance upon completion of the project. Artists will also receive a materials stipend of up to $X to cover material and construction costs of the artworks.

Fundraising Plan

The costs of *Artists in Action*, including artists' fee and materials, administrative, marketing, technical, and production costs for the artists' presentations, will be covered by grant monies raised by BAM from donors such as XYZ and other funders. Based on the success of the original Planning Grant, it is anticipated that XYZ will take a leadership role in supporting this project. BAM will also seek funding from ABC Foundation and the RST Foundation, among others. The visual arts partners involved in this project will be responsible only for the indirect organizational costs (including personnel) involved in mounting the artist presentations at their sites.

National Expansion

The national expansion of the program will take place over two years (Years 3 and 4 of the Initiative). The first year of the expansion, National Planning Year I, will involve the development of a National Advisory Committee of up to fifteen representatives from museums and visual arts facilities located in cities across the country. The National Advisory Committee will be assembled by BAM and *Artists in Action* Project Director in accordance with recommendations from the Initiative's New York City Advisory Committee, representatives from the XYZ, and other national performing and visual arts organizations.

The National Advisory Committee will convene at least once during the first Planning Year to make recommendations for the national implementation of the Initiative. The objectives of this meeting will include: (1) evaluation of *Artists in Action*'s first program year in order to make recommendations for the future operation of the program, (2) development of selection criteria to identify cities and institutions outside New York City where the program can most easily be replicated, (3) discussions with potential "organizational partners" in the recommended cities to determine interest and ability to participate in this program, and (4) development of a strategy for implementing *Artists in Action* in the targeted city. As a result of this year-long planning process, a target city and participating organizations (including the performing arts institution that will serve as the lead organization for the Initiative in that city) will be selected for implementation of *Artists in Action*.

During the second year of the program's national expansion (Year 4 of the Initiative), BAM will work with the selected visual and performing arts institutions to develop *Artists in Action* in their city. *Artists in Action* Project Director and BAM staff will work side by side with the lead organization's staff members to: (1) develop a local Advisory Committee which will nominate artists and locate visual arts partners, (2) utilize the experience of two years of program development in New York City to design an ongoing structure for *Artists in Action* in this second city, and (3) design and develop artists' contracts, fundraising and marketing plans, and other program elements that can be used by the participating organizations.

During the National Planning Years I and II, BAM will offer participating organizations direct and indirect support by providing the following: (1) stipends for travel to New York City for meetings, (2) re-granting of monies to cover direct expenses related to the planning meetings, (3) the services of *Artists in Action*'s Project Director to facilitate the developing program, and (4) program documents and other assistance resulting from BAM's previous experience with the program. At the end of National Planning Year II, the targeted city will be poised to launch its Visual Arts Initiative the following year. Based on the successful installation of *Artists in Action* in this city, BAM will duplicate this process in other cities.

Conclusion

The Visual Arts Initiative is an exciting and timely project for several reasons. The program encourages visual and performing artists to develop different ways of looking at and thinking about their work. It also recognizes the fact that many visual artists no longer limit their activities to the creation of discrete two- and three- dimensional objects. Instead, contemporary artists utilize a "fusion aesthetic" to create emotionally-charged installations that combine painting, sculpture, audio and video technology, as well as performances by the artists themselves.

In addition to creating new relationships between visual and performing artists, *Artists in Action* promises to create a unique model for collaboration between visual and performing arts centers in the development and presentation of collaborative projects. For the institutions involved, the project provides an opportunity to develop new audiences, to offer artists expanded opportunities, and to form relationships with other arts organizations. For BAM, a presenting organization that works primarily with performing artists, the project provides a special opportunity to understand and serve the visions of visual artists.

As the program develops nationally, it will provide a chance for fruitful exchange between artists and organizations in different cities across the country. Ultimately, the Visual Arts Initiative hope to provide a new model for collaboration that can be utilized by other performing and visual arts centers both nationally and internationally.

Because *Artists in Action* and its works-in-progress mini-series will be marketed through visual and performing arts publications and institutions, audiences will be encouraged to visit new venues and to experience new forms of art. As the "art partners" rotate from year to year, audiences will have the opportunity to visit and become acquainted with a variety of new institutions. Ideally, *Artists in Action* will lead to new visitors and members for each of the organizations that participates in the program over time.

At this time, the Brooklyn Academy of Music respectfully requests that the EFG Foundation support the 1996 program year of *Artists in Action* with a grant at the level of $00,000. As a major supporter of this innovative initiative, the Foundation will play a significant role in helping to create a new dynamic for exchange in the arts.

Brooklyn Academy of Music/*Artists in Action*
Page 5

(Courtesy of the Brooklyn Academy of Music)

AFFINITY CARD MAILING

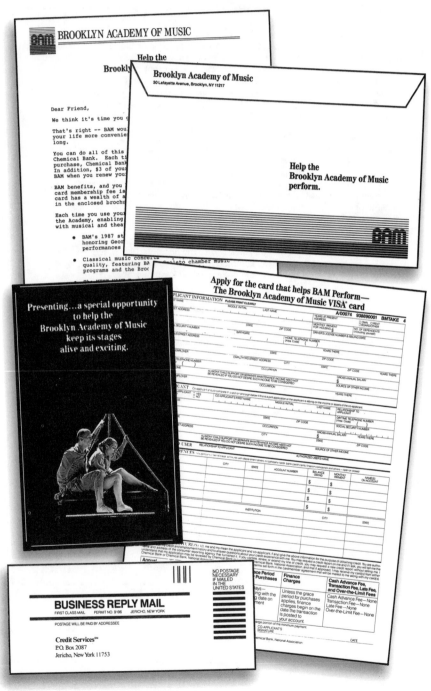

(Courtesy of the Brooklyn Academy of Music)

ANNUAL FUND MAILING: PRIVILEGES AND PLEDGE FORM

Museum of Contemporary Art
Annual Fund
Donor Recognition Privileges by Level of Support

Contributor   **$250 - $499**

◆   MCA's base membership benefits for one year
◆   MCA Donor Card
◆   Listing by level of support in the MCA's Annual Report
◆   Personal copy of the MCA's Annual Report
◆   Invitations to attend the Curator's Tour of each major exhibition

Friend   **$500 - $999**

All the above listed privileges plus:

◆   Invitation to attend one Contemporary Art Circle exhibition preview
◆   Invitation to attend the annual Donor's Lecture and Reception
◆   Invitation to attend the annual Behind-the-Scenes exhibition tour

Circle Fellow   **$1,000 - $2,499**

All the above listed privileges plus:

◆   Membership in the MCA's Contemporary Art Circle including:

        -     Invitations to Circle Exhibition Previews
        -     Invitation to the Circle Lecture and Dinner
        -     Invitation to the Circle Annual Meeting

Circle Patron   **$2,500 - $4,999**

All the above listed privileges plus:

◆   Invitation to a Circle Patron Reception
◆   Copy of an exhibition catalogue selected by the Museum

Curator's Circle   **$5,000 & Above**

All the above listed privileges plus:

◆   Invitation to attend a Curator's Reception
◆   Listing on the MCA's Annual Fund lobby plaque
◆   Copy of an exhibition catalogue for each major exhibition

Director's Circle   **$10,000 & Above**

All of the above listed privileges plus:

◆   Invitation to attend the Director's Dinner
◆   Invitation to attend a Meet-the-Artist Reception

MUSEUM OF CONTEMPORARY ART
Annual Fund Pledge/Gift Form
Fiscal Year 1996
[July 1995 - June 1996]

I/We (full name) _____ hereby pledge/pay support in

the amount of $ _____ to the Museum of Contemporary Art's Annual Fund.

METHOD OF PAYMENT
(please circle the appropriate number and complete)

1. Enclosed is my/our check for $ _____ representing the full amount of my/our pledge.

2. I/We will send my/our donation in full by _____ (date). Fiscal Year 1996 Annual Fund contributions are due by April 30, 1996.

3. I/We prefer to contribute according to the following schedule. All pledges must be paid in full by April 30, 1996. You will be billed automatically.

    $_____ $_____ $_____ $_____
       amount   amount   amount   amount

    _____   _____   _____   _____
       month   month   month   month

4. I/We prefer to charge $ _____ on my/our Visa or Mastercard, representing the full amount of my/our pledge.

    Visa/Mastercard account number _____

    Expiration date _____ Cardholder Signature_____

DONOR RECOGNITION INFORMATION
(please check & complete one)

_____   Please list my/our name as _____

_____   I/We wish to remain anonymous. Do not list my/our name.

Signature _____ Date _____

Please make your check payable to: **The Museum of Contemporary Art**.
Please return this form in the envelope provided.
For more information call 312.280.5176.

08/01/95

(Courtesy of the Museum of Contemporary Art, Chicago)

ANNUAL FUND RENEWAL LETTER

November, 19XX

Dear Friend of BAM,

All of us at BAM have so much to thank you for this holiday season. With your generous membership support, you have made 19XX an extraordinary year.

Your support helped bring the world to BAM's stages: exceptional opera from the *Kirov* and *Les Arts Florissants*, dance from *Twyla Tharp* and Taiwan's *Cloud Gate Dance Theatre*, new work from our greatest living theater directors—*Peter Brook, Giorgio Strehler, Ingmar Bergman,* and *Robert Wilson*—and much more. All this, with *Mark Morris* and *Cheek by Jowl* still to come!

Now, with the expiration of your membership soon approaching, **we are writing to ask you to renew or increase your support for 19XX**. All it takes is a few minutes of your time to ensure more of the extraordinary programming you enjoy at BAM season after season.

With your generous support, BAM brings you the world's best companies, many of which would otherwise never be seen in New York (where else but BAM could you see theater from Sweden, Italy, Israel, France, England, and Germany—all in one year?) Your support also brings you the world's best artists—iconoclasts and innovators like *Robert Wilson*, cutting-edge choreographers like *Pina Bausch*, and extraordinary musicians like *William Christie*. **Your support now ensures that BAM will continue to surprise and challenge you again and again.**

We like to say that being a Friend of BAM brings you the **best of BAM**. Of course you will continue to receive the best benefits we offer—the best discounts, the best tickets, the best enjoyment (including six working rehearsals each year), and the best service. But most importantly, your membership support will ensure that BAM continues to be a home for the world's **best contemporary performing arts** year after year.

Whether the stage is filled with the dance of *Mark Morris*, the wonderful theater of *Cheek by Jowl*, or a new discovery, you can always count on BAM to invigorate your entire year with excitement and imagination. **With ticket sales meeting only 40 percent of our expenses, and drastic reductions in government support, we must count on *you* to provide the funding that enables BAM to continue its unique mission.**

Please take a few moments and renew your membership support. Thank you in advance for your continued kindness and generosity.

Sincerely,

Karen Brooks Hopkins
Executive Vice-President

(Courtesy of the Brooklyn Academy of Music)

ANNUAL ACQUISITION APPEAL PACKAGE

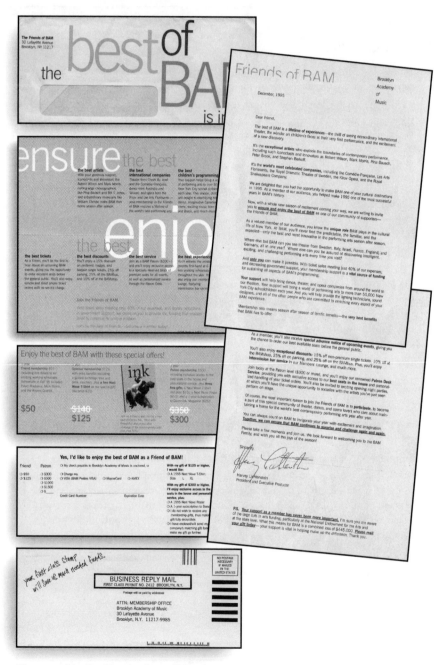

(Courtesy of the Brooklyn Academy of Music)

TELEFUNDRAISING RENEWAL SCRIPT

Good evening, Mr./Ms._____. This is _____ calling from the Brooklyn Academy of Music. (How are you this evening?)

We're calling, Mr./Ms. _____, for two reasons. First, we'd like to thank you for the support your Friends of BAM membership brought us this past year. Even with sold out performances, ticket sales meet only 40 percent of our expenses. The remaining 60 percent is met by grants and gifts from private individuals like yourself. Your generosity has been especially uplifting as we face a critical loss of government funds that we have depended on. BAM's combined losses total $445,000 this year! The contributions we have received from members have never been more appreciated. Thank you very much for your kindness.

The second reason we're calling is to personally invite you to renew your Friends of BAM membership. As we reach out to our renewing members for your continued support, we are asking that you consider an increased gift to help us make up for our loss of government funds. We have set a goal of $100,000 for December and January, and your renewing now during our phone campaign will help us in reaching our goal.

By renewing at the _____ level (two levels above previous gift), you'll receive all the benefits you're familiar with, like invitations to working rehearsals, plus some great additional ones as well. (EXPLAIN RELEVANT BENEFITS) To show our appreciation for your increased support, we'd also like to send you a special gift. (RELEVANT PREMIUM)

I can renew your membership at the _____ level with a gift of $____. How does that sound?

(GO TO CREDIT CARD CLOSE, DROP, OR OBJECTIONS)

(Courtesy of the Brooklyn Academy of Music)

TELEFUNDRAISING ACQUISITION SCRIPT

Hello, may I speak to (USE FULL NAME) please?

Good evening, MR./MS. _____ . This is (YOUR FULL NAME) calling from the Brooklyn Academy of Music. (How are you this evening?) (LISTEN FOR RESPONSE)

(FOR INSIDE LISTS)

We're calling to thank you for making BAM one of your cultural destinations this year and helping make this one of the most successful years in our history.

MR./MS. _____ , I understand you attended (our Next Wave Festival; our past spring season; our production of *Alice*, directed by Robert Wilson, etc.).

—Is that correct? (LET THEM RESPOND, DEVELOP A CONVERSATION)

—And what else did you see here?

—And what did you like about it?

—Have you seen other (theater, dance, music) events here at BAM?

—What do you enjoy about BAM?

—That's great to hear!

—Thank you, I'll pass that information along.

MR./MS. _____ , we're also calling this evening to invite you to enjoy the very best of BAM by becoming a member of our community of supporters—the Friends of BAM.

Are you familiar with the Friends of BAM?

(IF RESPONSE IS YES, BEGIN WITH "Well, then you probably know that . . . ")

(IF NO) Support from our Friends of BAM members ensures that we can bring dance, theater, and opera companies from around the world to our theaters, season after season. As a member, you help provide the lighting technicians, sound designers, stage crews, and all the other people who are committed to bringing you innovative performing arts.

Membership support also allows us to continue our important education programs, which serve over 50,000 school children every year. With ticket sales meeting only 40 percent of our expenses, membership support is a vital source of our funding, and it has never been more important than right now. I'm sure you're aware of the drastic decreases in government support to all areas of the arts. What this means to BAM is a combined loss of $445,000 this year alone. To make up this difference, we are increasing our efforts to build membership at all levels, and for December and January we have set a goal of $100,000.

As we ask for your support, we also want you to know that a Friend of BAM membership will bring you a whole series of benefits and privileges to enhance your BAM experience.

Close and Ask

Let me highlight some of the membership levels for you.

By joining at one of our Patron levels, you will receive exclusive access to specially reserved Patron seats (the best seats in the house) and personalized handling of your ticket orders. You will also receive advance notification of all programming, plus invitations to backstage events and opening night parties throughout the year. In addition, you can witness the artistic process first hand at six working rehearsals, free and available only for members. Your name will also be listed in the *BAMbill*, as an special acknowledgment of your support.

These benefits are available by joining at our Supporter level with a gift of $300. How does that sound? (PAUSE)

(IF HESITATION)

To make it more convenient, it is possible to charge a gift of $300 or more by using our installment schedule, which lets you enjoy all your benefits right away while making two, three, or four well-spaced payments. For instance, you can charge an initial amount now and your next payment will not be deducted until March 1. Plus, as a bonus for joining at the Supporter level during December or January, we would like to send you both a Next Wave T-shirt and your choice of three great CDs of music heard here at BAM by either Richard Einhorn, Philip Glass, or Les Arts Florissants. Your gift now will also put us that much closer to reaching our goal of $100,000 and will give us the valuable support we need as we look ahead to our spring season and Next Wave Festival in the fall.

So, shall I put you down for a gift of $300? (PAUSE . . . LET THEM SAY THE NEXT WORD!)

(IF NO)

I understand that this gift level may be too sizable a commitment for you at this time. We have various giving levels that are all equally important. At the Sponsor level, you would still receive advance notification of programming and invitations for four to our working rehearsals and backstage tours. If you join now, over the phone, we have a special savings on our Sponsor level. Ordinarily available with a gift of $125, you can become a Sponsor member for $105 and save $20 when you join today through our phone campaign. In appreciation for your contribution, we would like to send you a Next Wave T-shirt.

Would a gift of $105 be possible for you at this time? (PAUSE)

Great!

(IF NECESSARY, YOU SHOULD DROP DOWN BY INCREMENTS, US-ING GIVING LEVELS, NOT JUST DOLLAR AMOUNTS. IT IS ALSO IMPORTANT TO GIVE A REMINDER THAT A GIFT PROVIDES SUP-PORT TO BAM. FIND A GIVING LEVEL THAT IS COMFORTABLE FOR THE DONOR BY NAMING SPECIFIC AMOUNTS.)

ANOTHER EXAMPLE : For a gift of $105, you would be helping BAM enormously and you would receive the benefits at the Sponsor level.

Credit Card Ask

Now, I have your address as (CONFIRM ADDRESS, SPELLING OF NAME, LISTING IN BAMbill, AND OTHER INFORMATION)

Is this correct?

Good! We're processing our contributions with any of the major credit cards.

Which card will you be using?

(IF RELUCTANT, GO TO SECOND CREDIT CARD ASK OR USE OBJEC-TION RESPONSES)

Second Credit Card Ask

If you could put your gift on a credit card, it's another way you can support BAM. It cuts down on additional clerical and handling costs, and we can put your gift to work right away as we prepare for our upcoming seasons. Using a credit card increases the value of your gift! So, would it be possible for you to use your credit card tonight? We would really appreciate it.

Thanks.

Which card are you using?

And what is the card number?

And the expiration date?

And the name on the card is _____?

Let me read that back to you. (READ BACK)

OK, you're all set. MR./MS. _____, I want to thank you for your generous gift of $_____. We'll be sending out your receipt, along with your membership card, benefit package, and gifts, within the next few weeks.

Pledges

(IF DONOR MUST SEND PLEDGED AMOUNT BY MAIL, SPECIFIED PLEDGED AMOUNTS ARE IMPORTANT—USE OBJECTION RESPONSE IF NECESSARY)

OK, you're all set. MR./MS. _____, I want to thank you for your generous pledge of $____. We'll be sending out your pledge packet with a return envelope today. Would it be possible for you to send in your gift within 2 weeks? It would really help us with this phase of our campaign. Thanks, I'll note that you'll be sending in your gift soon.

Matching Gift/Referrals

There's one last item I wanted to mention to you. Do you (or your spouse) work for a company that participates in a matching-gift program for donations to nonprofit organizations? Often gifts can be doubled or tripled by these matching funds. BAM receives additional support and you receive the benefits from the combined gifts given in your name. If you know you have this available, I'll mark down your company name and note that matching funds will be sent. All you have to do is to notify your company that you have made your contribution, and they will send the appropriate forms to BAM. Thanks for your consideration and support. By the way, would you know of any friends or relatives who also might be interested in supporting BAM? (RECORD NAMES AND PHONE NUMBERS)

Thank you again, and have a good evening.

(Courtesy of the Brooklyn Academy of Music)

TELEFUNDRAISING OBJECTION RESPONSES

I PREFER TO SEND A CHECK

I understand. Of course we can accept checks. The reason we prefer to use credit cards is that they're much easier to process and thereby cut down on the additional costs we incur in recording and tracking pledges, and we can put your gift to work right away, putting your support into action! Of course we will send you a receipt for your charge, which you can use for tax purposes. In addition, by charging your gift you can begin your membership benefits right away. You can call our Ticket Services Department tomorrow to order any single tickets you may need without a surcharge. Just tell them you were signed as a new member by (GIVE YOUR FULL NAME) and they will take your order.

So, would it be possible for you to use your credit card tonight?

Thanks so much, we really appreciate it.

I NEED CANCELLED CHECK FOR TAX PURPOSES

I understand. It's easier to keep all your tax records together. All gifts we receive are confirmed by a receipt, whether you give by check or credit card. You may not be aware that you need a valid receipt to claim your gift for tax purposes. As far as the IRS is concerned, a cancelled check to BAM could have been for a ticket purchase! Considering this, would it be possible for you to use your credit card?

I'M WORRIED ABOUT CREDIT CARD FRAUD

I understand, it's smart to be cautious about the use of your card. Most consumer reports on credit card use over the phone emphasize that you should know the organization to which you are giving out information. If you would like to confirm that this call is from BAM, I can give you our office number, and you can call and ask to be transferred to my extension. Or you can call and give your number to my supervisor. My name is _____. My supervisor is _____. Would you like the phone number here?

I'M AFRAID OF UNAUTHORIZED CHARGES

I understand completely. I can assure you that we are just as concerned about the proper handling of credit card information as you are. We have to be! We take every precaution to insure confidentiality and security around the use of credit cards. Your number is seen by the fewest people necessary to quickly process your charge, and your number is not saved in your file, unless you request that we do so for installment payments. Each time you charge at BAM, you must give your credit card information again. If you ever question a charge from BAM on your statement, please contact our ticket services director or membership manager immediately. I hope that having this information makes you feel more comfortable using your credit card at BAM. It really helps to expedite any payment you make and affords us the most efficiency in handling your requests. If you use your credit card tonight for your contribution, I can process your membership right away. Would that be possible?

SEND ME SOMETHING; I DON'T WANT TO GIVE A SPECIFIC AMOUNT

Since we have a goal of $100,000 in this campaign, if I could put you down for a specific amount, it would really help us in knowing how close we are to reaching our goal. Even if you commit to a lesser amount, something you are comfortable with, and then decide to send more later, this would help us know how we're doing. If $____ would be a comfortable amount for you, I'll note that as your pledge and we'll count that toward our goal. May I put you down for $____?

Great!

$125 ($105) IS TOO MUCH FOR ME

In that case, you may be interested in a basic Friend Membership. You will still receive advance notification of all events, your Friends of BAM newsletter, invitations for two to all working rehearsals, direct phone access for single ticket orders without a surcharge, a 15 percent discount on nonpremium single tickets, 25 percent off on parking and the BAMbus, a 10 percent discount at the BAM Boutique, discounts at local restaurants, and access to the Friends hotline for help with ticket concerns. At $50, it's really quite a value, and you'll be helping BAM and our education programs. How does that sound?

$50 IS TOO MUCH FOR ME; I CAN'T AFFORD TO GIVE

I can understand that, MR./MS. _____. Actually, a gift of any amount would be doubly appreciated. First, because it would bring us that much closer to our goal, and second, because when we apply for grants from foundations and major corporations, they look to see not only how much money we are able to raise on our own, but how many people have made donations when deciding their level of support. So, a contribution of any amount makes a difference far beyond your gift. Would, say $25, be an amount you'd feel comfortable with?

I FEEL I SUPPORT BAM BY BEING A SUBSCRIBER OR PURCHASING TICKETS

And we appreciate you for it! Unfortunately, even with sold-out performances, ticket sales provide only 40 percent of our operating budget. You can imagine the expense of bringing entire companies from Milan, Paris, Stockholm, or

Taiwan to our theaters along with technicians, crews, and designers! We still try to maintain our low-ticket-price policy despite the decreases in government support we face. Membership is a vital source of our funding, now more than ever. Frankly, we need more people like you, who appreciate what BAM offers, to support BAM as a Friend of BAM. Your support helps ensure the quality performing arts you expect from BAM.

I DIDN'T ENJOY PROGRAMMING OR EVENT ATTENDED

I'm sorry to hear that. What didn't you like? You know, the BAM experience involves both artist and audience taking risks with works that are cutting edge and experimental. Not everything will always work, although we've received a very enthusiastic response from both critics and audiences alike for the majority of our programming this past year. What else did you see this year? And how did you like it? I'm sure you'll agree that BAM will always be successful as long as we continue to present innovative performing arts that surprise and challenge.

I DIDN'T LIKE MY SEATING

It's true that for certain performances it was very difficult to get the very best seats. *Salome* was virtually sold out right away. Other artists and companies, such as Robert Wilson, Ingmar Bergman, Les Arts Florissants, and Cheek by Jowl have such a strong following here at BAM that demand far exceeds our ability to give every patron the choice of the best seats. That is why becoming a Friend of BAM is such an advantage. If you join as a Patron level member, you can use our Patron Desk Service and have exclusive access to specially reserved seats (our best seats in the house) for any performance and personalized phone handling of all your ticket needs. As a member, you'll always be among the first to be notified of our upcoming events, including our Next Wave Festival or our spring theater season, so that you can place your orders early. For this convenience alone, membership makes a lot of sense. Wouldn't you agree?

I HAD PROBLEMS GETTING TICKETS OR WITH A TICKET ORDER

Due to overwhelming demand for tickets, especially this past Next Wave season and recently for our opera season, there is a chance that some human error may account for a few problems. But please be aware that we take steps so that problems don't occur, and any mistakes that may happen are corrected right away when you notify us. It is always best to keep a copy of your ticket order, including dates and times of performance and theater. Check with our Ticket Services Department or with the person who takes your order to find out when tickets are scheduled to be mailed. If you are ordering close to the date of a performance, tickets will be held for you. You'd be surprised how many people don't check their tickets as soon as they receive them! If there is an error, we can usually solve any problem if you let us know right away. If your problems have resulted from purchasing tickets from an outside agent, members can call in all orders directly to our Ticket Services Department and avoid a surcharge on each ticket. Additionally, members are entitled to a 15 percent discount on all purchases of nonpremium single tickets, based on availability. By becoming a member, we can guarantee you the best service and the most enjoyment of your experience at BAM. What do you think?

I DON'T GO TO BAM THAT OFTEN OR ANYMORE

I can appreciate your busy schedule (your change of lifestyle) (how far you come to get here). Many of our members do visit often and see most everything offered. However, many members don't attend often or see only one artist or company whenever they are here. What our Friends of BAM have in common is being part of our community of supporters—people who support BAM each year as a unique cultural voice in New York and who ensure that the best and most innovative performing artists from around the world continue to present works at BAM that excite and challenge, season after season.

I GIVE TO OTHER CULTURAL INSTITUTIONS AND CHARITIES

That's great, MR./MS. _____. Then you're among those who appreciate the fact that institutions and organizations depend on private support from individuals. BAM is no different in that we also depend on individual gifts for support and we hope you'll include us in your giving this year. (RETURN TO SCRIPT AT POINT OF INTERRUPTION)

I'D RATHER SUPPORT PEOPLE, NOT INSTITUTIONS

I can appreciate your caring about human needs. MR./MS. _____, have you ever heard of our education programs? (PAUSE) Well, I'm not surprised. I don't think we tell enough people about the 50,000 school-aged children we reach every year with BAM's daytime Performing Arts Program for Young People. Many thousands of our city's youth depend on BAM for their first exposure to the magic of live performing arts, and have for a generation. Today, with cutbacks in school programs, this is often the only arts education they receive, giving a balance to the influences shaping their outlook and their future. The point is, without support from many people like you, we might be in danger of losing one of New York's oldest and finest offerings in performing-arts education. This is an opportunity for you to help benefit thousands of young people in a unique way. Can we count on you for your support?

(Courtesy of the Brooklyn Academy of Music)

SPECIAL EVENT INVITATION AND PATRON LETTER

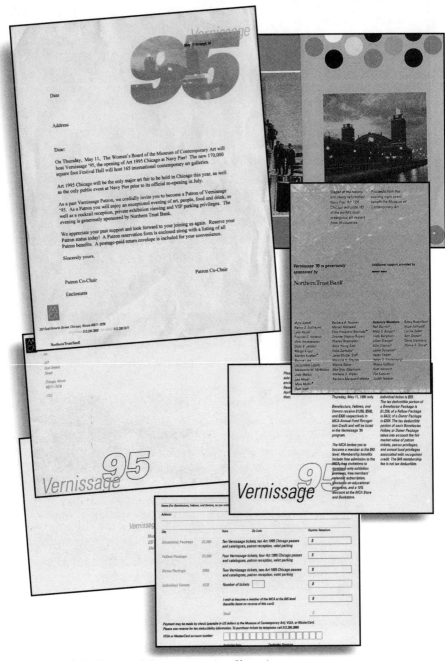

(Courtesy of the Museum of Contemporary Art, Chicago)

SPECIAL EVENT INVITATION

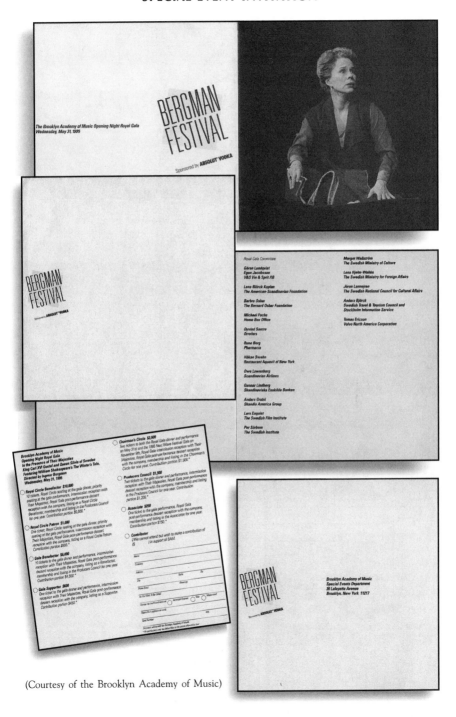

(Courtesy of the Brooklyn Academy of Music)

Capital Campaign Materials

ENDOWMENT CAMPAIGN BROCHURE

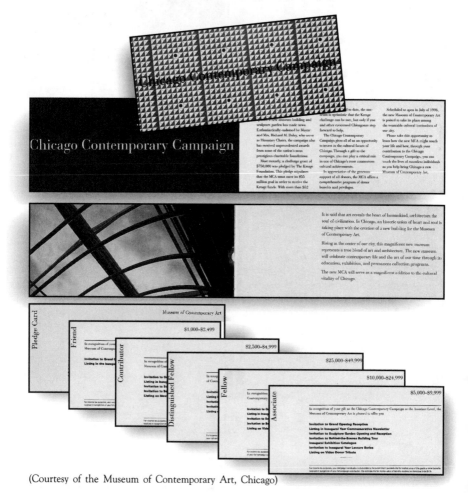

(Courtesy of the Museum of Contemporary Art, Chicago)

NAMING OPPORTUNITIES AND PRIVILEGES

Museum of Contemporary Art
Chicago Contemporary Campaign

Founding Campaign Contributors
Recognition Privileges *

Associate ($5,000 - $9,999)

Listing on Video Donor Tribute
Listing in Inaugural Year Commemorative Newsletter
Grand Opening Reception
Sculpture Garden Opening and Reception
Behind the Scenes Building Tour
Inaugural Exhibition Catalogue
Inaugural Year Lecture Series

Fellow ($10,000 - $24,999)

Listing on "Fellows" Donor Plaque (Education Center Lobby)
Commemorative Tribute Book (Soft Cover)
Listing in Commemorative Tribute Book
...Plus all "Associate" Level Privileges

Distinguished Fellow ($25,000 - $49,999)

Listing on Distinguished Fellow Donor Plaque (Great Entrance Hall)
Inaugural Year Exhibition Catalogues
New Museum Construction Tours
Preview of Inaugural Exhibitions
...Plus all "Associate" and "Fellow" Level Privileges

Patron ($50,000 - $99,999)

Listing on "Major Gifts Donor" Plaque (Great Entrance Hall)
The Gala Grand Opening Dinner
Inaugural Year "Evening with the Artists" Dinner Series
New Museum Lithograph (signed & numbered)
New Museum Video
New Museum Ground Breaking Reception with Commemorative Gift
...Plus all "Associate," "Fellow," and "Distinguished Fellow" Level Privileges

* Campaign contributions can be paid over a three to five year pledge period.
Founding Donor status requires pledges to be made prior to the campaign's conclusion.

November 1995

Major Naming Opportunities

The very nature of creating a new world-class museum lends itself to providing recognition opportunities for families and corporations to name various parts of the new museum and endow programming activities for generations to come. The following major naming opportunities are offered as suggestions by early leadership donors and may be combined to meet the interests of our donors.

Principal Building		$15,000,000
Education Center	(Ground Floor)	$ 7,500,000
● Orientation Hall	(Main Floor)	$ 500,000
● Multi-Purpose Facility	(Ground Floor)	$ 1,000,000
● Classrooms (2)	(Ground Floor)	$ 250,000
● Conference Rooms (2)	(Ground Floor)	$ 150,000
Sculpture Garden		$ 5,000,000
Theatre	(Ground Floor)	$ 5,000,000

Galleries

Main Floor North	(Main Floor)	$ 3,000,000
Main Floor South	(Main Floor)	$ 3,000,000
Vaulted Gallery A	(4th Floor)	$ 2,000,000
Vaulted Gallery B	(4th Floor)	$ 2,000,000
Vaulted Gallery C	(4th Floor)	$ 2,000,000
Vaulted Gallery D (half)	(4th Floor)	$ 1,000,000
Vaulted Gallery D (half)	(4th Floor)	$ 1,000,000
Galleries (7) (2 remaining)	(4th Floor)	$ 500,000
Projects Gallery	(4th Floor)	$ 500,000
Lake Gallery	(4th Floor)	$ 500,000
Visitor Information Gallery	(Main Floor)	$ 400,000

(Key: 1 Cube = $500,000)

Video Gallery	(Mezz)	$ 500,000
Media Gallery	(Mezz)	$ 500,000
Plaza	(Exterior)	$ 3,000,000
Great Hall	(Main Floor)	$ 3,000,000
Atrium Lobby	(Main Floor)	$ 1,000,000
Permanent Collection Lobby	(2nd Floor)	$ 2,000,000
Library	(Lower Level)	$ 500,000
Lakefront Cafe (A)	(Main Floor)	$ 250,000
Lakefront Cafe (B)	(Main Floor)	$ 250,000
Terrace Garden	(Main Floor)	$ 250,000
Private Dining Room	(3rd Floor)	$ 250,000
Museum Store	(Ground/Main Floor)	$ 1,000,000
Main Conference Room	(Top Floor)	$ 300,000
Conference Room (South)	(Top Floor)	$ 200,000

Chair Naming Opportunities

Director Chair $1,500,000

Art Chairs

Chief Curator	$1,000,000
Curator of Special Exhibitions	$ 750,000
Curator of Permanent Collection	$ 750,000
Curator of Performance, Performing and Media Arts	$ 750,000
Curatorial Chairs (2)	$ 500,000

Education Chairs

Curator of Education	$1,000,000
Curator of Public Programs	$ 750,000
Curator of School Programs	$ 750,000
Librarian	$ 750,000

Endowment Naming Opportunities

Exhibition Endowments

Major Annual Exhibitions (2)	$3,000,000
Special Exhibitions (3)	$1,000,000
Permanent Collection Exhibitions (2)	$ 500,000
Permanent Collection Exhibitions (2)	$ 250,000

Education Endowments

General Educational Programs	$2,000,000
Community Educational Programs	
Adult Programs	$1,000,000
Contemporary Issues Programs	$1,000,000
Multicultural Programs	$1,000,000
School Programs	$1,000,000
Senior Programs	$1,000,000
Children's Programs	$ 500,000
Contemporary Art Courses	$ 250,000

Publications Endowment $1,000,000

Sculpture Garden

Inaugural Exhibition	$ 500,000
Spring Program Endowment	$ 500,000
Summer Program Endowment	$ 500,000
Fall Program Endowment	$ 500,000

Special Exhibitions: Inaugural Year Exhibits

Grand Opening I	$1,000,000
Grand Opening II	$ 750,000
Major Exhibits (2) (1 remaining)	$ 500,000
Significant Exhibits (4)	$ 250,000
Special Exhibits (5) (3 remaining)	$ 100,000

Permanent Collection: Inaugural Year Exhibits

Initial Installation	$ 500,000
Significant Exhibits (4) (3 remaining)	$ 250,000
Special Exhibits (3)	$ 100,000

Permanent Collection: Inaugural Year Exhibits

 Initial Installation $ 500,000
 Significant Exhibits (4) (3 remaining) $ 250,000
Special Exhibits (3) $ 100,000

Special Exhibition: Research and Publications

 Publication Endowment $ 500,000
 Research Funds (2) $ 250,000
 Poster and Special Exhibition
  Reproduction Funds (2) $ 150,000

Video Gallery Endowment $ 500,000

Media Gallery Endowment $1,000,000

Theatre Programming

 New Music Endowment $1,000,000
 New Music Series $ 200,000
 Film Endowment $1,000,000
 Film Series $ 100,000
 Performance Art Endowment $1,000,000
 Performance Art Series $ 100,000
 Lecture Series Endowment
  Art Criticism $ 150,000
  Chicago Artists $ 150,000
  Contemporary Architecture $ 150,000
  Critical Thinking $ 150,000
  Electronic Art $ 150,000
  Film $ 150,000
  Permanent Collection $ 150,000
  Photography $ 150,000
  Sculpture $ 150,000
  Works on Paper $ 150,000
  Contemporary Writers $ 150,000
  Symposium and Lecture $ 150,000

Theatre Facilities   (Ground Floor)

 Light/Sound Booth/Projection Room $ 350,000
 The Docent Room $ 150,000
 Dressing Room A $ 100,000
 Dressing Room B $ 100,000
 Grand Piano and Stage Equipment $ 100,000

Library   (Lower Level)

 General Acquisition Fund $ 500,000
  Acquisition Fund $ 100,000
  Exhibition Fund $ 100,000
  Library Office/Reading Areas (2) (1 remaining) $ 150,000

Office Suites:

 Director's Office   (5th Floor) $ 300,000
 Public Programs Office Suites   (4th Floor) $ 250,000
 Development Office Suites   (5th Floor) $ 500,000
 Visitor Services Suite   (Mezzanine) $ 350,000

<u>Management Information Systems</u>

Computer Equipment and Programs	$ 500,000
Management Information Systems Endowment Fund	$ 500,000

<u>Art Preparation and Conservation</u>

Art Preparation Center	(Ground Floor)	$ 500,000
Art Storage Vaults (2)	(Ground Floor)	$ 200,000
Carpentry Workshop	(Lower Level)	$ 100,000

<u>Grand Opening Week</u> $ 500,000

During the course of the campaign, additional naming opportunities will be developed for gifts at these and other levels. These opportunities are offered as of September, 1993.

09/93
A:\workdoc4.OPP

(Courtesy of the Museum of Contemporary Art, Chicago)

LETTER OF INTENT

Museum of Contemporary Art
237 East Ontario Street
Chicago, Illinois 60611
Telephone 312 280-2660

Museum of Contemporary Art　　　Telefax 312 280-2687

Letter of Intent

To assist The Chicago Contemporary Campaign for the Museum of Contemporary Art (MCA), and in consideration of the gifts of others for the same purpose, I/we,

_____

(please print full name(s) as it should appear in official records)

hereby subscribe and agree to pay to the MCA the amount indicated below in accordance with the schedule noted. I/we agree that this commitment will be binding on my/our estate in the event I/we do not complete this pledge during my/our lifetime(s).

$_____ Total Pledge

Preferred Payment Schedule

____ Annually　　　　　____ Semi-Annually

____ Other: _____

over a period of ____ years, beginning: _____
　　　　　　　　　　　　　　　　　　　　　　　(date)

Amount: $_____ each payment Herewith: $_____

_____ Or, I/we prefer to make payments as follows: _____

_____

_____　　　　For income tax purposes, you may check here if you do **NOT** wish to receive any of the Donor Privileges offered to you in recognition of your Campaign gift. By declining to receive these privileges, the full amount of your contribution will be tax deductible.

Special Instructions: _____

_____

Legal Signature: _____

Date: _____

CHICAGO CONTEMPORARY CAMPAIGN

(Courtesy of the Museum of Contemporary Art, Chicago)

NAMED GIFT RESERVATION

Museum of Contemporary Art

237 East Ontario Street

Chicago, Illinois 60611

Telephone 312 280-2660

Telefax 312 280-2687

Museum of Contemporary Art

Named Gift Reservation

Having pledged a gift to the Chicago Contemporary Campaign in the amount of $_____, and having studied the program of "Named Gift Opportunities" commensurate with the size of my pledge, I hereby reserve the following named opportunity:

Name of Gift Opportunity:_____

_____

Please indicate how you wish your name to appear in print regarding this designation:

_____

_____

I understand that name recognition of a component of the <u>new</u> museum in no way implies ownership or control over such building or endowment components.

As the design for the <u>new</u> museum develops, some conceptual changes may occur in the scale and size of the building components. All donors will be kept apprised of such developments.

To maximize visibility and increase public awareness of the Chicago Contemporary Campaign the museum will manage all public announcements of Campaign gifts. All gifts except any specifically designated by the donor as "anonymous/confidential" will be considered eligible for public release in a manner to be determined by the museum.

Signature: _____

Date: _____

C H I C A G O   C O N T E M P O R A R Y   C A M P A I G N

(Courtesy of the Museum of Contemporary Art, Chicago)

CAMPAIGN UPDATE NEWSLETTER

Chicago Contemporary Campaign Update No. 9

Museum of Contemporary Art
January 1995

On an evening in March of 1986, at a dinner party hosted by MCA Trustee, Mrs. Beatrice Cummings Mayer, nine trustees made verbal pledges totaling the first $5 million to create the MCA's new building. Back then, 1995 seemed very far away! I'm sure we did not fully realize the enormous impact our plans would have on the city of Chicago and the world of contemporary art. By 1991, those original pledges were dramatically increased to $37 million by the entire board when the trustees finalized the more ambitious scope of our building and operational needs.

Now, as February of 1995 approaches, we have raised $51 million toward the $55 million goal of the Chicago Contemporary Campaign. Considering the great success we have enjoyed to date, it may seem an easy task to take the campaign over the top. In truth, we now face one of our most critical challenges. As volunteers prepare to launch the General Gifts Phase of the campaign, the challenge is punctuated by an impressive and timely Challenge Grant of $750,000 from the Kresge Foundation. This Challenge Grant stipulates that we must reach our campaign goal in full in order to receive the Kresge grant.

Having celebrated the topping out of our magnificent new building on December 10th, we are confident that Chicago is fully aware of the impact of the plans that were laid nearly a decade ago. What began as a dream soon became a groundswell of enthusiasm that overflowed from our own board of trustees and close friends into the entire community. I believe the endorsement of the Kresge Foundation will add considerably to that enthusiasm. I also believe that all Chicagoans now stand ready to welcome the new MCA, with its strong architectural presence and its unique influence on the life of our city.

It is also gratifying to note that, even with the campaign goal in sight, the leadership example has not waned. At the Topping Out celebration, MCA board chairman Allen M. Turner announced a $500,000 gift from the Robert R. McCormick Tribune Foundation as well as an additional $500,000 gift from the Turner family to bring their total gift to $1.5 million. These generous gifts give us a good start toward meeting the challenge of the Kresge Foundation.

I hope the example of these MCA friends and the opportunity to be part of this historic achievement, now tangibly on display, will inspire all who have not yet been asked to join in supporting this exciting project. There are a number of appealing named gift opportunities available which allow donors of $100,000 or more to associate their names in perpetuity with one of the world's great museums of contemporary art. There also is a full range of donor recognition programs for gifts of $10,000, $25,000, and up. When our volunteers contact you, I encourage you to talk with them about these opportunities and select the area that interests you most as a means of associating your name with the new MCA. I also invite you to contact me at my office (312) 580-4605 if you have questions about any aspect of the campaign.

The success we have enjoyed throughout the course of the campaign is attributed to a major commitment on the part of a very significant number of people. But, reaching the final $55 million goal will require an ongoing effort and further commitment on the part of many more. As the new MCA building and sculpture garden continues to take shape, I urge you to step forward and take your place among those whose contributions will take the Chicago Contemporary Campaign over the top in 1995.

Jerome H. Stone, Chairman
Chicago Contemporary Campaign

Far left: Members of the trustee new building committee pause for a picture as they celebrate this milestone in the MCA history and acknowledge the culmination of their efforts. From left to right: Jerome H. Stone; J. Paul Beitler; Dr. Paul Sternberg; Richard Tellinghuisen, manager new building project; Marshall Herlsler; Richard Cooper; Kevin E. Consey, MCA director; and Buddy Mayer.

Left: Students of the Farren Middle School at the Chicago Housing Authority's Robert Taylor Homes take time out from their ascent training to sign the new building's final beam.

concluding with the admonishment, "Now that we've built it, they better come!"

Throughout the morning, the jovial mood was pervasive as celebrants munched on muffins and shared congratulatory toasts of hot mulled cider. Contemporary music permeated the air and eyes were magnetically drawn to the five-story skeleton of the new museum towering

overhead. It was easy to imagine climbing the massive concrete stairs to the second-floor entrance, and easy to see the spaces inside where treasured works of art soon will reside. Expressions on faces attested to the fact that the new museum had never been so real, and that optimism for reaching the $55 million goal of the Chicago Contemporary Campaign had never run so high.

Construction Progress Report

Now that the structural work of the new museum building is completed, bypassers can begin to envision how the building will look a year from now when it is finished. Structural steel and concrete clearly define the five floors of the building, and the giant staircase leading to the second-floor main entrance is already an imposing presence.

During the remainder of winter and into spring, rough-in plumbing and electrical installation will continue on the inside as the aluminum panel skin is applied to the exterior of the building. Erection of the skylights on the roof will no doubt provide a great deal of interest to residents of the neighboring high-rise buildings.

On December 9th, the MCA hosted a lunch for the construction crew and key building committee members served workers on the new building.

Chicago
Contemporary
Campaign
Update No. 9

(Courtesy of the Museum of Contemporary Art, Chicago)

EVENT INVITATIONS

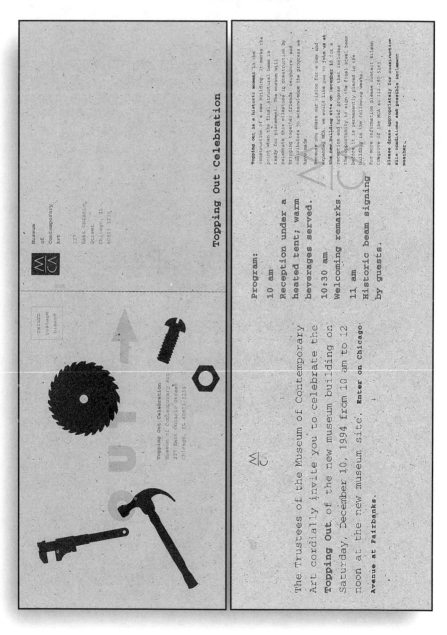

Museum of Contemporary Art
237 East Ontario Street
Chicago, IL 60611-3216

return postage please

Topping Out Celebration
Museum of Contemporary Art
237 East Ontario Street
Chicago, IL 60611-3216

Topping Out Celebration

The Trustees of the Museum of Contemporary Art cordially invite you to celebrate the **Topping Out** of the new museum building on Saturday, December 10, 1994 from 10 am to 12 noon at the new museum site. **Enter on Chicago Avenue at Fairbanks.**

Program:

10 am
Reception under a heated tent; warm beverages served.

10:30 am
Welcoming remarks.

11 am
Historic beam signing by guests.

Topping Out is a historic moment in the construction of a new building. It marks the point when the final structural beam is ready for placement. The museum will celebrate this milestone in construction by bringing together friends, neighbors, and contributors to acknowledge the progress we have made.

Because you share our vision for a new and expanded MCA, we would like you to join us at the new building site on December 10 for a reception and brief program that includes the opportunity to sign the final steel beam before it is permanently placed in the building in the following weeks.

For more information please contact Eileen Cosgrove of the MCA at 312.280.5163.

Please dress appropriately for construction site conditions and possible inclement weather.

APPENDIX M

Teaching Ideas for Arts Administration Students

CHAPTER 1

I. Get the Basics
a. Describe the institution-building process.
b. What are the categories of funding sources?

II. Stretch Your Skills
a. Choose an arts institution in your community and write a mission statement that might pertain to it. Create some hypothetical goals, objectives, and tasks for that organization. (This organization will be used throughout the course to develop fundraising skills.)

CHAPTER 2

I. Get the Basics
a. Describe the responsibilities and composition of an effective board of trustees.
b. How does the board participate in fundraising?

II. Stretch Your Skills
a. Create a manual for the board of "your" organization. Develop two profiles of the kind of trustees your organization needs to serve on its board.

CHAPTER 3

I. Get the Basics
   a. What are the types of information sources used in prospect research? In what ways is research helpful in fundraising?
   b. What are the five basic types of financial support fundraisers are concerned with?

II. Stretch Your Skills
   a. Select a project from "your" organization's list and run it through the fundability index, creating a careful analysis of that project's likelihood of being funded.
   b. Create one corporate and one individual research profile of funding prospects your organization might pursue.

III. Field Trip
   a. Visit the foundation center library in your city and go through the orientation process. Familiarize yourself with relevant books, IRS forms, periodicals, etc.

CHAPTER 4

I. Get the Basics
   a. Why do businesses support arts and culture?
   b. What are the types of business support available?

II. Stretch Your Skills
   a. Create a corporate general support proposal for "your" organization including a solicitation letter, a proposal, and attachments.
   b. Create a sponsorship package for a special project to be carried out by "your" organization, including selecting the appropriate potential sponsor, the letter of request, the project proposal, and a description of all of the sponsorship benefits the funder will receive. Be as creative as possible in designing the package.

CHAPTER 5

I. Get the Basics
   a. What is the history of foundation support for culture in the United States?
   b. What are the types of foundations that currently make grants?
   c. What are the most important issues foundations consider when evaluating grant requests?

II. Stretch Your Skills

a. Create a proposal to a foundation for the funding of a special project for "your" organization. Describe the project in terms of how it addresses issues of concern to the foundation and how it relates to their guidelines. Include in the proposal a solicitation letter, a project budget, and relevant attachments. (Example: An after-school arts-education program serving young people in an economically disadvantaged community.)

b. Identify specific types of foundations (in your community) that would be likely prospects to fund "your" organization.

CHAPTER 6

I. Get the Basics

a. What do you think motivates individuals to support cultural institutions?

b. Describe the steps in a direct-mail fundraising campaign.

II. Stretch Your Skills

a. Create a direct-mail package for an acquisition campaign for "your" organization, including: outside envelope, appeal letter, descriptive brochure, reply device, and reply envelope. Create a similar package for renewing a donor.

b. Design a phone solicitation script for "your" organization.

c. In class, set up a role-playing workshop in which students act as phone solicitors and respondents.

CHAPTER 7

I. Get the Basics

a. What is the history of government support of the arts?

b. What are the various options for government support—from the federal to the local level?

II. Stretch Your Skills

a. Research project: Describe the conflict that has caused the controversy about the National Endowment for the Arts and that has resulted in massive budget cuts to that agency.

b. Fill out an NEA grant application for "your" organization. The application should pertain to one of the allowable categories for funding.

CHAPTER 8

I. Get the Basics
a. What is the chain of command in the leadership for a major special event?
b. Who are the members of a special-events team, and what are their tasks?

II. Stretch Your Skills
a. Create a special event for "your" organization. Describe the event, the leadership, budget, and fundraising goal. Be as creative as possible!
b. Design an invitation and appeal letter for the event.

CHAPTER 9

I. Get the Basics
a. When should an organization consider an endowment campaign?
b. Describe each phase of a capital campaign.
c. Explain the various ways of making a planned or deferred gift to a not-for-profit institution.

II. Stretch Your Skills
a. Create a job description for a campaign director for "your" organization.
b. Write a case statement for a capital or endowment campaign for "your" organization.
c. Create a solicitation manual for volunteers to use on a fundraising call.
d. In class, set up a role-playing workshop in which students act as solicitors and respondents in personal campaign visits to request leadership gifts.

GENERAL

I. Speeches
It would be an advantage to have guest speakers attend classes. These could include board members; foundation professionals; contribution officers from corporations; public relations professionals; and campaign, special-events, and direct-mail consultants. Most important: Be sure your class has opportunities to meet artistic, managing, and development directors of effectively run arts and cultural organizations.

II. Creating a Casebook

In addition to having students compile all the proposals and materials suggested in the above-listed excercises, have them also read various magazines, periodicals, and newspapers. Ask students to clip appropriate articles that:

a. Are relevant to fundraising

b. Indicate economic trends that effect fundraising

c. Describe prospect opportunities—businesses, products, and individuals that could be potential funders

INDEX

• • • • • • • • •

by James Minkin